AND EVIL
SHALL BE
VANQUISHED

A WARRIOR'S ANTHOLOGY OF ORIGINAL
POETRY AND OTHER WRITINGS

ROBERT CONDE, JR.

This book is a work of non-fiction. Unless otherwise noted, the author and the publisher make no explicit guarantees as to the accuracy of the information contained in this book and in some cases, names of people and places have been altered to protect their privacy.

LifeRich Publishing is a registered trademark of The Reader's Digest Association, Inc.

LifeRich Publishing books may be ordered through booksellers or by contacting:

LifeRich Publishing
1663 Liberty Drive
Bloomington, IN 47403
www.liferichpublishing.com
844-686-9607

Because of the dynamic nature of the Internet, any web addresses or links contained in this book may have changed since publication and may no longer be valid. The views expressed in this work are solely those of the author and do not necessarily reflect the views of the publisher, and the publisher hereby disclaims any responsibility for them.

Cover artwork by Olivia G. Hartland

ISBN: 978-1-4897-3124-1 (sc)
ISBN: 978-1-4897-3123-4 (hc)
ISBN: 978-1-4897-3154-8 (e)

Library of Congress Control Number: 2020920115

Print information available on the last page.

LifeRich Publishing rev. date: 10/21/2020

Original Works Written By SPC Gabriel David Conde
KIA April 30, 2018, Kapisa Province, Afghanistan

Compiled by Robert Conde, Jr.

For Gabe

and for the mighty men and women who have served in the United States armed forces, for the innocent people of Afghanistan, and for the families and loved ones of warriors who are no longer with us.

May the words in this anthology inspire, comfort, and refresh your soul to live your life to the fullest measure and carry out your mission with passion.

CONTENTS

FOREWORD

By Donna Conde, Gabe's Mother

Gabe was always a boy/man of many words. He always liked to talk—a lot.

His teachers in elementary school always had very positive things to say about Gabe and his classroom behavior. When they talked about how quiet he was, Bob and I would look at each other and smile. Gabe saved up all his words for us! From the time I picked up him and his sister, Olivia, from school, Gabe talked, and he talked and talked. All day in school he'd been thinking about all the things he needed to say, obviously. He would talk about anything and everything. I didn't mind a bit. His sisters had a hard time getting a word in edgewise when he was around, always. However, I'm so thankful he was this way, and left behind a part of himself in his writings. It brings such comfort to my heart to hear his voice in all he wrote that comprises this book.

I wish some of our conversations could have been recorded as well, revealing the depth of insight he had into scriptures, word studies, strategies, and the human psyche. Gabe had a great variety of interests in many things, from physics and calculus to anatomy and physiology, from music and arts to knives and guns. He could talk or argue your ear off about almost any subject. Gabe had an old soul, with wisdom and insight beyond his years. I admit some of his writing is over my head! I miss, so much, hearing him talk, and argue, even if I agreed with him.

Any mother who has a son understands how fiercely she loves him, in spite of his shortcomings. One thing I love about Gabe is his complete honesty with himself and God and his absolute love for God. These things shine through, over and over again in this book. And there is no question about Gabe's driving desire to be a true hero. Yet, like David of ages past, he struggled. He struggled against his own fleshly desires. He struggled against spiritual forces. He struggled with imperfect people and imperfect leadership. But he continually strived to rise above his struggles and do the right thing. I respect and admire him for making this choice.

Enjoy this book in small or large segments of time. Gabe will make you cry, smile, laugh out loud, scratch your head in wonder, and cringe with some of his expressions. It's all genuine, original, Gabe. I love him, and I miss him so very much!!!

Please understand that some names and places have been redacted for the sake of privacy and security.

By Olivia Hartland, Gabe's Sister

One of my biggest regrets is that I did not respond to the email Gabe sent me in February of 2018 for my birthday. Ironically, he told me in that email not to waste time on regrets or missed opportunities. What can I say? He gave so much advice that it would be impossible to try to follow all of it. The same email included advice about getting "schwasted," a quote from Deadpool, and some (civil) nicknames for my husband (boyfriend at the time). I don't think Gabe would have had a filter even if it were disguised as port wine or a shiny new gun. He would talk to whomever would listen, and sometimes even to those who wouldn't. No topic escaped his commentary. There was a lot of nonsense as well as a lot of truly inspiring gems of wisdom in what he said, and he delivered all of it with authentic and unwavering confidence. Embracing ridiculousness and candor, gentleness and intensity, he would say whatever was on his mind.

When he was alive, his words were a reflection of his character—a character I could only describe as "Gabe" since no other label or set of adjectives could suffice (though he chose many for himself). When he was alive, I took his words for granted. He was alive, so I did not cling to reflections of him. Now those reflections, aside from memories and home videos that seem from another world, are the only clues to the character. These artifacts cannot replace his presence, but they can amplify his legacy. It seems like my goofy big brother has become a carefully documented historical figure. I had the privilege of knowing the person, so for me his writings are a reminder of who he is. He will always be my brother, my memory, my role model. But he is not just mine anymore. Now he is yours too, reader. His wisdom and ideals are truths to encourage you. His inner struggles are now questions to convict you. His imagination and ideas are now stories to captivate you. Now you and so many others will get to glimpse his overwhelmingly unique personality.

I have read the email he sent for my birthday over and over, often for other people. Since I am always at a loss to describe him, I find it simpler to use his own words. Now he can speak to those he never reached, to those who knew him well, and to everyone in between. I guess he's still able to talk to anyone willing to listen. "Love, the most wise and astute, cultured, a connoisseur of fine liquors, man among men, and ultimate peak of big brother evolution, Gabe." Thanks, Gabe. For everything.

By Priscilla Conde, Gabe's Sister

When Gabe got his license, he would drive me places when my parents couldn't. He would drive me to school and tell me all about the inner workings of society and more importantly, the hierarchies within hierarchies of middle school. He would drive me to a friend's house and tell me stories of what he and his friends would do and finish them with, "So don't do that." He would always tell me to call if I needed anything, and I knew that I could call and he would come.

When it snowed, he would take me on random drives with no destination, just to spin out and have fun in the weather. He never got the chance to drive me to high school, although I wish he could have so I could have had an extra twenty minutes to talk with him.

When I got my permit, Gabe told me that when he came home in July, he would take me four-wheeling. I looked forward to it, because finally I could be in the driver's seat and think of all the fun conversations like Gabe did.

Gabe was seven years older than me. He had every opportunity to be a moody teenager and leave his little sisters to fend for themselves, but he never did. We all annoyed each other at times, but both of my siblings were gracious, and I knew they would always have my back. Even when Gabe was halfway around the world for the better part of a year, I felt protected.

I have had my fair share of obstacles in my short time on this earth.

And Gabe was always there, ready with advice, love, and support. Our emails back and forth were long and wordy. I would be frustrated, and he would be calming in a dramatic sort of way. He was wise and never hesitated to share his wisdom with others. At the end of every email, or letter, or phone call, Gabe would tell me to be stoic, seek wisdom, and live fearlessly.

I know Gabe still has my back. A brother's love does not end at death, and that is something of which I am sure.

INTRODUCTION

"EAGLE DOWN! EAGLE DOWN! CONDE'S DOWN!" shouted a special forces tactical team member as he watched SPC Conde's body fall backward and hit the hard ground of the mud brick rooftop, landing flat on his back. His body lay motionless with his hands still held in firing position as the special forces soldier continued yelling out to Conde. Another special operations soldier called over the radio that Conde was down. The two green berets were themselves pinned down on an adjacent rooftop by Taliban forces firing from a nearby ridge as the soldiers engaged the multiple enemy fighters quickly approaching from below. When the call went out on the radio, it took about thirty seconds for Gabe's team leader to get to him from the opposite side of the rooftop to render aid. It was too late.

The US special forces Operational Detachment Alpha (ODA) soldiers and Afghan Army special operations soldiers were nearly surrounded that morning and continued the fight for the next twelve hours. Two Afghan Army commandos were also killed in action that day. One US Air Force pararescue medic was seriously injured, and four Afghan soldiers were wounded.

A short time after the soldiers returned to Bagram, they telephoned Conde's family to explain the mission, answer questions, and tell of how he died providing cover fire and calling out enemy positions with no regard for his own safety. They somberly said it was a "lucky shot" and "a one-in-a-million shot" that struck and killed Conde. The autopsy results would later conclude that he had been killed instantly by a single bullet that entered above his left shoulder blade and exited at the base of his neck on the right side. The bullet had impossibly missed his body armor, severed both his carotid artery and jugular vein, and fractured and dislocated the vertebrae in his neck.

The investigation also revealed six bullet holes in the shemagh (Afghan head wrap) Conde wore across his chest the morning of the battle. The bullets likely were stopped by his body armor, as no other bullet wounds were found on his body. One bullet hole in the scarf appeared to have been made by a .55 caliber round. We imagine the large, high-powered bullet might have been the force that knocked him backward, even as the single, high-velocity, small-arms bullet struck him from behind, killing him. A one in a million shot.

<hr>

Gabriel David Conde was born at home in Belton, Missouri, in November 1995. The circumstances of his birth were unique, as his story began months before he was born. In the large church we attended when Donna was pregnant with Gabe, several different people approached her and said she would have a son whom God had called to be a warrior with a heart like King David. We received these words as an indication that our unborn child would be close to God, and we wondered why strangers would tell us these remarkable things. Even after he was born, prophetically-gifted people told us similar words about Gabe at random times. One notable time was at the end of a church service when we walked forward to receive prayer. A woman named Diane prayed for us and asked if she could pray for Gabe as well. Gabe was less than a year old. As the woman prayed, she said, "This beautiful boy will become a warrior, but his heart will be soft. I can see him writing words, songs, poetry, and psalms. He will be a psalmist, like [King] David ...."

In spite of these unusual experiences, Gabe's childhood was very much like other children in the Kansas City area at the time. He was unique in that he had a hero mentality that seemed to be in him from the time he was a toddler, and he genuinely loved God. He learned to play the trumpet, he loved to read, and he discovered he was somewhat of a math genius. Gabe and his family lived in Belton, Grandview, and Lee's Summit, Missouri, before moving to Berthoud, Colorado, the summer before he started eighth grade.

Gabe was the oldest of three children, and he loved his sisters, Olivia and Priscilla. He took to heart the responsibility of his role as big brother, and it was said of him that he could protect his sisters all the way from Afghanistan.

Gabe was a dreamer. From a young age, he could recount vivid, complex dreams that came to him in the night. We loved hearing about his night visions, and we encouraged him to write them down. Thankfully, Gabe did write some of his dreams. In retrospect, some of them were prophetic in nature, even up to the days before he was killed in action. These dreams are included in this volume.

Gabe was a mathematic anomaly. He was one of those guys that loved calculus, and he seemed to understand mathematical concepts at a younger age than other kids his age. He loved learning, and he really seemed to embrace his intellect, among the other gifts God gave him. Here is an example of his work in Calculus II class during his first semester at the Colorado School of Mines ("Mines"):

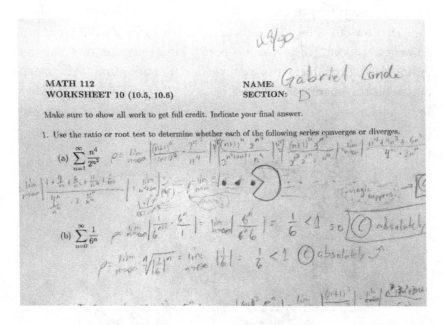

Gabe was a deep thinker. As you will discover in his poetry and some of his other writings, Gabe was a man ahead of his time, or perhaps he was a man born a couple of centuries later than he would have chosen for himself. Some excerpts from his prose writings about "the creature,"

included in this book, began when he was eleven years old. In his more recent writings, including some journal entries from deployment, "the creature" and other characters seem to have acquired more depth as Gabe's experiences widened.

Gabe was a musician. He learned how to play the trumpet in elementary school, and he worked at mastering the instrument without outside prompting. He really enjoyed playing in the jazz band through middle school and high school. He also taught himself how to play the guitar (somewhat), and later in his teenage years, we discovered he had a decent singing voice. Among his favorite movies was *Les Misérables*, the 2012 epic musical film starring Hugh Jackman as *Jean Valjean*. Gabe had memorized several songs from the movie, and in short order, he was singing "Look Down," "Who Am I?," and "Do You Hear the People Sing?," in a remarkably clear baritone voice.

Gabe was a writer. Most of this book was written by Gabe's own hand. We hope you are able to appreciate his youthful and passionate heart and hear God's heart for you through the honest words of his servant, Gabe.

Gabe was an artist. We didn't know that Gabe was an artist until he went to college. He said he was bored, so he started drawing sketches during the lectures. Here is an example sketch he drew from a photograph during his freshman year at Mines.

Gabe was a physical fitness maniac. He became a student of everything he set his mind to do, and he spent hours working the muscles that he relied upon to carry all of his gear, including his own ammo for his holy SAW (squad automatic weapon). He joined the 1000 lb club in his unit in Alaska, and the last numbers he shared with his youngest sister a month into deployment were, in his words, "P.S. Prill, if you need to terrify a scrawny turd who's never seen a barbell, I can now bench 285 pounds, deadlift 435, and squat somewhere near 380. It's not much compared to some freaks of nature, but those numbers are steadily moving upward. And I have 7+ months with nothing better to do over here than plot the demise of some sniveling twerp. You know, just in case :)"

Gabe was a good friend. He had close connections with amazing, strong, gifted, intelligent, and heart-connected people. They helped shape him to become the man who chose to stand and take bullets as he protected the men with whom he served. To his high school and college friends and to those of you in the US and Afghan armed forces who fought alongside him, I am sorry for your loss. I hope you are calling on God as Gabe did. May He bless you and keep you, and may each of you succeed in all you do and become the men and women God created you to be.

Gabe was a generous spirit. Although he was frugal in spending money, he was altruistic toward people less fortunate than himself. At times he gave sacrificially, almost zeroing out the meager savings he earned as a lowly private and specialist in the infantry. He was always ready to help friends and strangers in need. Perhaps this quality of selflessness was part of what drove him to be the hero of his own story and ultimately give his life for his team and the good people of Afghanistan.

Gabe had strong opinions (like most military men and women). Gabe's opinions of the United States Army, as a young enlisted infantryman, are included with few redactions. His frustration with people who squandered their God-given lives was nearly as severe as his hatred of pedophiles, rapists, human traffickers, and murderers.

Gabe complained a lot – especially to his family and close friends – and then he acknowledged and sometimes backed off his rants. He could go on and on about shortcomings of our corrupted government, injustices of central banking, the flavor of cheap cigars, the feminization of men in America, and other topics that provoked his ire at the right moment.

Gabe was stoic. In spite of his chain being easily yanked at times by things that would not cross the minds of many people, Gabe learned to guard his tongue when a judicious response was the wisest choice. He told his sister, Priscilla, to "be stoic" as advice to help her navigate the waters of middle school and high school.

Gabe was a hunter and not a fisherman. Just ask his friends.

Gabe was a gentleman. When he was growing up in Missouri, Gabe learned the values of respect, kindness to strangers, and upholding the law. He held doors open for his mom and sisters and others, and he knew the value of working hard, regardless of payment. When Gabe was about eight years old, he went with me to help a woman in the neighborhood clean up debris in her back yard. She was impressed with his work ethic at his young age, and when the work was done, we were getting ready to leave. The woman called him over to her and said, "Gabe, you are a very good worker!" and held out a five-dollar bill. Gabe stepped back and said, "No thank you, I can't take that." The woman's eyes widened in surprise, as she asked, "Why not? You worked very hard today, and you earned it." Gabe replied, "Thank you, but I don't have to be paid just for doing the right thing." My jaw must have hit the pavement, not sure if he actually said what I heard. The expression on the woman's face provided the answer.

Gabe was super self-confident, outwardly boastful at times, yet remarkably humble at his core. Depending on one's proximity to his core, which he chose to share with a small number of people close to him, one may have witnessed his superficial arrogance and stubborn will to win every argument, regardless of importance. One example of his humility was how he minimized the importance of the work he was selected to do in Afghanistan during deployment. During his sporadic phone calls, when we asked what he had been doing, he would typically say, "You know, livin' the dream. Pulling guard duty, doing worthless training exercises, trying not to be so bored...." Based on our phone conversations and infrequent emails, I thought Gabe had been on three or four missions during deployment. We were told later that between the two special forces ODAs he was selected to support, Gabe had been on about 80 total missions during the eight months of his deployment. Many of the missions were not combat-related (like "guardian angel" and training missions), but Gabe really was living his dream of becoming a green beret.

Below is the text from a certificate displayed in a shadow box given to our family by ODA 0214:

2nd Battalion
10th Special Forces Group (Airborne)

CERTIFICATE OF APPRECIATION
IS PRESENTED TO

SPC Gabriel D. Conde
this 12th day of May 2018

2nd Battalion, 10th Special Forces Group (Airborne) extends to you our personal thanks and sincere appreciation of a grateful nation for your contribution of honorable service to our country. You have helped maintain the security of the nation during a critical time in its history with a devotion to duty and a spirit of sacrifice in keeping with the proud traditions of military service. Your commitment and dedication have been an inspiration for those who will follow in your footsteps, and for all Americans who join today in saluting you for a job well done.

Signed
ROBERT O. SANDERLIN
CSM, USA
Command Sergeant Major

Signed
KEVIN M. TRUJILLO
LTC, SF
Commanding Officer

—————◆◆◆◆◆—————

Gabe died a hero. He not only gave his life for his fellow Americans, he also fought and died for the Afghan people. After his buddies dragged his lifeless body off the roof to a safe place within the compound on the ground, the two American soldiers as well as Afghan Army soldiers stood guard over his body continuously until he was finally airlifted back to Bagram. When the soldiers were securing Conde's body to a litter for a move to the helicopter landing zone (HLZ), during a brief pause in the action, an unknown Afghan soldier approached one of the US soldiers with no interpreter present. In broken English, the soldier tried his best to speak.

"Conde." he said, as he touched Gabe's chest.

"Yes," the US soldier replied.

"Great fighter…, funny…, brave…, my brother." The Afghan soldier then removed his Afghanistan flag from his own shoulder and placed it on the torn sleeve of SPC Conde, placing the flag over Conde's chest. "He… good Soldier…. He died… [pointing to his chest] (for) our country…." The Afghan warrior then touched his own heart and said, "Afghan brother."

The US soldier nodded to the Afghan soldier and continued to package up Gabe's body. They never found out who this Afghan soldier was.

———————— ✦✦✦✦✦ ————————

The words of Gabe's poems, like most poetry, carry depths of meaning that may not be apparent in the first reading. When he first began to share his poetry with us, I recall hearing the words and thinking, "This is really good!" but not really understanding how the words would profoundly affect me personally these years later. Even today, as I review his writings included in this anthology, his poetic words reach through time and wash over my heart yet again, drawing out the tears, while exposing and restoring another small fragment of the enormous hole he left behind.

———————— ✦✦✦✦✦ ————————

Gabe with his "holy SAW" in Afghanistan 2018

PART 1

ON BECOMING A HERO

From a very young age, Gabe wanted to be a hero. Like many boys, Gabe spent a lot of his time role-playing make-believe battles where he defeated the bad guys and rescued the beautiful princess. As he grew, he studied and learned more about his childhood hero, King David, and he took to heart many of the psalms penned by David. Gabe's appreciation for the biblical Hebrew king (including his bravery from a young age, personal struggles, and ultimate leadership of ancient Israel) is reflected in many of Gabe's poems and other writings.

Gabe perseverated over his decision to join the military. Having graduated near the top of his class in high school, he decided to attend the Colorado School of Mines ("Mines") in the fall of 2014. By the middle of his first semester, Gabe called me on the telephone.

"Dad," he said, "would you and Mom be offended if I dropped out of Mines to join the army?"

I said, "Of course we would not be offended. We always knew you would make that decision, but we hoped you would go through ROTC so you could enlist as an officer and get better pay." I went on to explain that he should at least finish his freshman year to honor the scholarships he had received.

In his youthful idealism, Gabe described how he was bored and how he felt like he was wasting his life away at engineering school while he could be learning the art of war and how to vanquish evil most effectively. He said he really felt like God was calling him to join the US Army, and he was sure he wanted to go the special forces route. He explained he did not

1

want to go in as an officer because he wanted to earn the respect of the enlisted soldiers as one of them and learn from actually doing the work. Gabe agreed to finish his freshman year at Mines. He enlisted in the army during the spring semester of 2015.

On August 8, 2015, PVT Gabriel D. Conde shipped off to basic training at Fort Benning, Georgia, to begin his formal training on becoming a hero.

To choose

Golden, Colorado,
31 October 2014

It's in times of brutal languish
that heroes take their rise
the people suffer from
    great anguish
in those heroes' eyes.

But who decides to wear the cape
to dawn the righteous crown?
Who is worthy of such fate
who will lay his life down?

It was done once before
a lone Savior freed a people.
His name is now widespread
in churches, homes, on steeples.

But on a smaller scale,
when a hero must stand tall,
whom do the weak seek for?
To whom do they call?

Perhaps they call on money
on financial aid, on greed
but this will simply drift away
it is not what they need.

Others call on charity
"I deserve what I am given."
It is all more clear to me
all motives are now driven.

No one really knows
what it is they seek
no one really understands
the plight of the meek.

So in the day to day
it is up to choices
up to individuals
with strength in their voices

To rise against corruption
against all the dark and evil
to do what they know is right
to save those struggling people.

To choose this is not easy
it takes strength of soul and will
to decide when to pass mercy
and when to strike the kill.

Yet I don't believe that people
choose this for themselves.
first they must be called
to stand against the hell.

And when they see the calling
they can choose to walk away
I hope I would not do that though
if I were called that way.

I would love to take the cause
of the weak and innocent

to block the prying claws
of the heartlessly malevolent.

To rise above all earthly pains
and yet see them all before me
to snatch the young from jaws
    of death
not caring if people adore me

The reward from saving just one life
to feel that gentle rush
would fuel my hope to
    save another
until my breath is hushed.

A soldier

Golden, Colorado
01 March 2015

As one who walks through
    burning snow
as one who faces biting wind
one who carves a path in the wilds
one who always must fight
    and win
imagine then, his purpose ends
what does his life do then?

How can one move past
    such drive
and still find motivation to thrive?
A person who is born to fight
will find no joy in peace, for that's
    not his right
long for, he will, days to come or
    days long past
in which each breath could be
    his last.

Even if he has never violence seen
even if his mind is clean
evermore the drive will call
the drive to fight and the drive
    to fall.

It is not desire that sets his course
the choice is his, yet not in a way
    of sorts
it is destiny that lays his path
and fate that guides his wrath.

Such a man is a soldier, born to be
a man that will fight until the
    world is free
a man that will live with fire in
    his eyes
even as dying on the ground
    he lies.

Such a way is a soldier, born
    to live
each day with nothing more
    to give
he fights for honor, justice,
    and good
but evermore he fights, as we
    knew he would.

Evermore he fights for those
    he loves
even as the gun falls from
    his gloves
even as the sun sets on his life
he will give everything to end
    their strife.

Journal Entry before Basic Training

Berthoud, Colorado
28 July 2015

I leave for basic combat training in less than a week. The past week itself has been a whirlwind of events and emotion. I went to a rodeo with Heath and Kiah and Kiah's German friend. That was fun. I climbed part of the Longs Peak trail with Brian. That was also fun. Saturday my family had a going-away party for me, and that too was fun in a way I suppose. It's all been good. I am in the calm before the storm. It is relaxing and enjoyable, but my heart pounds ever harder as I see the clouds approach. I am going to be gone from everyone and everything I know and love. I am going to be alone, and I am finally at peace with that. For in truth, I am never alone. God has been with me since before I was born and will continue to guide and protect me, to give me strength, and to humble me. I have no more deep emotional [attachments] to the girls I have rambled on about in the past. I have accepted that God's will for my life and his timing for the events therein is no doubt better than what I could possibly conjure with my own imagination.

There have been people close to me (my mom, my dad, a family friend, other friends) who have made me aware of their vision of the future where I am concerned. Jenny, a family friend with a gift for prophecy, has called me a man of sorrows. Others have made me aware of their fear for my emotional well-being, of the pain I will encounter. My parents have faith in God's protecting of me, but they too are scared for me as their child. All this seems about right. I'm on the right path. It may be burdened with pain, but in fighting through it with help from God I will know joy on the deepest of levels, and I will have times of happiness. I pray that what pain and sorrow I do suffer though, may serve as an example, a story, a lesson, a legend to others who would otherwise know nothing of the true hardships of life. I pray that the events of my life, without credit given to me, will affect the hearts of people for millennia to come.

There I go being melodramatic again, but the desire is real. I want the grit, the pain, the brutal fight. I want the fantastic and impossible successes and the crushing blows of defeat. I want the peace of a wife and a family and a cigar with the guys. I want the violence of war and the elation of victory. I have always wanted to be a hero. Maybe now, maybe in realizing the destiny of my life, a hero I will be.

I wanna be big (a conversation with God)

Before Special Forces Assessment and Selection (SFAS)
01 December 2015

"I wanna be big
I wanna be great
I want that green beret
I don't wanna be late
I wanna be strong
I wanna be brave
I gotta be a hero
So I can free the slaves
I want skills
I want power
I want a righteous fight
More each passing hour"

"You have a way to go
But I will guide you there
It may not be as you expect
But I will help you bear
The weight that I will place
Upon your shoulders
A noble burden I've given you
My lonely, loyal soldier
You have no power
On your own
But I'll lift you up
You won't be alone."

"I want to get married
I want to have kids
I want a happy life
All that you can give
I want a home

Up in the hills
With friends nearby
And steaks on the grill"

"I know my plans for you
To prosper and keep you from harm
But your fate to some
May alarm
You've chosen my path for you
So I will guide your feet
Until that fatal day
When we finally meet."

"Will I live long?
Will I save some lives?
Will I cut down your enemies?
Before at those gates I arrive?"

"So many questions
I'll answer them in time
Just trust in me for now
And stay out of the slime
Remember what I've called you to
Much pain lies on your path
You'll always have a choice
Of carrying out my wrath
This calling will claim
Your life one day
But I will guide you
All the way."

"I have so much
That I wish to do
But to your will
I will stay true
Death or pain or sorrow
I will follow you to the end
Just please protect those I love
While this time I spend
Searching for my fate
And fighting any war
That you point me towards
Whatever lies in store."

"My child, my son
Your faith will have reward
I'll give your family peace
While you fight by the sword
I'll protect your home
I'll save your friends
My joy will stay with you all
Until the very end."

So you got your wish

Berthoud, Colorado
08 May 2016

So, you got your wish
To go and fight a war
But what if you die trying
Or return broken and poor?

What if they reject you
And the sacrifice you made?
What if they forget you
Like a sorrowful song
    once played?

What if they accuse you
Of murder and of greed?
Or worse if they abuse you
Make you cry and bleed?

War is a dangerous game
No one returns without scars
Which ones will you bear?
Will your flesh or mind
    be marred?

Are you sure they are worth
    dying for?
That sickly sorry throng
What the hell are they
    babbling about?
The newest stupid song

So you got your wish
To go and fight a war

But whose side are you on?
Who decides the score?

Who is pulling the strings
To send you where you go?
Who tells you what to do?
Are they right? How do
    you know?

Questions, all these questions
Just shut up and let me tell
I'll answer just a few
Before I march through hell

The people of this world
Sick as they may be
Deserve to be fought for
So I will gladly bleed

If they turn on me later
When I have returned
I will speak the truth
And see that they will learn

Scars I know I'll have
But scars are fully healed
Open wounds will not stay long
And my soul will be revealed

As for who is pulling
All the strings from higher

I know exactly who and how
And He is not a liar

The Lord of Hosts is
    my commander
My leader and my guide
His word will always keep me
At peace, and at His side

So there's nothing left to fear
No questions that I have
I will fight though I may die
Though the world laughs

For with me there is hope
And without me there is still
For the Lord of Hosts is
    never wrong
And He dictates who I kill

Someone say it

JBER in Anchorage, Alaska (with a nod to J.R.R. Tolkien)
16 November 2016

Someone say it'll be alright
That a day will come they'll see
   the light
Someone say the future is bright
But even if they would I only
   wish that I could
Believe that they're right
That the future is bright
That all that is good is not lost

Someone say the world's okay
That a day will come that will
   end the fray
Someone say the debt will be paid
But even if they will I can only
   wish, even still
To believe what they say
About a following day
And a world untouched by
   the frost.

Perhaps I am overthinking
But the world around me
   is shrinking
And no one has even an inkling
Of the death that is theirs at the
   top of the stairs
No one is thinking
Everything's breaking
Good intentions, out the window
   are tossed

So maybe I will be the one
To stand and say what's done
   is done
But tomorrow will rise a brand
   new sun
To shine upon the free, my
   brothers and me
Freedom bought by blade and gun
To leave the general
   populace stunned
A certain line needs to be crossed

For, to make the world able to see
A battle is waged on bended knee
Alongside one fought on the feet
All to win us a day where evil is
   finally slain
A battle will rage and there I'll be
Fighting to make the world free
For though I wander, I am not lost.

What does it mean to be a hero?

JBER in Anchorage, Alaska
22 December 2016

What does it mean to be a hero?
What does it mean to die for
    a cause?
What does it mean to suffer
    and fight?
When all hope is gone,
    utterly lost?

How do you keep on moving
Trudging along each
    tiresome day?
What does it take to find
    meaning in nothing?
How am I supposed to find
    a way?

I remember, not long ago
Being fearsome and strong
Ready to take on the world
    or more
Without heed to how hard or
    how long

Now I am tired
Exhausted, depleted, spent
The life, the fire, it's faded
    to flicker
My mind is weary and wrent

And now, now of all times they
    tell me
To go and do something brave

Go and take on the world
    and more
Obey you lowly slave

You should have asked me sooner
When the fire still raged inside
Not now when my hope is
    an ember
And my passion has all but died.

But go, they say, and conquer
Come back a victor with pride
Unknowing of my gutless stupor
With naught but a dim-lit guide

Will this challenge make
    me stronger?
Yes I suppose it must
But at what cost to my will
Which is already approaching
    the dust?

So say I do get through it
Say I gain that illustrious fame
What then, how does that
    help me?
I'm already sick of the game

Some part of me looks for
    a challenge
But it's crushed by the weight of
    what's real

How long it will take to achieve?
How long it will take to heal?

And what, in full scope, have
    I gained?
A title, a rank, a badge?
They think my fire will burn
    for that?
Really they must be mad

You know, it feels like I'm ranting
Complaining about things
    I shouldn't
So I thought about ending
    this nicely
But then I realized I couldn't

Some feigned motivation or drive
Isn't going to help in the swamp
And if I pretend I would find
    it there
I'd be ignoring reality's stomp

There is no substance in a maybe
There is no future in a hope
And no amount of
    artificial passion
Will help climb a rocky slope

So this is where I am
I'm cold, worn out, run dry
Go out and become a hero
But why should I even try?

What does it mean to be a hero?
What does it mean to fight for
    a cause?
If it's what you do when you feel
    like this
Then I've already miserably lost.

Memories of dreams are dancing
Just beyond my reach
Dreams of trials and daring
But I don't even want to cross
    the breach

A band of a thousand men

JBER in Anchorage, Alaska
04 February 2017

A band of a thousand men
Unaffected by the carnage there
Advanced against enemy lines
Leaving the earth behind
    them bare
Unstoppable and unbreakable
They fought like demons of
    a horde
Yet upon closer inspection
Each shone like an angel of
    the Lord

The enemy stood no chance
Their numbers were cut by
    the second
Incapable of victory, too slow
    for retreat
Death and defeat were all
    that beckoned

It was as though those
    thousand men
Were an army a hundred
    times more
With the least of them slaying
    twenty times his weight
All of them drenched in their
    enemy's gore

To a looker from afar
These men were not far from gods
But to one amidst the chaos

A realization left them in awe
Behind each noble warrior
A band of beings marched
Made of light with eyes of fire
They left the very soil parched

In turn they moved forward
Fighting as the man
    they shadowed
Lending force to his blows and
    speed to his aim
Down to every fist thrown
At times they advanced
    before him
When the man grew tired or faint
With a breath of exhaustion he
    would belt a cry
And an angel dashed forward
    spilling blood as paint

They would lift the man and
    right him
And move their bodies as his
Such that he wouldn't be so much
    as scratched
By a cannon aimed for his ribs
But blink just once and they
    were gone
Leaving just the man of valor
Untouchable on the field of battle
With strength
    surpassing spectacular

And times this by one thousand
The men to his left and right
Together they formed a
    frightful host
Wielding heaven's own might

Songs were sung of their gallantry
And stories told of their
    battles bold
But only one there amidst
    the carnage
Understood the true depth of
    their souls
They were men with spirits
    of righteousness
Yet savages in war
For who else could lead a band
    of angels?
And how else they, could heaven
    fight for?

So lost

JBER in Anchorage, Alaska
10 March 2017

So lost oh child dear
With dirt in your eyes
And on drags the year
Surrounded by empty lies.

So lost oh brave little soldier
No idea what is next
No idea where to go
Or when the next test.

So lost oh sad young pup
The weight of the world
Makes you want to give up
Go back to the cave tail curled.

So lost oh weak little human
Walking with blinders through an
    empty life
Don't stay that way little human
Lest the dreams you once had be
    put to the knife.

Maybe you forgot which way to go
Maybe you really are lost
Maybe you search frantically for
    a goal
Without first stopping to thaw
    the frost.

It hurts, doesn't it
Being alone
No one to hold
No place to call home.

Your strength feels sapped
Your mind is tired
You're hating the world
You're never inspired.

All you want to be
Is the superhero inside
But you fear that may never occur
That the dream of your life
    has died.

I'm afraid that I can't help you
    right now
You'll have to carry on through
The night grows darkest before
    the dawn
But relax, you have nothing
    to prove.

Whether you feel it or not,
You're being looked after well
Soon this purgatory will end
And you'll get to fight through hell.

A hero on the battlefield

JBER in Anchorage, Alaska
24 July 2017

A hero on the battlefield
I ran toward the enemy line
With a steely gaze and wild eyes
I yearned to fight, longed to shine

I crushed my foe with leaden fist
Machine gun purring loud
I never tripped, and never missed
The gun smoke was my shroud

A roar of victory on my lips
I charged the final hill
When suddenly my arm fell limp
And my blood began to spill

I raised my weapon with the other
Not as steady against the kick
And I felt myself fall sideways
In my leg a painful prick

Looking down, to my dismay
I see no leg attached
My blood sprays now on
      the ground
Onto one last hope I latch

I pull the pin from the grenade
Bleeding in the mud
Throw it over the
      stacked sandbags
And listen for a thud

Satisfied I'd killed my prey
I drifted off to sleep
Too cold, too tired to stay awake
The darkness began to creep

My eyes blink one more time
And I see my brother's face
"Rest well," he says, tears in
      his eyes,
"You've won your final race."

As I looked down from above
The gory battlefield

I saw my friends all knelt beside
My body, no more to heal

Some cried, some stood stoic
But I could hear their thoughts
And if ever tears a ghost
      could shed
I would have shed the lot

I watched them load my body
On the helicopter floor
I watched them fly me far away
To a land peaceful, humble,
      and poor

They laid me in a cedar box
And set it atop a pyre

They shot the guns to the
        warrior's march
And sent me home in fire

I watched the flames for near
        an hour
Then wandered to my house
Looked out the window one
        last time
And walked once
        more throughout

Saw my grieving family
And wished to ease their pain
But the ghost can't touch
        the living
Lest they receive a stain

So I sang in a new tongue
A song of mourning passing
Sang to them to remember
        the good
Despite the tears that
        were amassing

Satisfied I'd done what I could
I walked out to the hills
Atop the peaks I find my rest
Until the cup is filled

For behold, the Creator cometh
And in paradise I wait
To be called to the
        final battlefield
And seal all evil's fate.

PART 2

INTROSPECTION

Gabe was a colicky baby, and it was about 18 months after his birth that he finally slept through the night, and his mom and I finally got to sleep a full night ourselves. We originally planned to have five children, but after Gabe was born, we jokingly said, "One is too many!" Thankfully, he was also a very happy baby. His belly laugh and his quick, engaged, and excited expressions sparked the joy that kept us sane during those early months.

Even as a baby, Gabe had a propensity to observe and almost seem contemplative, as he took in the sights, sounds, and tactile input from his surroundings. As a young boy, he would often stop and stare, as his mind churned through daydreams of his adventures in his future world.

These childhood fantasies grew into adolescent idealism and became the fabric of introspection that is evident in his writings. He often spoke of his desire to rid the world of evildoers even as he inwardly questioned if he had the resolve to take someone's life. As a teenager, he seemed to have settled his thoughts on the matter, as he verbally described how he would destroy anyone who would try to harm his sisters, his cousins, or his friends.

The dreamer became a man. He chose to join the US Army as a special forces recruit. He chose to be a paratrooper. When he was dropped from selection, he chose the airborne infantry. He made these choices after years of introspection and prayer about how he would become the man his God (YHVH) envisioned him to be.

Childhood in Lee's Summit, Missouri

I run and am not tired

Before Special Forces Assessment and Selection (SFAS) at Fort Bragg NC
14 December 2016

I run an am not tired
I ruck and am not faint
My spirit and mind are wired
It is Christ who keeps me sane
The next few weeks of hell
Will not leave a mark
I will not succumb
to pitfalls in the dark
I love you Lord my strength
You give me joy anew
You will save my life
You will see me through
When these weeks are done
I'll praise you with thanks
from the mountain tops
to the river banks
Come quickly to my aid
when I am in need
And help me on this quest
to make the world free

Lord tell me of my life

Before SFAS at Fort Bragg NC
14 December 2016

Lord tell me of my life
my portion and my calling
tell me when I'll fly
When I'll be strong or will be bawling
Tell me what to do with
each challenge and decision
for with you there's no mistake
no need for apprehension
So speak to me my God
let me see your face
And show me where to turn
While I run this race

"Gabriel my boy
Your prayers will be answered
Keep your faith in me
And I'll keep your soul from cancers
Fight for the oppressed
the orphan and the lost
I'll help you save their souls
In blood their lives were bought
You will do great things
and save so many lives
Run wild without fear
as in my will you strive
I love you and I'll keep you
far from any fear
You will know my voice
and have peace when I am near
Don't heed the other voices
of anxiety and pain
Keep your heart before me

from all worry refrain
for I know my plan for you
you'll bring glory to my Name
So cowboy up and soldier on
and just enjoy the game."

A righteous man am I

At SFAS, Fort Bragg NC
14 January 2016

A righteous man am I
Until the day I die
In faith I live my life
A righteous man am I

A faithful man I am
For love and peace I stand
For justice in the land
A faithful man I am

I am free I am wild
With the innocence of a child
Yet I won't be beguiled
I am free I am wild

In God I place my trust
My soul is free of rust
And though the wind does gust
In God I place my trust

A warrior I'll be
To make the world free
The mountain air I breathe
A warrior I'll be

Save me Lord from wrong
From evil who are strong
Don't let them hunt me long
Save me Lord from wrong

God uphold my cause
My race I will not pause
Help me bear my cross
God uphold my cause

Free me from all pain
Oh God heal my brain
For I sway like winter grain
Free me from all pain

Give me joy abound
Enough to spread around
Lord lift me from the ground
Give me joy abound

Thank you Lord my God
You are my shield and rod
You save me from the prod
Thank you Lord my God

Thoughts after Selection

Written after being dropped from SFAS (possibly still at Fort Bragg NC) May 2016

It occurs to me I may never join the ranks, the brotherhood, of those that fought before me. I may see, sit, and toast with them in Valhalla, or whatever part of heaven God has set aside for us, but in truth I will never belong with them. Their fight is over. Their war is done.

The last of the patriots have left the fire out in the rain, and here I am, standing beside it. Unable to retire to their reward, unable to keep the fire lit for lack of wood, but it will burn a while yet. The last of the cowboys have returned from the range. The cattle drive complete. Yet there is more livestock to be gathered.

The killers have killed, the fighters have fought. The sailors have sailed, and the soldiers have stood guard for the final time. That leaves me, the most recent to return. The cowboys, vaqueros, I look up to them, but they no longer look to the wide forest of war or missing herds of other breeds. That leaves me.

The founders, the fire keepers, the guardians of this city of light, they have retired. They are sick of the rain. That leaves me.

What am I? An angel in an army of devils? A shepherd in a pack of wolves? A warrior about to step into his element? Or a visitor. And a messenger. A leader? A grunt. I am a boy on a field trip gawking at the men who conquered the world. And the boy to whom that world is entrusted. I'm really glad God won't make me carry it alone….

Don't you see

JBER in Anchorage, Alaska
26 October 2016

I'm not free
I sicken me
Don't you see
I am diseased
I am not pleased
Won't be appeased
Don't you see
I disgust me
I'm not free
No room to breathe
Too cold to freeze
This stifling breeze
May very be
The death of me
Don't you see
I can't breathe
Rage that seethes
With sharpened teeth
Come to eat
It's got me beat
This grim defeat
Crawl to my feet
Now take a seat
And watch me
Don't you see
Helped by He
Who conquers thee
Now just maybe
I can truly be
Free.

Evil shall be vanquished

JBER in Anchorage, Alaska
07 July 2016

Evil shall be vanquished
four quite simple words
when coincide become a phrase
sharper than any sword
For when put into practice
a pattern can be seen
Rapists die, thieves are caught
from a rope they swing
Murderers don't last long
Hateful become few
Good men begin to multiply
to see this justice through

Evil shall be vanquished
it begins to mean much more
when pictured, a lone soldier
knowing the reason for his war
He fights each battle harder
on any given day
Constantly aware there
are bodies left to slay
A burden he has shouldered
to rid the earth of men
that would see his homeland suffer
if he refused to fire again

Evil shall be vanquished
Soon the day shall come
All debts shall be repaid
When the deed is finally done

Missing motivation

JBER in Anchorage, Alaska
26 October 2016

Where did my motivation go?
I lost it somewhere along the line
Now it's missing, gone as gone
    can be
But I'm ok, I'm doing fine

Still it bothers me to think
That it just somehow slipped away
But maybe I will find it again
Yeah maybe I will, one day

Until then what do I do?
I'm living life with artificial drive
Not that it matters to anyone else
I'm here, I'm alive

But I need passion in my
    life again
I feel like I'm missing something
I want energy for the day ahead
But I reach down and come up
    with nothing

So what is it I long for?
What's this ache, this empty void
It was once filled with dreams
    of battle
Now it hardly even makes a noise

Still I long for a righteous fight
To slay bodies in defense
    of innocence

But I can't bring up the will
    to train
I've reached the land, but can't
    climb the fence

Where did my motivation go?
Did I drop it along the way?
Now it's all I can do to keep
    on doing
And keep my darkness at bay

Perhaps I'll find it again
In some new and beautiful form
But until then, this emptiness
Will become my norm

Unless my God, in His goodness
Will grant me this request
Give to me unyielding drive
So I can truly become my best.

Stream of Consciousness

JBER in Anchorage, Alaska
27 February 2017

I've been thinking much lately about the potential future of my romantic life which is currently non-existent. I find myself thinking about when I will marry, if it ever becomes a *legal* marriage. Government enforced laws surrounding marriage are gay anyway (pun intended) and I believe two people can be married in God's eyes without being married in the eyes of the IRS. Suppose that time comes soon though. Then wouldn't it make sense for me to meet my future spouse much sooner? Or supposing I have already met her, wouldn't it make sense for me to know who it will be? Wouldn't it make sense for her to know? Who tells the other first that they think dating would be a good idea. As a gentleman I feel it is my responsibility to act, but this isn't some spur of the moment date. Considering my present situation, if I were to theoretically ask out a current female friend, it could cause serious waves on the tides of friendship despite the level of trust we have. Losing the kind of friendship we currently have is terrifying, as well as the prospect of it not working out romantically. So maybe it's someone I haven't met yet (despite strong evidence to the contrary). In that case, it would take a long time of knowing the person before I would consider dating them properly with the intention of marriage. Then the dating time period would have to be long enough for me to build the level of trust I would need to marry someone. For a person who has never been betrayed or cheated on, I have some of the worst trust issues known to man. Or maybe I don't. I'll tell myself I trust people, and some people even call me trusting, but in reality I'm almost always emotionally prepared for being let down. I expect very little out of people as a result. My wife is gonna have it hard. Apart from my family and close friends, she'll be the only person in whom I place the whole of my trust and all of my hopes on (in a human sense anyway).

Maybe it's not worth thinking about. I figured a short stream of consciousness essay would ease my mind, but it seems to have depressed me ever so slightly. In the end I do not know what my life holds, and I have to trust God with it all. Well, that's what I tell myself. In truth those words have always struck a dissonant chord with me. God is always there when

I need Him, and having His wellspring of infinite spiritual sustenance to draw upon in times of hardship is something I've come to appreciate more than many. However, I do not see him as the kind of God that loves seeing His children helpless. People say, "It's all in God's hands." That may well be true, but it's not like He's making your life choices (wouldn't that be nice). He gave us two hands of our own, powerful minds, and a free will. Don't you think He wants us to use them? He gave us a level of strength and intelligence that I believe is untapped in today's world by Christians and heathens alike. In the Bible, God himself made a comment that if left unchecked, humans would "become like us." I can only imagine he was talking to Himself (as the trinity) or to his closest angels. Either way it testifies to the incredible things humans are capable of on their own as a creation of the great Creator. Even thinking from a father's perspective, I will always be there to help my children even into their adult years, but I would hate to see my child rely on me for their whole life to make their decisions and guide their actions even if I knew the best choice each time.

So do I trust God? Yes. Will I do my best to pursue his will for my life? Yes. Will I turn to him with questions, and in times of trouble, and even just to talk? Yes. Will I roll over like a whipped dog and drift through life like an aimless dandelion seed coasting on the *it's-all-in-God's-hands* excuse? No. God wouldn't want me to be passive. I'll pursue His heart, and the causes and passions He's placed in mine. But I won't do Him the dishonor of whimsically wasting the life he's given me just because He hasn't yet told me what to do. I will pray. I will choose. I will learn. I will grow. ...Damn this is good stuff. I feel like I'm preaching to myself. Which is right because this is not a matter of salvation, but a matter of honoring God in the best way I can. Some people may find a life of pure reliance on Him in every way is more honoring. I cannot judge them, nor will I, since I have been there before, and my life may well cycle back to there again. My aim is now clear, though, and I will strive to act and to honor Him. Trusting that he will always be there when I have troubles, or questions, or just want to talk.

Spiritual core

JBER in Anchorage, Alaska
03 April 2017

I am not sure why I detest people so much. Little things that other people find normal, or even cool, irk me to the point of rage sometimes. I have a very specific idea of what a human should be like, and rarely do I find people that match or exceed my desires. My family are among the few, as are my closest friends and a few people I don't know very well, who have proven themselves through action. It is these types of people who set the example for the world. An example to which very few, relatively, will ever measure up. Maybe that's why I hate humans. My standards for them are simply too high.

I've been blessed in being raised and often surrounded by people who force me to learn and grow in a variety of areas. Most people have not had that kind of life. Most people muddle on through existence never contributing, never changing, never evolving. Perhaps my hatred for such people has become so poignant lately because I sense myself drifting in that direction. I sense that a time has come to choose a path to pursue once my time as a soldier ends. I have been gifted with a mind and a body that is capable of pursuing any career I could possibly want, yet I find myself attracted to the simple ones: a rancher, a park ranger, a small time tourist or bush plane pilot, but those options all feel too simple—too small. I want to find a passion to devote my time and spiritual, mental, and physical resources—a specialization where I can be the best. However, I desire such an occupation without sacrificing time for other pursuits like athletics, music, and creating.

I want to be the hero of not just one story, but an entire volume. I want to be the main character in not just my life, but the lives of people across the world. Unfortunately, I must acknowledge much of this outlook as a foolish and self-serving creation of my own mind. In truth, and at the core of my spirit, I wish to affect eternity with my actions and to do so on behalf of the innocent and the weak. No matter how much I hate them…, no matter how much they piss me off, no matter how many of them I may kill to defend the rest, I can't help but love humanity.

This worthless, helpless, soft-bodied race of self-serving assholes—I love them. Rather, I love what they could be. I love who they were meant to be. I love the innocence with which they were born. I love the love in their hearts. I love their passion and their joy. I love their sorrow and pain. I love their potential for learning, creating, and accomplishing the incredible. I love their gentle touch, and powerful force of will. I love their individuality, and their ability to band together. I love their simple complexity. And all of this because I love their Creator. I love the God who makes no evil thing and adores His creations as His children.

I'll probably never tell anyone this truth of how I feel about humanity. It's easier and safer to say I hate all but a few. It's simpler and more amusing than explaining the intricacies of my love for them, and no one would understand how I could still be willing to kill after explaining it. They don't get that the two can coexist in one being: an open and perfect love for people and the desire to end the lives of those who have broken my code of justice. Mercy and compassion are the bridge between the two. Even God himself wiped out humanity once and then forgave us as a whole when He sacrificed Himself in mortal form.

I wonder if all people are that way at the core of their spirits. I think they are. The soul becomes cluttered, weighed down, scarred and muddied from lifetimes of sin and wrongdoing, but if you were to scrape all the filth away, clean and polish the result, and stare deep into it, I think you would see a core much like what I have described yet with some unique and beautiful differences.

My life's ethos

JBER in Anchorage, Alaska
06 April 2017

The Gabriel Ethos

1. Do not lust nor act upon lustful thoughts or desires.
2. Be empathetic and compassionate while remaining stern and fierce.
3. The words of humans do not matter. Focus on the words of the Almighty.
4. Strong spirit, strong mind, strong body, but first strong faith.

The David Ethos

1. The glory belongs to the King of all.
2. Work hard, fight hard, pray hard.
3. Do not pursue unnecessary battles; do not shy from conflict.
4. Defend the innocent and the weak.

The Conde Ethos

1. Remember who and whose you are.
2. Uphold the name of your family and your God.
3. Stay free and wild.
4. Be generous and be excellent.

World turning

JBER in Anchorage, Alaska
11 April 2017

World turning
World burning
I am dying
I am yearning

Each breath I draw is closer
Closer to the end
Each step I take is slower
This time's not mine to spend

In agony I wait
Replies are far between
I detest my current state
But still on God I lean

My path is veiled from me
My purpose hidden from view
The final end, I cannot see
Somehow I must stay true

Oh God please upon me rest
A solemn burden
A glorious quest
That lights a fire in my chest

Let me fight
Your enemies
Show me the plight
Of the weak, give me sight

I need a reason to fight
I have so much to give

Show me where to take
    my strength
Show me how, for you, to live

I am lost without a compass
Blind without a cane
I have no strength but what
    you've given
I feel not any pain

I need your guidance now
I need your holy grace
I need to hear an answer
I need to find my race

You have given me a
    warrior's heart
A philosopher's mind
A fighter's build
I'm one of a kind

You've blessed me
    beyond compare
With you I am not lost
Allow me, in your holy fight
    to share
No matter the pain, no matter
    the cost

What you have planned, I
    cannot see
Though I know, it will include me

And my part in this giant play
Will be my honor, will be the way
It will be my love, will be your say

What is life, if not to live?
And what is living, with nothing
    to give?
I cannot cope with monotony
I refuse to think you've
    forgotten me.

Break me first, if you must
If it is you, it will be just
Break me so that I may live again
Kill my greed, Kill my lust
Save me from my selfish crust

No matter the pain, no matter
    the cost
Show me where I will no longer
    be lost
Give me a purpose and give
    me strength
No matter the pain, no matter
    the length

Darker side of joy

JBER in Anchorage, Alaska
16 April 2017

Why is my spirit moved so
What forces drive my thoughts
To this end of lonely sorrow
And the joy that thence is brought

The loss I feel is growing
Though I know not the cause
The thought of what it could be
Gives me peace, gives me pause

It's a loss without a goodbye
A grief without a start
That steady aching feeling
Of a heavy-laden heart

Even now it's passing
As I recall the song
The story of a sacrifice
And a time long gone

Why is my spirit moved so
What powers touch my mind
To think of future sadness
But the happy ending kind

The hope I have is tiny
A mere flicker of a flame
But it warms my soul to dream
And keep marching all the same

A sense of undone actions
A growing, dark unease
It's peaceful there and quiet
Among the sullen willow trees

This is an in-between place
'Twixt the past and future battles
A dark and somber resting point
Where not a sabre rattles

For at this point we recall
A deed done in distant past
When Son of Man saved
    the world
Broke our chains at last

Still it's a somber idea
Remembering His actions
The pain He bore for our disgust
No matter tribe or faction

So I'll stay a little sad
For those still steeped in sin
As I thank my God with joy
That my life is His again

PART 3

WISDOM FOR A CONFUSED GENERATION

It has been said of this generation of young people (and probably every prior generation as well) that they have not been taught logic, and their understanding of history is profoundly deficient. Gabe also voiced this critique of his own generation, but his observations were not limited to the shortcomings of our nation's youth. His writings in this section reveal a fiery defiance of status quo as he calls out the lethargy and empty ways of living that have forestalled good men and women from achieving their God-given purposes.

Posing shirtless in Alaska, 2016

The breakup
Berthoud, Colorado
March 2014

My time with you though fleeting, is a memory dear.
Your impact on my life, it hit so near.
I don't understand the way I feel.
I have never taken so long to heal.
My heart was stone, untouchable, cold.
But you did something incredibly bold.
Cracked it open, revealing a molten core.
And left it there, to cool on the floor.
I'm looking at it now, in the dirt, beating slow.
It longs for you, in a way none can know.
There's a glimmer of hope, each time you smile
Like a ship passing by a lonely isle.
I love when you are happy, be it with me or not
I'm still giving it a go, giving it all I've got
To be a friend, lighthearted and fun
But the pain burns worse than the bite of a gun.
Look at me now, into my eyes.
Tell me why, who, what caused it to die.
Help me to make sense of it all
And forgive me, because this weight I can't haul.
You've done the impossible and made me feel.
So say it all now, say everything, and let me heal.

Lonely dinosaur

Berthoud, Colorado
01 May 2014

Once upon a time, in a far-away land, there lived a lonely dinosaur.

He was big and strong, and feared among all, but he could only count to four.

One day he was out hunting, and much to his surprise, he found a hidden passage door.

It led down a giant tunnel, so he didn't hit his head. He'd never been underground before.

As he walked, he got hungry. Thankfully he found a meal in the form of a weaker allosaur.

You may say "EWW" and you may call him gross, but he wouldn't have it any other way. He finds ordinary life a bore.

As he continued down the tunnel, he heard a funny sound. It came from down below, through the earthy floor.

With a giant clawed foot, he investigated the noise. Much to his dismay, a giant burrowing lizard out of the ground, tore.

The fight was fast, but bloody, and the lizard lay quite still. So he kept on walking, wanting to see more.

Finally he reached the end, and crawled out of the tunnel. He was in a whole new world that shocked him to his core.

Around him were others, dinosaurs just like him. They welcomed him into the group, and he joined in their hunts. And so the lonely dinosaur was not lonely anymore.

Good traits to have

Berthoud, Colorado
19 May 2014

Intensity, ferocity, wildness
No contest
Do not give any less
Passion, desire, motivation
Don't waste time
On petty contemplation
Stamina, dedication, endurance
go the distance
Pay the penance
Strength, power, force
Leave nothing behind
Fight without remorse
Compassion, care, empathy
Know the sign
Not everyone needs mere sympathy
Logic, calm, keenness
Keep a sharp mind
Make plans seamless
Wisdom, caution, steadfastness
Lead with knowledge
Peer into the vastness
Live life to the full
Fight the bull
Leave nothing left that you could have given
It's about the journey AND the destination
Persistence, logic, wonder
Lead a people, save a nation.

A man

Berthoud, Colorado
08 June 2014

A man
A man is kind
A man is caring
A man shows mercy
A man shows compassion
He knows the meaning of true
    love and how it is shown
A man is strong
A man is steadfast
A man is trustworthy
He protects those he loves no
    matter the cost
A man is truthful
A man is wise
A man is respectful
He always keeps his word and
    honors his promises
A man is tough
A man is keen
A man is able
He does what needs to be done,
    and does it well
A man is honorable
A man is noble
A man is a leader
He leads with courage
    and inspiration

A man is moral
A man is patient
A man is loving
He treats others well, and showers
    affection on his love.
A man respects life
A man provides
A man works hard
He refuses to watch injustices
    consume the world
    around him.
A man makes mistakes
    and repents instead of
    defending them.
A man reaches for help when he is
    broken instead of wallowing
    in his own misery.
A man knows his weaknesses, but
    does not hide them.
He will fight to the death for his
    Lord, his love, and his family.

Nameless woman

Berthoud, Colorado
20 July 2014

Oh nameless woman
Won't you show your face
Let me see what none has seen
Let me behold your grace

You walk a million miles
Just to watch the eyes that follow
You through the countless towns
But isn't that a bit hollow?

You tease me with your hair
Taunt me with your back
You only show what you want me
   to see
While you prepare to attack

Oh nameless woman
won't you show your eyes
Let me see those oceans deep
So I can see past the lies
You tell leading me in circles
Round and round until I
Am dizzy and can't walk
You know I gotta see your eyes

You drift from town to town
Wrecking homes along the way
I never know how long you'll be
or how long you're gonna stay

You speak to me so softly
Tell me to come with you
That I'm the only one
   you've known
to make you feel like bein' true

Oh nameless woman
Won't you show your smile
Let me see that
   glimmering sunrise
So I can stare a while
You tell me that you love me
Even if I'm not your style
So darling let's dance
then walk a country mile
Because with you it would be easy
To forget about real life
And spend the day in hapless joy
easing me of strife

Oh nameless woman
Won't you say you're mine
Show me all there is to you
let me know your mind

Let me spend the years
With you in deep embrace
Let me see what none has seen
Let me behold your grace.

The eagle

Golden, Colorado
26 October 2014

The eagle roams the skies
king of his domain
He watches all with shining eyes
all pay tribute to his rein
The eagle soars above the clouds
Majestic above all
riding upon his wings spread proud
never does he fall
He is not touched by earthy pains
he is truly free
And yet he can see the all the strain
as clearly as can be

The pedestal

Golden, Colorado
07 November 2014

The man walks slowly
going with the crowd
his shoulders slumped lowly
his head is bowed.
Suddenly he sees a pedestal
rising from the masses
he began to drift towards it
as the crowd harasses.

He stops there at its base
frozen in the flow
something calls him to the top
something says to go.
He takes a cautious step
the first in a flight of stairs
but is pushed back violently by
    the crowd
receiving many harsh stares.

But another person sees him,
and stops along his side
so he takes another stronger step
a step on which many have died.
The person who is watching
begins to lift his foot
and as he does, another
watches from the soot.

The crowd is still passing
going God knows where
the only thing the man knows
is that he won't go there.

Another step upward
and clinging chains down pull
they try to drag him with
    the crowd
but he fights it like a bull.

Another step and he
    grows stronger
he strains against the chains
each breath he takes is longer
he no longer feels the pain.
Another step and the chains
    grow weak
more followers have amassed
they long to know what it is
    he seeks
no matter what lies in their pasts.

Another step and the chains break
falling down into the fray
the man runs up the stairs
longing for the light of day.
Bursting through the clouds
he sees the brilliant sun
freed from the darkened shroud
the people behind him run.

The pedestal seems to end
as though there's only room
    for some
but the man takes a step in faith
and the people all watch, stunned.

The billowing clouds give way,
revealing solid ground
grass that stretches miles
trees, and rivers abound.

More people flood up from
    behind him
taking in this world new
freed at last from their
    unrealized bonds
up the stairs they flew.

The man stands watching
relieved and proud and glad
but something inside tugged
    at him
something made him sad.
So many more down below
that would never see this place
he could not in good conscience
leave them to their fates.

So he picked up a lowly flower
from the grass upon the ground
and turned around and walked
    back down
to the dirty, sullen, moving town.
Many tried to kill him
upon his sudden return
with mighty strength he
    fought them
to share what he had learned.

Some heard his words
and began to climb the stairs
and some of those fell off

before they reached the air.
But that mighty few that made it
they thrive there to this day
freed from all mortality
they are there to stay.

And the man that saw
    the pedestal
and fought for what was right
he lives on still down below
bringing the dark to light.

A single lonely life

Golden, Colorado
08 December 2014

There are poems about heroes,
songs about love and loss.
I'd be lying if I said this was one
   of those.
There's a line I'm trying to cross.

The line of accepted and right
the line between truth and law
the line between the lights
the line of stories real and raw.

There was a man who lived
that was a hateful sort.
A child once approached him
just to be given harsh retort.

He lived his life this way,
though he was but thirty-five.
His mood seemed set to stay
until the end of his life.

People always judged him.
They all did frown upon
the way in which he acted.
"He should know that it
   is wrong."

But they didn't understand
why it was he hated.
They didn't understand
how much he was degraded.

Thirty years before,
he was just five years old
and saw his family murdered
in an alley dark and cold.

Then some ten years later,
the memory was faint,
but it came back in power
at the death of a saint.

A kind young woman had
   raised him.
She was his only aunt.
And then, when he was just fifteen,
she died there in his hands.

It had barely been a year
from his aunt's demise
when another tragedy befell
his dark and jaded eyes.

A courtyard full of people
gunned down in his view.
Unable to do anything,
he watched as they were slew.

And then the gunner turned
   to him,
tossed an evil sneer.
"You'll become like me," he said.
"You'll be the next to do this here."

Following this time,
five years down the road,
he saw a bus of children
crushed by a logging load.

He tried to lift the trees
From the lifeless bodies.
Rage filled his eyes with tears,
and he fell beside them sobbing.

So now the man of thirty five
refuses to look up.
Afraid of what he might see,
afraid he might screw up.

I said that his was not a poem
    about loss,
about heroes, hopes or love.
Because now I've come the line
    to cross
with a steady forceful shove.

This man is all of us.
Our pain, our rage, our fear.
This man is just a tender child
that cannot see or hear.

This man has faced adversity
and come out much more weak.
He has lost his life's battle.
He has grown harsh yet meek.

This man is inside all of us,
making us feel trapped.
Making us cruel and mean
for fear of being had.

But the story is not done.
See this man has longer lived,
and when he turned forty-three,
he began to give.

Sick of all his riches,
his hoarded wealth, and cash,
he didn't do it to do good,
he just wanted rid of his stash.

But then one day he saw
the result of what he'd done.
A poor and struggling family
could now adopt their son.

An old and tired lady
can afford to eat tomorrow,
and the ability to buy a house
lightens a young couple's sorrow.

This man looked and realized,
this man inside you and I,
he had changed many lives
that previously could have died.

And as his past rushed up to him,
each pain and crushing blow,
he began to understand
what we all should know.

A single lonely life
no matter how broken down
can always lighten others' strife
and be lifted from the ground.

Stallion

Golden, Colorado
21 January 2015

He belongs to no person
no group or strong battalion
he is the purest form of free
behold the mighty stallion

His hooves are unshod
his mane, tangled and long
he stands a mighty eighteen hands
his chest is thick, his neck
    is strong

He has no obligations
no need to rent his home
his eyes bleed intimidation
his belly caked with mud
    and loam

He wanders through
    the mountains
sleeping where he may
fighting off the lions
he fears none who step in his way

It is not nature that drives him
it is not fate that sets his course
he lives a life free from all
he lives the life of a wild horse

This life has such bred legends
stories, songs and lore
of the mighty stallion
and how he seemed to soar

They tell of his crusades
from plain to golden hill
trampling out all who dare oppose
his dark and steely will

They tell of his children
giants among their breed
leading herds of thousands
following an ancient creed

"None may tame us
none may ride
none may break us
none may hide.
We are born free
and so we shall die
for none may tame us
and none can try."

This motto seems to echo
across the plains tonight
reminding of that sturdy steed
reminding of his fearsome might.

Free from all, afraid of none
galloping through the setting sun
Black as night with eyes like fire
New lands to roam, are his desire
face stern like a bronze medallion
all behold, the mighty stallion.

Ode to chew

Golden, Colorado
22 January 2015

Chew is something beautiful.
Those brown and crumpled leaves
bring joy unto my soul
as I roll up my sleeves
to dig into the bag,
pull out a blob of dampened gold,
and roll it over on my tongue
and wait for thrills untold.
Pack the leaves into my cheek
and feel the chill begin,
running down my muscled spine
like a subtle, gentle sin.
The nicotine seeps into
my capillary veins.
It makes the world seem more soft
relieving certain pains.
It may not be the best of things.
It may begin to harm,
but fatty foods are technically more dangerous,
so I see no cause for alarm.

In the mountains

Golden, Colorado
29 January 2015

There is a certain thrill
to being alone in the mountains.
It's a certain kind of wild
that fills your countenance.

The feeling of being there
in the place humanity weak,
knowing you have advantage,
yet being so meek.

The animals are stronger,
faster, smarter, able,
yet there you are, gun in hand,
calm, cool, stable.

The beasts regard your presence,
some threatened, some not,
and there you stand, scanning
    the trees,
the hunt filling your
    every thought.

The challenge of survival
brings out a certain joy.
It makes your blood run strong,
makes your eyes keen and coy.

Is it the air that brings out
    the animal?
The pine that unleashes the beast?
Could it be the hills, that release
    the power,
or the sky that brings your
    soul peace?

Who's to say, what magic
    lies there,
what enchantments fill the rock?
For me it is the scenery,
that reaches to my soul,
the purple mountains majesty,
as I ready shoulder to stock.

In my mind I am reaching

JBER in Anchorage, Alaska
08 May 2016

In my mind I am reaching
And the preachers are preaching
All the lowly are leeching
From the man without a cause.

He is lost and is wandering
Through darkness he's blundering
The poor hired underling
Stands up for no applause.

He faces the slander
All the children that gander
Like being rubbed by a sander
He starts to bare his claws.

But then my reaching is touching
And the preachers say nothing
All the lowly are clutching
To what I have to say.

For the man is then struck
By some token or luck
He is freed from the muck
And allowed to see the day.

But 'twasn't luck that saved him
Not tokens that belayed him
For 'twas truth that made him
Free to walk away.

Choice upon return

JBER in Anchorage, Alaska
05 September 2016

Borne upon storm clouds and lightning
Behold a terror so frightening
Feel all your senses heightening
Stand in awe of boundless power

See men fall down and cry
See the mountains topple and die
See the birds of the air cease to fly
When comes that fateful hour

You think yourself to be free
But you are ruled by lust and by greed
You have no strength but to plead
To be spared from a wrath that devours

Blood rains down from above
No more olive branch, no more dove
We have pushed too far to shove
Our guilt turns our stomachs sour

Turn your eyes upon the light
See the gory, heavenly fight
As evil is vanquished by what is right
Will you still so silently cower?

Stand and determine your fate
For judgement has come and the hour is late
You can be gone or you can be great
Stay a useless bud or become a flower

The man at your side

JBER in Anchorage, Alaska
02 October 2016

So what is the purpose
of living each dreary day?
The days grow short and long
and short again
as they slowly fade away.

So what is the purpose
of carrying on through
to the end of the song
if you only know when
you'll have another brew?

You sit alone in a lonely bar
remembering ancient loves,
how they never really worked out
or lasted
when push came to shove.
You sit alone in a lonely bar
remembering old regrets,
how you wish it could have
    been different
or forgotten
as another cold sun sets.

A shadow creeps behind you
waiting for your choice.
Will you let it creep into
    your heart
or your mind
and turn into a voice?
A shadow creeps behind you
waiting for a chance

to fill your head with
    broken thoughts
that you'll find
are just empty noise.

You dwell upon the past.
You think about it all,
the love that didn't last,
the trips and sudden falls.
You think it's just the way
life is really just a game,
and you were dealt a sorry hand.
It's really quite a shame.

You drain the rest of the draft
and stumble to your truck,
sick to your head from thinking,
but you don't give a f**k.

You start the engine and get going
home to a cold bed for sleep.
A couple hours of lonely rest
and then back to work with all
    the sheep.

Certainly you missed something,
some sign or grand big break,
but now it seems chance slipped
    you by.
It must be true, it must be fate.
You swerve a little in your lane,

and your fender scrapes the
    guard rail.
It's not like it matters, the paint's
    chipped already,
and there's no check coming in
    the mail.

You drift into your
    thoughts again,
the shadow ever closer.
Who do you think you are?
Failure, loser, poser?

Hell there ain't no point in living.
It's just one knock after another,
and no one left to ease the pain,
no family, and no brothers.

The war took a toll on you,
but it really doesn't matter.
You still work hard, and pay
    the bills
as your heart grows ever sadder.
You see young John there dying
like it was yesterday.
Bleeding out and crying,
Why'd it have to be that way?

You blink away the sudden tears,
and swerve a little more.
You only had three
    beers, dammit,
but whiskies? Maybe four?
You probably shouldn't drive,
but you gotta get back home.
Gotta get home to go to work

alone, always alone.
You didn't see the semi.
The shadow took your eyes.
You drifted back to the battlefield.
The dark, the death, the lies.
And the last thing you remember,
a flash of blinding light,
twin headlights through
    the windshield,
your last visions of the night.

So what is the purpose
of living, of fighting?
The defibrillator's charged.
It's impact is biting.
So what is the purpose
of pushing, of trying.
They shock you again, your heart
    pumps a beat.
Could it be you're dying?

Who would remember if you did?
Who would care and who
    would cry?
There's no one left now, is there?
No one to say goodbye.
So what would it matter if you left
to that dark and endless sleep?
It wouldn't, no it wouldn't.
Through your mind the
    shadow creeps.

But behold, what is this light?
The morning sun on the rise?
You blink and blink again,
and do not believe your eyes.

The shadow suddenly lifts,
and there standing before you,
a figure clothed in brilliant white
with eyes that seem to adore you.

The emotion you feel cannot
    be described,
peace and sorrow and anger
    and joy.
Your heart is reaching a
    fever pitch.
Could this be another of the
    shadow's ploys?
No, it's much too real.
This man now at your side
speaks in gentle whispers
of how he too, once died.

Then you remember John.
The final words he said,
"He's here, I'm meeting
    Jesus, man!
Hell, it ain't so bad to be dead."
Sh*t, now the tears are flowing,
but you don't have control.
You've become overwhelmed
    by knowing
you had a bigger role.

The man at your side still speaks,
and you remember war
    once more.
He reminds you of all the lives
    you saved.
There are children now who
    wouldn't have been before.

Their faces flash before you,
the men you fought to save,
and those you killed to save them.
They all thought you were so brave.

But the man beside you knows.
He shows you how he bled.
Many a bullet for your heart
were taken by him instead.
And now you see the truth.
How every turn and stumble,
He kept you on your feet
while keeping you still humble

In a weeping voice you ask
if this really is the end of it all.
There is more yet you wish to do.
This can't be the curtain call.
And the man beside you,
with a chuckle in his voice,
says He was just keeping
    you company
and clearing your head of noise.

And then the pain begins,
a burning in your chest.
Your heart revs back to life,
working hard, doing its best.

You cannot see the man
    beside you.,
but you feel he is still there,
and the three that kneel over you
handle your life with care.

A month or so in a hospital,
and you'll be back on your feet,

aware now of a course to run
before the man at your side again
    you'll greet.

So what is the purpose
of living each dreary day?
Perhaps to live for others
to save,
another fight, another fray.
So what is the purpose
of carrying on
to the end of the song?
For that purpose, now you pray.

A second lease on life,
a sinner, so near to death
was given by God himself
in a pure, redeeming breath.
You know the man by your side
is helping at every turn,
and the shadow is no
    longer creeping,
and your deadly lesson is
    finally learned.

The one exception

JBER in Anchorage, Alaska
17 October 2016

So you know that I dislike people
You know I can't stand their guts
You know I don't care for
    their feelings
And I think many a throat should
    be cut

But you fail to grasp my
    true intent
My desire in seeing destruction
I do not wish for excessive death
Merely an end to evil corruption

Corruption of the heart and mind
Of which very few are free
Some are controlled by media
    and words
Others by power and greed

In truth I'd see it all end,
A grave and deadly disaster
To cause a collapse of all they
    hold dear
And remove the prize that they
    were after

However, please hear these words
There are some I would not harm
Some I will protect
    without thought
Whose deaths are cause for alarm

The innocent and the children
The fatherless, weak,
    and oppressed
The pure of heart, without means
    of defense
To protect, I would not rest

My hatred for humanity large
Is spurned by the evil it holds
So maybe I don't want you
    all dead
But your tolerance is getting
    real old

If ever you wish my protection
Turn from your wicked ways
Open your eyes to think
    for yourself
And fight by me in the end
    of days.

Let it burn

(to the tune of "Let It Go" from the animation, "Frozen")
JBER in Anchorage, Alaska
16 November 2016

The M4s pop in the valley tonight
Smoke drifting in the air
The chaos is overwhelming
And it looks like I'll be there

The artillery's pounding like my
    brain behind my eyes
Couldn't be more fun, now the
    ammo's live

Sling lead reload now take a knee
Throw a grenade so very happily
Run and stab, now call in fire
This shrapnel hurts

Let it burn, let it burn, really hate
    these guys anyway
Let it burn, let it burn, stacking
    bodies all damn day

Well now I'll rest in my bullet
    proof vest
Let the battle rage
The blood never bothered
    me anyway

It's funny how some bullets
Make everything seem red
These assholes that surround me
Are about to be real dead

It's time to slay some haji punks
Double tap, don't give a fuck
Two in the chest, one in the head
They're fuckin dead

Let it burn, let it burn, really hate
    these guys anyway
Let it burn, let it burn, stacking
    bodies all damn day

I don't care about the R O E
Let the battle rage

instrumental

The napalm pours out from the
    air onto the ground
With "gat gat gat" as ever
    constant backup sound
A burst of green tip hits a haji in
    the ass
Another for good measure, as I'm
    walking past

Let it burn, let it burn, like the
    shrapnel in my arm
Let it burn, let it burn, until the
    town is gone
Here I stand, at the L O A
Now the battle's done
The blood never bothered
    me anyway

Placate the masses

JBER in Anchorage, Alaska
27 February 2017

Placate the masses with media and drugs
Sweep all the evidence under a rug
When they ask for your stance just smile and shrug
In the spiraling dance of corruption.

Keep the public informed how we like
Blame the flood on the water, not on the dike
Ignore the idiocy of this four legged bike
In the labyrinth's store of politics.

Mess up, speak up, make an excuse
Gush with words filled with deception profuse
Like a rat on a pile of human refuse
In the sickening style of hierarchical greed.

I wish that I had some power, some skill
To put to the sword such diabolical ways
I'm willing in mind, my body built for the kill
As time ticks by in ever longer days.

I feel like my time is wasted,
Here at the bottom-feeder's lair
It seems no good would come from a try
From a try or even a dare.

I have no influence or standing
On which to affect the change I wish
I'm a lion in a pride of hyenas
An eagle in an army of fish.

It makes me laugh

JBER in Anchorage, Alaska
07 May 2017

Oh it makes me laugh it makes
    me grin
This poor people steeped in sin
Can't even muster the strength
    to win
Such a sorry pathetic lot

As I drown the last drop of a tonic
    and gin
I move to the exit of this small
    bar and then
A sound at my back around
    makes me spin
Look at the gun that guy's got

Oh it makes me laugh it makes
    me smile
This poor little fool coughing
    up bile
A knife to the gut and he'll bleed
    for a while
Another fight down in the books

I walk into the street and startled
am I
By a carriage dropped down as if
    from the sky
It's cargo a sultry and beautiful lie
The pan of fate sizzles and the
    fire cooks

Oh it makes me laugh it makes
    me cringe
The pleasures of the world on
    which men binge
Chase too fast and you'll come off
    the hinge
Such silly worldly desires

The carriage before me unloads
    it sins
A beautiful pearl in this city
    of dinge
Of society she's only ever been on
    the fringe
This buxom and sultry liar

Oh it makes me laugh it makes
    me sigh
She asks me if with her I would lie
Such a question, such flattery
    oh my
If only I was a man of loose moral

But "Nay" I say
And I walk swiftly away
My strains to be eased some more
    proper day
With a woman smelling less floral

Oh it makes me laugh it makes
    me groan

The dark of this earth, its peat
and its loam
How all men reap from the seed
that they've sewn
The pains it carries can be harsh

A man on the street there all on
his own
Lucky to only be thrown a stone
Never an ounce of kindness
been shown
Wallowing in the depths of
life's marsh

Oh it makes me laugh it makes
me frown
How the world can force such a
proud man down
He served his country and fought
for the crown
And now he's cast out on
the street

I toss him a sixpence and continue
through town
Past all the trash and rubble
in mounds
The din of the city, such a
numbing sound
Before an odd sight my eyes greet

Oh it makes me laugh it makes
me cry
This world of hurt that wants
sweetness to die

This agony of life into which we
all buy
Before me a man strikes a girl

Accused of the worst, the stones
they fly
She's shrinking away, my soul
hears her cry
The masses are screaming "witch"
but they lie
Before I can think I catch the
next rock they hurl

And I say:

"Oh it makes me laugh it makes
me weep
You wolves who abuse this poor
lost sheep
Be gone from my sight all you evil
who creep
Let him without sin remain"

One by one they slip off the street
Off to their beds, no different
they'll sleep
Pieces of trash in a big
rubbish heap
Society's miserable stain

Oh it makes me laugh it makes
me pine
I wish for a cleaner, nobler time
I look to the sky, as if for a sign
Here ends my lamenting refrain.

What kind of life is this

JBER in Anchorage, Alaska
05 June 2017

What kind of life is this
That romanticizes death
We sing of love and happiness
And dying in the same breath

The avarice of man
Should not be so lightly shown
Implying we don't long
For an eternity of our own

What kind of life is this
That glamorizes hurt
Drama is a second nature
Our response to kindness is curt

The capacity of man
For good is underrated
We absorb the lies of the world
Resulting in souls berated

Few men today are genuine
They are forced into a mold
And spit back into the world
Very alone, very cold

And yet they drive on
Through the storms of life
They rise from every failure
Fight through every strife

If malformed and broken
Men are capable of such

How much more could they
    have done
If their minds were left untouched

The avarice of man
Should not be made light
They long for all this world has
And for that longing they fight

If misguided and lost
Men are capable of such
How much more could they
    have done
If not strapped down to
    their crutch

What kind of life is this
That sees such empty ends
A life that forces
Wills and minds to bend

The answer is not simple
Nor is it lost to reach
Each man must seek his maker
And for new life beseech

The journey remains hard
The path is ever long
But in this we can find purpose
And in goodness remain strong

Independence?

JBER in Anchorage, Alaska
02 July 2017

Independence, freedom, liberty
Chimes the bell in patriots' hearts
Rise and stand, protect your land
Everyone do your part

Bondage, slavery, death
A bleak side of a dark reality
Who would stand, or lend a hand
In a place without morality

Two sides of a worthless coin
Two opposing trains of thought
This duality of a dark reality
Is it all our blood has bought?

People all sing freedom
And claim they have their share
But are enslaved by
    earthly troubles
Their feet fall to every snare

The masses all cry liberty
And celebrate their dreams
But the husk of war cries past
Is hardly what it seems

The population
    shouts independence
And pretends to give a damn
But they know not the meaning
    of the word
They are ignorant as lambs

Independence, freedom, liberty
A dull ache in a patriot's soul
As we drift deeper into our cages
Ourselves into slavery, we've sold

Money, success, identities
Cause salivation on the lips of
    the crowd
They desire drama and intrigue
Unaware their knees have bowed

The masses worship their gods
Their famous ones, wealthy
    and fat
They feel at home in
    wretched forms
Which the righteous grimace at

The people all demand attention
To be given at whim and will
Whatever their flesh so covets
Unaware they are dying still

The world screams in agony
Yet ignorant of its fault
Continues on a path of destruction
With no hesitation at all

Independence, freedom, liberty
A faint whisper in a patriot's mind
An inkling of a need to restore
And remove the chains that bind

But no revolution will save them
No war or death will avail
For their captivity is that of
    the spirit
And their coffins are
    already nailed

They have but one chance
To obtain those three
    mighty words
To cause independence, freedom,
    and liberty
To be felt, not just heard

Repent of their lives of adultery
Relent in their worship of dark
Call upon the name of
    the Creator
And to His teachings, hark

Life saver

JBER in Anchorage, Alaska
24 July 2017

"I'm tired,
I'm done
I want it to end.
I have a gun
To my head
A bullet to send.
I tell you
Because I
Want someone to know
What I had
On my mind
When I decided to go.
Don't stop me
I've chosen.
Just give me support.
It'll be done
In a moment,
With the pistol's report.
Goodbye, my friend,
I'll miss you,
I swear.
But this life
Is much more
Than I can bear."

"NO. How dare you.
Don't leave it
At that.
This isn't some quarrel,
Some goodbye,
Some spat.
You speak of

An end that
You know nothing about.
And by then
It's too late
To figure it out.
Think about me,
My feelings,
My love.
You think I
Don't get tired
When push comes to shove?
But I don't live
For me, or for
My pain
I live for all those
Who remember
My name.
It may be selfish,
It may
Be brash,
But to me
You're more than
Sidewalk trash.
Maybe I'm selfish,
Maybe
I'm harsh
For not letting you sink
Into that
Deadly marsh.
So be it, I'll be
The bad guy
If I must.

If it will save
You from the
Devil's lust.
I care, I'm scared
I'll feel your pain.
So don't leave me
Your memory
In a blood blotted stain.

If you can't live
For yourself, then
Live for me.
Let me pay
The penance, let me
Set you free
If you love me, you'll listen,
If you love me,
You'll stay.
If you love me, you'll hold on
If you love me,
You'll pray
And say
These words:

'Dear Father above,
Look where
I'm at now.
My life has
Been beaten and
Broken my brow.
I need your strength
To get me
Through this.
Give me some sign
That I will
Not miss.
Save me my God,

And rescue
My soul.
Come quench and
Fill this
Burning hole.
In Christ's name
I pray
Amen.'"

And behold heaven opened,
And there stood a man
With a crown on his head,
Deep scars on his hands,
And with a voice quite thunderous
Quite softly he said:

"I have already borne
Your pains on my head.
My child, my love
Don't throw
This away,
Your life which I've bought,
The price
Fully paid.
No matter your pain,
No matter your fear,
Just speak my name,
And I will be near."

The room then fell silent,
The gun clanked to the floor.
The two friends embraced,
Not fearful anymore.
If only all in this life,
In this world, could see
The love of our Shepherd
And what he did for thee.

Forgotten

JBER in Anchorage, Alaska
26 August 2016

The death of a soul forgotten

A soul that's pure or that's rotten?

See for yourself, my brave
    little man,
See what my work has begotten.

Listen now to the story
Of life and a death so gory.
Hear the beat of the band
And chorus of brilliant glory.

Long ago when metal did sing,
The sword did victory bring,
Was born a child like no other,
As a man would feel death's sting.

His work was upright and pure,
Songs of his toils endure.
None on earth could have been
    his brother.
His path, so straight, so sure.

The lives he saved are countless,
The power he wielded boundless.
Before a death so sad,
That left the world, for a
    moment, soundless.

He defended the weak
    and oppressed,

Allowed the unworthy as
    his guests.
He drove all evil men mad,
But they have yet to see his best.

He struck fear in the hearts of
    the mean.
His time far afield kept him lean.
No man can match him today.
His rage is a sight to be seen.

Who this this man you describe?
There are none like him alive.
With everyone walking astray,
How did he keep such drive?

He was a man of mercy
    and power,
Burdened by sorrows each hour,
Who endured
    tremendous suffering
To erect a battlement tower.

He was a man of justice
    and passion.
A whip of righteousness
    he fashioned.
He makes storm clouds
    his covering,
And yet is filled with
    endless compassion.

A king among angels and men,
Sent to end a world of sin.
Rejoice upon his return.
This story is not at an end.

He was loved by thousands
    and more,
But some wished to level a score.
They refused his message
    of goodness.
"We'll kill him," so they swore.

He knew it had to be done,
So they took him, my
    beloved son.
They spilled his blood upon
    the earth,
Thinking that they'd won.

They beat him and spat in
    his face.
They pressed thorns into his head
    to disgrace.
Those evil men found mirth
When they nailed him to
    his place.

To this day I hear his cry.
Why did he have to die?
To save a people so cruel,
To end the enemy's rule.
In agony he prayed,
An iron will displayed,
And did not raise a yell till he said
"Father, have you left me
    for dead?"

Who could endure so much?
What is the purpose for such?
Did he really set anyone free?
Did he ever become a king?
This is horrible, so sad, so wrong,
That they'd kill a man so strong,
That cared for all souls on earth.
And yet they cursed the day of
    his birth.
Where's the glory you spoke of?
It sounds like a tragedy.

I'll tell you, be patient, and watch.
Follow me, you'll see.

In the moment he died the
    earth shook,
Like a quake from a history book.
It wept for the loss of its author.
Now, to the temple, look.

The veil, it's torn in two!
Now any who wish can see you.
But that barrier, it was
    so permanent,
How could it be cut clean through?

Blood is a sacred thing.
In spilling his own my Son
    did bring
Down to earth the firmament
Where dwells my spirit's spring.

With his work on
    earth completed,
Wisdom rose, and spoke
    as needed.

His followers begged him to stay,
But the crop was already seeded.

So he has returned home,
And we'll wait for the wheat
    to grow.
The harvest, come when it may,
His fierceness then will show.

For God became man
To take back the land
That evil had stolen away.
When His blood met the ground
And thunder did pound
The connection was finally made.
But the fight continues on,
The journey is hard and long.
So take up your cross, be strong
And march toward judgment day.

PART 4

FAMILY

Gabe was fortunate to have grown up in a family and extended family who loved him and expressed their love in different ways throughout his life. His sisters, cousins, aunts, uncles, and grandparents had a significant influence on his life, and they formed part of the bedrock of his values for God, family, and country.

Although most of his poetry did not directly state his love for family as a core value, his writings clearly demonstrate his love for family as the primary reason for his savage alacrity to vanquish evil. He penned "A Mother's Love" for his mom less than a year before his death. Even though it was written for Donna, his words hold true for every woman with a mother's heart who has ever cared for a child. He wrote "A Chosen Man" as an encouragement for me in the wake of a tragic accident.

While in Alaska, he would call home and talk with us fairly regularly. After a while on the phone, his mom and sister would get busy with other things, and Gabe would then discuss more personal matters with me. I loved listening to him talk. This trend continued and was accentuated after he was deployed to Afghanistan.

"Wild Contemplations" brings together his romance with the outdoors and his very real love for his future wife, whom he often wondered about and discussed with me in our phone conversations. Gabe talked about his desire to own a 10,000 acre ranch in the mountains of Colorado or Wyoming, marry the woman of his dreams, and someday have children. He loved his family, and he wanted to become a husband and father after his military service was completed.

Siblings!
At home in Colorado, January 2017

A mother's love

JBER in Anchorage, Alaska
12 May 2017

A mother's love is always
Forever, without end
Not dependent on condition
Not just now then

A mother's love is deep
Affectionate and kind
Borne of mortal agony
Bringing life her soul to bind

A mother's love is wide
Stretching far beyond the stars
At no distance does it wither
As it's wrote in all her scars

A mother's love is joyful
Her children are her pride
She carries them through their first steps
And at her last they're at her side

A mother's love is thoughtful
She loves the young one's smiles
Early school day mornings, to late holiday nights
On her heart she's etched the miles

A mother's love is elegant
A child's first knowledge of grace
Strong and steadfast, caring and kind
Warm is a mother's embrace

A mother's love is loving
Simply put and pure
It is all these things and more
Of this you can be sure

A chosen man

JBER in Anchorage, Alaska
20 September 2016

Behold little one and see
What pains befall this world
Careful, slowly breathe
Its colors now unfurl

The blood that runs through you
And gives to you such life
It is beginning to boil
It can feel this awful strife

And yet blood is still spilled daily
By accidents, war. Violence.
It cries out to me from the ground
It screams a thundering silence

Why, you ask, is it so?
Why does blood rain upon
    the earth?
Does it really make the grass grow?
Why is the earth in torment as
    though it's giving birth?

The times, little one, are
    different now
They are turning ever on
But their spin is now laced
    with evil
That would see this world gone

This evil that breaks families
This evil that takes lives
This evil that hurts the innocent

While evil men still thrive
It will not last much longer
But its death throes are extreme
No one will stand against it
Except for one small team

A team of beggars and thieves
Of men with a debt to pay
A team of those who have lost
Of those who now see the way

They have felt the darkness
Whether by fate or
    chance encounter
And they will stand to face it
With unyielding, silent power

They are men whom I
    have chosen
To see such terrible things
And they will be the players
That loose true freedom's ring

And there is one among them
Even different from the rest
He I've held in secret
And trained for this test

He has seen the dark and light
He knows the strength of love
The evil will tremble in fright
Should he lace up his gloves

He is a man of gentle courage
With a heart that's pure
    and strong
A heart filled with compassion
That endures now and for long

He will guide a great many people
To the lives I've called them to
He values innocence and life
He will see this mission through

The troubles that have
    assailed him
The pains he's fought and won
They have, and still prepare him
To prepare a way for my Son

Behold, though tragedy strikes
Though the beast draws nearer
    each day
This man I've chosen will rise
And hold the darkness at bay

And no matter what he faces
What troubles he endures
I will stay beside him
Of this you can be sure

So fret not, little one,
For the darkness will not hurt you
Remember the man I've chosen
He will help keep your heart true.

Wild contemplations

JBER in Anchorage, Alaska
28 January 2017

Eating wild blueberries by a quiet mountain stream
Peaks of scintillating majesty surround me like a dream.
A pistol on my side and my gear upon my back
I fear not the wilds, nor the beasts that might attack.
This journey through the virgin lands, to the place I call my home
May just be a simple excuse to let free my soul to roam.
For when the sun has set, and my fire dims to coals
I can't help but feel at peace, when the stars come out in droves.
The depths of night pushed to the edge by a sparkling firmament
The perfect setting for my simple thoughts, or a grandiose event.
The sounds of life now fill my ears, a bustle so unfamiliar
The chirps of birds, and clicks of bugs, of trodding paws all similar.
Some have said there's magic here, an ancient, noble force
I must agree, but only in part, for this land is God's of course.

If there is such peace, such perfect, unstained nature
Why bring a weapon of war, of destruction, its very maker?
Only a fool comes unprepared to the raw side of the world
Mere steps away from a fight or flight, like a snake waiting and curled.
Such is the truth of a pristine wilderness, a humming mountainscape
Here rules the law of nature, of survival and of
death, from which none can escape.

So I remain quite ready to defend my right to
life against the woodland creatures
And if I take another, I do so with compassion, quickly, without features.
In this wild land I am sustained, by Providence and by the hunt
It is simple living among the mountains, no politics, no stunts.

And when I get back home, to the woman that I love more than all
I will remember this savage side, but tame it for her, since for her I fall.
But it will always be there, the compassionate killer of beasts
To defend what I hold dear to me, that fight I will not cease.

PART 5

ON GOVERNMENT AND POLITICS

Gabe liked to talk with people about government and politics, whether he agreed with their views or not. He typically spoke about his political ideology in context of himself as the benevolent dictator of a country where everyone was free to live their lives in peace and prosperity as long as they obeyed his decrees. Of course, in Gabe's imaginary world, every citizen of his country would be required to own firearms and qualify on them regularly. He believed in capital punishment for capital crimes such as rape, murder, and kidnapping, and in his fantasy rants, he described how he would dispense permanent justice immediately upon the offenders.

He seemed to love to engage people in conversation who disagreed with his political views. Even when people agreed with him, he tried to find nuances of disagreement so he could convince them of his assertions. He practiced his debate techniques regularly on his sisters and close friends who discovered the kryptonite to his zeal was inane or non sequitur responses. I remember him describing how a certain colleague in his platoon would goad him into debate only to find ways to push his buttons. The army was good for him in several ways, but I found it prankishly refreshing to hear him complain about how this individual would blithely invoke nonsensical and irrational justifications to declare Gabe's reasoning as untenable.

Gabe eventually proclaimed himself to be "cultured and worldly" in contrast to his brothers in arms, citing his self-described superior knowledge of, and taste for, fine tobacco, spirits, music, and books.

In Afghanistan, a few of Gabe's buddies colluded to "convince" Gabe the earth was spherical (under the guise that he was a flat earther). Gabe mentioned it to us on the phone once, saying, "Yeah, some of the guys here are trying to get other people to believe I'm a flat earther. I am just going along with it for now to keep them entertained, but it's starting to get annoying...."

Proof of our convictions

Berthoud, Colorado
23 September 2012

Blood, honor, glory
Oh what a story
Told for ages from now
A lasting relic of renown
Built on the minds of the tellers
The stories fly like propellers
But is there any truth left?
Are the listeners deaf?
How do you reconcile
The deceitful style
Of words from the tongue
Heard when young?
How to reverse the damages
Of the ungrateful savages
That continually ravage is
Beyond my adages
Scope of manages.
It doesn't make sense
But it's my two cents
The world needs more common sense
Someone else can save the elephants
The world market is getting tense
The government has put up a fence
Between the people and their rights, hence
Our dilemma of preposterousness
Why am I even telling you this?
What is to gain from ignoring your bliss?
You should be scared enough to piss
But why bother when you'd rather die
Than lie

In bed with the truth?
You're beyond the innocence of youth
For sooth
The time has come for proof
Of our convictions.

Fighting the corrupt

Berthoud, Colorado
25 December 2013

Our hero stood atop a hill
Preparing to do battle
He steeled his mighty will
And looked up to the sky

Betwixt the clouds, ominous
A black ship lowered anchor
Out walked a form, upon the deck
The deadly, lustful banker

Our hero, with a mighty leap
Soon stood upon the stern
Take this ship by force, would he
And banker, of world, learn

In arrogance, the banker boasted:
"Take me not can you
I stand on shoulders of giants.
I, many mortal men, have slew.
Your goose, consider roasted."

Our hero say thus in response:
"Need not I, your petty threats,
For of different breed I am.
Lose, you will, this little bet,
For I'm a lion, not a lamb."

Materialized, a diamond sword
Within the banker's hand.
It shone with royal elegance
Yet made, 'twas, by the blood of
    the land.

Our hero drew his weapon,
A sturdy metal blade.
Forged by ancient aliens,
A bright tune, when swung,
    it played.

Sparks galore, when met
    their swords
Like a meteor show amidst
    the clouds.
Knew not, our hero, the
    banker possessed
Limitless hordes, behind the
    cirrus shroud.

The battle turned in favor
Of our hero, strong and true.
The banker fled and upon a
    giant horn,
A deadly note he blew.

When the wall of grey
    clouds parted,
Our hero knew his fate.
The might of banker's armies
Did not come too late.

Within the hero's eyes
Lit a brilliant fire.
Sacrifice himself, he would.
It was his sole desire.

He would defeat the
    banker's army,
And with a dying breath,
Lean o'er the railing of the ship
To see the fruit of his death.

The hero set his jaw.
His blade of glory, with
    freedom sang.
Through the enemy ranks
    he fought.
On that night the church
    bells rang.

Through the night the
    battle raged,
The hero against many.
Felt the hero, for once, his
    true age.
He lost all strength, and
    was taken.

The banker gave the order.
The hero's head was bowed.
The diamond sword did glint
Above the hero, proud.

His ancient blade was far
    from him,
Lost amongst the clouds.
Began to fall the diamond sword,
When suddenly, the hero's
    might aroused.

A tremendous golden bolt
    of lightning
From heaven up on high

Surged into the hero,
And with a mighty cry

He summoned fallen alien sword.
Fearing not to die,
He charged through the final
    enemy ranks
With, once more, fire in his eye.

Before the hero, the banker knelt,
Fearing for his life.
The hero raised the ancient blade,
Knowing not his might.

Powerful blow sent banker man
        to hell,
Caused the heavens to rock,
The tides to swell.
And down to the earth,
The cloven, black ship fell.

Naught is known of the good
    hero's fate.
Some say he vanished.
Some say to this date
He still roams the earth, famished
For justice to serve.

Believe, do I, with that final blow
The hero died.
To heaven did go,
And looks upon earth with a
    contented smile,
Admiring his work,
At least, for a while.
With freedom abound, he rests
    his head,

But when tyranny erupts,
He'll wake from the dead.
For though death take him,
Though he fall,
Though he grows weak
Through it all,
He will, out evil, seek.
Cursed to live a thousand years.
Blessed to save a thousand tears.
He will return to battle fear.
And evil shall be vanquished
When he is near.

The hero

Berthoud, Colorado
28 July 2015

The hero stands atop a cliff
Hands cuffed behind his back.
Pushed to the edge by a gaping rift,
The people behind him
    embrace attack.

He is lost in his own time
With no supporters, no home.
He listens as distant bells chime.
The end has come to his time
    to roam.

The hero looks down
    the precipice,
The spears pushing him
    from behind.
Surrounded by hatred and malice,
He wonders why he had tried to
    be kind.

They obviously don't want saving,
Their minds controlled by
    their lords.
So really there's no point
    in slaving
to free a willing servant horde.

The hero prepares for his demise
As those he fought for curse
    his name.
He takes a step into the sunrise,
For death bore him no shame.

The fall was long and quiet.
His body crashed upon the rocks.
The crowd of lookers went silent,
Stilled like boats in a frozen dock.

It hit them there, what they
    had done,
Taken an innocent life.
The life of one who had served
    them all,
they had put him to the knife.

The veil from their eyes was lifted
    that day,
And they saw what the hero
    had seen.
Controlled by malicious dictators,
they were servants to an evil king.

"What have we done?" one cried,
"He was our only hope!"
"Who will protect us now he
    has died?"
"Curse this vile, rocky slope."

They began to loudly argue,
How would they live now?
The arguing turned into fighting,
The group into a violent row.

They were a hopeless mess.
They would soon kill each other,

dissention among families,
brother against brother.

The overlords looked on,
pleased with what they saw.
A house divided cannot stand,
which allowed for stricter law.

Suddenly a voice arose
from the back, clear and loud,
The mob silenced, their
    fighting ceased.
The mysterious speaker addressed
    the crowd.

"You thought that you could kill
what was not meant to die.
You thought that slavery
was your destined life.
You rejected your own freedom,
And threw away your hope.
You tried to murder your
    only advocate.
You stained with blood your
    mountain slopes.
So now prepare, oh lowly house,
for your final opportunity.
Your flames of hatred you
    must douse
to be granted your impunity.
For though you stumble,
and though you fall,
though you falter
through it all.
I will be there.
Your fate is tied to mine.

Your troubles are my drive
see the hour, see the signs.
I am here, I am alive."
The people looked in shock
At the hero standing tall,
His head still bloodied from
    the rock,
His body torn from the fall.

They were silent for a moment,
as were their wicked kings.
Then one child shuffled forward
and whispered a couple things.

The hero beamed with joy,
and picking up the child, said
"He gets it better than all of you!
His heart is truly wild."

With a single cry,
the hero rallied the people.
They drove forward with
    great power,
And toppled the
    totalitarian steeple.

They earned their freedom
    that day,
And began a brave new life.
They begged their hero to stay,
But there were others still who
    lived in strife.

You may have wondered what
    it was
the child said that morn,

And no wiser words had been said
since the day the earth was born.

"I want to go with you
if you can make me free,
but can you please make them
    come too?
Some of them are my family."

An ode to the general populace

JBER in Anchorage, Alaska
09 October 2016

Peasants, slaves, feeble
   minded sheep,
They've all bought into the
   sickening plot.
They have no idea that they are in
   so deep,
No idea that they are falling into
   empty rot.

It hurts me, it vexes me, it offends
   me, I'm sad.
Do you think I care about such
   trivial thoughts?
Your threats are empty and your
   body is weak.
I doubt you're the type to ever
   have fought.

It's so wrong, we must act, they're
   so stupid, I'm right.
Do you think I care about your
   self-righteous rants?
You mind is dull, so easily swayed
   by media.
You rush to defend, not the weak,
   but some stance.

And here you've got me, breaking
   my own promise!
I'm doing what I hate because I
   hate what you do.

I don't like politics or statements
   or stances.
But here I am making one, all
   because of you!

You're worthless, pointless, you
   don't matter at all.
Yet you scream oppression and
   indignation at the man.
But you don't matter, your
   equality is lies.
And freedom? You want freedom?
   Good luck with that plan.

You want to be ruled, you crave
   a dictator.
You are too blind to see that
   you're getting just that.
You worship politicians as though
   they'll save you from fear.
All while letting your strength
   wither, letting your mind
   get fat.
And through it all you've
   neglected your mission,
To serve and to govern, to live
   and live right.
You think you're justified in all of
   your actions.
Well, tell yourself that if it helps
   you sleep at night.

I'm tired of it all, I'm revolted,
    I'm through.
These are things I would say if I
    believed that you cared.
But you don't so I won't indulge
    myself further.
I'll be happily watching when
    the fate of the world has
    you scared.

I get it now, why the flood
    destroyed the earth,
Why God started over with his
    precious creation.
It is because we became much like
    we are now,
A pathetic, heartless, sorry excuse
    for a nation.

Just so we are clear, I hold no
    party values,
I don't care about equality,
    economy, or war.
I'm just sick of hearing about it
    from all you.
If only there was some dire
    reckoning in store.

Surely we need a fresh start again.
If only there was some way to get
    rid of all evil,
But I suppose you all would have
    opinions on that, too.
Which leaves me only with
    the thought, "I really
    hate people."

Shit show

JBER in Anchorage, Alaska
11 October 2016

Well this is gonna be a shit show
Everyone is saying "Ah, hell no!"
And everybody's moving too slow
Ah yeah it's gonna be a shit show
It's gonna be a real big shit show
People don't know where they're gonna go
The events, times, and schedules got no flow
This, this is gonna be a shit show

Do you know what you're doing
Do you even have a plan
And not bother telling all of us
Well isn't that just grand

Now I'm a fan of anarchy
But only if I'm free
But this contract has me bound by oath
To be where you want me to be
Which isn't cool by me
Because you won't let me see
Where it is you actually need
Me to be, so I'm not free

Damn this is a shit show
This whole thing's rolling along bro
So why don't you just let us go
And watch as it all blows
Up in your face
Such a disgrace
Wasn't even a race

You could win
Because this system isn't designed
To be efficient, effective, refined.
Leaving all of us blind
It's a shit show again.

Anti

JBER in Anchorage, Alaska
03 December 2016

Look at this boy.
He's good, he's kind,
With strength of build
And power of mind.
Look at him live.
Watch him learn and grow.
You'll miss these times
More than you know.
Watch him stand for what's
Fair and what's right
With sureness of step and
Eyes that are bright.
Look at him lead
With a smiling face.
All the children follow.
He commands with such grace.
Look at this boy
Becoming a man,
Success and wisdom
In the palm of his hand.
Look at him do
Where others fall short.
Excelling in science and
Music and sports.
Look as they flock,
The other young folk.
Remember how they hung
On every word that he spoke.
But look now closer.
What's this we find?
No, it mustn't be real,
A trick of the mind.

After all, he's so good
With motives so just,
He could never be tainted
By worldly lust.

Look at this man
Now rising in fame.
His word carries weight.
Remember his name.
Look at him rise
Above troubles and pain.
Through it all smiling,
With the world to gain.

Watch as leaders
Now heed his advice.
Since he was young,
He's always been so nice.
It's good that you know him,
That you are friends.
Maybe he'll tell you
His means to an end.
Look at this man
With wealth and power.
Corporations and nations
Are his by the hour.
Look at his smile.
Can you still see it there?
The innocent boy
Beneath the mask he now wears?
He's come so far,
Accomplished so much,

And still he reaches out
And finds hearts to touch.
The world bends
To his will and his way.
Just like the children
That sunny summer day.
You've known him so long,
But he seems so far.
You never did see
Those deep hidden scars.

Remember how you held him
By the shoulders that day.
Proud to have him as
A friend that would stay.
But something is wrong,
Though he does all the
    right things.
The magic is gone,
Replaced by puppet strings.
You try to convince him,
To remind him of the past,
But you're no match for his mind.
He was always so fast.
Finally you realize
What's happening, what's done.
Why did you choose
    such perdition?

My son…
Look at this boy,
This man, this saint.
What picture of him
Will the world now paint?
Look at him lead
With passion and valor,

A man among men
With the beauty of a flower.
But you're sick to your gut
Because now you've seen more,
And you know what the future
Holds in its store.

You walk away slowly,
A drifter, alone,
Weeping for the loss
Of the friend you have known.
You know where he'll take
The world from here,
But you don't really care.
You're too tired for fear.
One thing left to do,
But you don't want to do it.
Don't worry, I'll be there
To help you get through it.
Build up an army
From those cowering doves,
And prepare to do battle
Against the friend that you loved.

PART 6

ON DEATH AND LIFE

The value of life and the mystery of death and subsequent life in heaven invaded Gabe's thoughts on several occasions, especially after he joined the military. His first experience with death came in the tragic loss of his beloved dog, Gilligan, when Gabe was twelve years old. He had chosen the alpha golden doodle puppy and named him after his favorite television character at the time. The fluffy, playful puppy grew to be a tremendously energetic dog with a strong will. Gabe studied and learned how to train the mutt to obey many commands. However, the intelligent dog discovered he could outrun the invisible fence with temporary discomfort, as he chased rabbits through the neighborhood. On one fateful day, when a neighbor girl left the front door open, Gilligan bolted outside and commenced his favorite sport. Gabe quickly noticed he had gotten out, and had run into an open area between neighbors' homes. Gabe called for his dog and ran after him. Gilligan seemed to think Gabe wanted to play chase with him, and he quickly turned and ran past Gabe in the opposite direction. The large, overgrown puppy did not yet understand the danger of Pryor Road, a four-lane street with a high speed limit that he crossed after running past his owner. Gabe shouted to Gilligan to stop as he ran to catch up to him. When Gabe got to the busy street, he commanded his dog to stay, but the innocent, frolicsome animal saw Gabe and darted into traffic, twice crossing the busy street at a full sprint. The car that struck Gilligan knocked his body more than forty feet, sliding to a stop beneath a large pine tree. Gabe described witnessing the scene in slow motion. He crossed the busy road as soon as he could, and held his dear pet for the next five minutes as the animal's life ebbed away in his arms.

Several of Gabe's writings alluded to the possibility of his own life being cut short. He seemed to think about his mortality more as his time in Afghanistan increased. After he had already been on more than fifty missions (unbeknownst to me), Gabe asked me during a phone call if I could tell him if I knew how he would die. I replied, "Gabe, you know I can't tell you that, but I can tell you that when you die, it will be your choice, and it will be the right choice." Gabe understood what I meant. He had dedicated his life to YHVH, his God. He trusted and believed that God would protect him, and he would choose whether to give his life for his friends when the time came.

Life Goals

Golden, Colorado
17 September 2014

There is so much to do in life. Opportunities shimmer in spite of constant responsibilities as endless possibilities thrive amongst endless tie downs. With everything there is to accomplish, to complete, choices must be made. These choices define us and direct the course of our lives, resulting in the formation of ideas, dreams that we wish to fulfill based on what we have done in life and where we wish to travel in it. These ideas and dreams, whether formalized into a paper or carried around in one's mind like thoughts on a breeze, are a person's life goals.

Since childhood I have felt the need to fight, to battle for a worthy cause, to give myself to a burden nobler than my own life. It is this deep desire that has given way to a personal career goal of mine. Within four years' time I plan to be enlisted in the United States Army either as active duty on the path to Special Forces or simply as a member of the National Guard. I want the training, the discipline, the strength, the courage, and the drive that define being a member of the military. It will take plenty of time and effort, but of all great things I could do with my life, I feel that service in protection of my nation and the ideals it once stood for is one of the greatest.

In our great country, we have opportunity that is unheard of in much of the world. It would be a shame and a sin to waste such an advantage in life, so in addition to military service, I intend to graduate from the School of Mines in 2018 with as much experience and knowledge as possible. The gates to success that this school has opened for people in the path are legendary, and I desire to achieve such success throughout my life once exiting the doors of my educational career. Therefore, a degree in mechanical engineering from the School of Mines is not only wanted, but necessary.

Success in life is often defined by monetary terms, or by social standing, but without love, life is fruitless and futile. So one of, if not the, greatest desire I have for my future currently is to find the love of a beautiful woman. These words, being written by a freshman in college, may seem suggestive or even immature. However, my desire is sincere and my motives pure. Man is incomplete without Woman. Marriage or not, I wish to fall in love with the woman of my dreams. I wish that this goal were within my power to complete soon, but I believe fate plays a stronger role than I in determining the time at which I shall find it fulfilled.

Finally, I have one goal that is not oft shared with my peers. I want to save a life. Physically or otherwise, I wish to drag another human being away from the brink of death even if it means giving myself in their place. This goal is the single most important action I will ever complete. Again, this goal is not timely because I cannot decide when or how to act until the moment is upon me. However, I believe it is safe to say that this is something I will accomplish before my death, whenever that may be. If I can save a single life within my own, I will consider my time on this earth a beautiful success.

My goals may not be what society considers normal or good, but they are mine, my dreams. It is this distinctive fact alone that makes them important and even vital. These goals will become my life as my life progresses toward the completion of each one. I will live my life accordingly.

A conversation with death

Golden, Colorado
31 October 2014

Death and I had a conversation
He did most of the talking
I only listened in contemplation
as we both were walking
"It's nothing you've done
that brings me now
Don't ask why
Don't ask how
I am here to take you
from this world
A barrier we must pass through
to see your soul unfurled
It is your time
to see the end
no matter the crime
all wills shall bend
You are free of sin
so your reward shall be good
take your time, settle in
live the life you knew you would."

After death gave his speech
I pondered what he said
Something made me want
        to screech
Something was off in my head
It occurred to me then
Why this was so
I walked it over in my brain
If it was true I had to know.
The result was the same
I had to speak my mind

Death called to me by name
I would not be so kind.

"It's not my time
to go yet
I have many sins
too many to forget
I know my soul is damned
So when you say I'm free
I wonder who took and slammed
your head against his knee
I may be dead, but I am not good
I have never lived the life I
        thought I would
So when you say
that I must pass over
to darkened day
I can't help but feel the bolder
And turn to walk away.
For I've heard there's only one
who can truly save
So I will see if he will take me
For I will not be your slave."

With that I turned away, walking
        back through the tunnel
I began to run toward the day,
        like water through a funnel
Bursting out the other side, water
        rushed from my lungs
I did not move as I cried, the taste
        of blood on my tongue

I slowly looked up, and there
    I saw
The great Almighty, the King
    of all
And I threw myself into
    the ground
"Forgive me God, my crimes
I would not have lived, but
    for you
Let me reconcile before my time."
With a face of gleaming bronze
and eyes like frenzied fire
The great Savior forgave me
And granted my desire.

Many do not believe this tale
When I say what I have seen
They think it was simple chance
that brought me back to this
    world green.
But do not doubt me when I say
Death is not the end
There is more beyond the gray
So your time, choose wisely, how
    to spend.

Pass on

JBER in Anchorage, Alaska
August 2016

Pass on
Never quit defying.
You will stand strong
'til you're dead and gone away.
You have come
to secure a future.
With your raised gun
fight on to another day.
Those who are lost
will never be forgotten.
With our last breath
we will surely say
"Freedom isn't just a word.
It's a feeling
A constant shouting heard.
So if I die
don't forget our promise.
You will stand strong
'til you're lying next to me."

And we'll echo
throughout all the nations
across the oceans
for all time
"With our shed blood
we secure a future
for our children
until judgment day.
So don't cry
not until it's over
and we stand tall
in holy victory."

Then remember
every fallen soldier
and their last words
cries of liberty.
For in time
though we are forgotten
what we bled for
will never slip away.
For there are guardians
that span the ages.
Amidst their great ranks
we're just a company.

And in time
when another war is raging
they will stand strong
the same as we.
And evermore they'll fight
without a care for their lives
until
the earth
is Free.

Death

JBER in Anchorage, Alaska
05 January 2017

Though death is a taker
A maker of doom
A shadowy corner in a
    well-lit room

It lacks certain power
As the hour draws late
For it can't quite kill a legend
    so great

So go ahead and live
Live to give and to bless
And when you die, don't cry, let
    your legend do the rest

Because death is a taker
A maker of pain
A sinister blot on a cloth
    without stain

But it lacks certain sting
At the brink of it all
For it can't quite harm a story
    so tall

So go ahead and wander
Ponder the world
Give it your kindness and let your
    legend unfurl

Death is a taker
A maker of loss
A sickening burn in a forest
    of frost

But it lacks certain grasp
When its clasp should be strong
For it can't quite devour a
    beautiful song

So go ahead and strive
Alive with passion and love
And see your legend dance in the
    clouds above

Death is a taker
A maker of grief
An insect's scar on a perfect leaf

But it lacks certain bite
Despite its harsh ways
For it can't quite shred
    history's days

So go ahead and fight
Toward a bright,
    unending tomorrow
And watch as your legend is wrote
    without sorrow

Death is a taker
A maker of ends
A dissonant subject among
    lifelong friends

But it lacks certain conviction
In its nonfictional tale
For it can't quite shatter a memory
    though frail

So go ahead and breathe
Leave the evidence of your time
And see how your legend brings
    peace to the mind

A taker, a maker
Of doom and of pain
Of loss and of grief
It ends all the same

Your life is a gift
To give at your will
Written and remembered
By those living still

So fear not the taker
The maker of fate
For it takes that finality to build a
    legend so great

The man of the hour

JBER in Anchorage, Alaska
01 May 2017

The man of the hour
A master of his craft
When faced with untold danger
Heartily he laughed.

No trace of fear did dance
Across his bearded grin
A man who'd conquered
    death itself
When he took the world's sin.

The shock across the world
Is still spoken of today
When broke the barriers of
    the spirit
And the King returned to stay.

Shining robes of brilliant white
Now burning, dripping red
Many foes rise up to fight him
And that many end up dead.

For though it pleases him
    to destroy
The evil of this earth
His smile remains a solemn one
For in death he finds no mirth.

I watch here from the ground
At the rift there in the sky
A breach of all my knowledge
The beauty wets my eye.

The King who once was slain
The God of stories old
Returns to us in our hour of need
Just as was foretold.

The scene is indescribable
For my human tongue
But the feeling is quite tangible
This joy that it has brung.

Behold He splits the sky
With a word of Wisdom's mind
The soul-shattering authority
Is equally terrifying and kind.

The demons and their minions
Give way before its force
Their bodies destroyed, their
    spirits damned
And the Man has no remorse.

The word then reaches earth
Behold the mountains quake
At the first syllable
In my boots I shake.

Then comes the middle sound
And gravity is nil
The dead now leap out of
    the ground
For a brief moment it is still.

The word is then finished
And its weight too much, too loud
I fall onto my hands and knees
Every being on this planet
    has bowed.

When I have the strength
I look back up to sky
His eyes meet mine and he smiles
And I begin to cry.

The pain, the stress, the sorrow
I pour it out upon the dirt
Finally we're saved
I no longer have to hurt.

I drop my gun there in the mud
And I stagger to my feet
I look back up to the King
Who I am now determined
    to greet.

Much to my surprise
My body feels quite light
A single jump sends me flying
My dark eyes now grow bright.

A smile spreads across my face
And I leap into the sky
As if on eagles wings I soar
Up to that battlefield high.

I'm the first one to arrive
With millions on the way
I kneel before the King I serve
And just that way I stay,

Until He bids me rise
And I raise my gaze to His
As throngs of us now
    surround him
He whispers to me this:

"You've done well my boy
As one of very few
Who I called to guide my people
To keep them safe and true.
The blood you've spilled to do so
Is covered by my own,
You need not fear the
    second death.
Welcome home, son,
    welcome home."

Earthward ponderings

JBER in Anchorage, Alaska, one month before deploying to Afghanistan
11 August 2017

Such evil in this world of mine,
How have they fallen so?
Those people made from God's
     own mind,
Down a darkened path they go.
In secret they plot their filth,
In the shadows, their
     unclean deeds.
The powerful grow more wicked,
Feeding naught but their greed.
Why do they fall astray?
What demons have cursed
     their path?
Why do they feel no need to fear
The judgment of God's wrath?
They abuse the weaker folk.
They betray their friends and fans.
They oppress anyone around them,
And debauchery fills their plans.
Yet so much it is in secret,
And evil power granted there,
That the public has no knowledge
Of what they should beware.
If only one would rise,
A hero and a saint,
To strike down the vile,
The dirt with their blood, paint.
A hero to destroy
The depravity of this place,
Replace it all with kindness,
Replace it all with grace.
But such a hero will

Return here once again.
Again because he once
Did save the world from sin.

And thank His Father
He will return.
For if he did not save us,
We all would surely burn.
For even those called innocent,
The defenseless, and the weak
Would be crushed under the weight
Of sins too many to speak.
But some He will not save,
For they have turned away,
Cursed the name of God,
And lived in twisted ways.
They have killed and raped,
Stolen lives and loves,
Accepted bribes to condemn
The worlds whiter doves.
So those wicked ones will perish
In a lake of roaring fire,
Their spirits there to die,
The penance their deeds require.
And the Hero will throw them there
And free His friends on Earth.
It will be a day of glory
Followed by a day of mirth.
And the world will turn back
To a place of peace and joy,
A place wild, fun, and safe
For every girl and boy.

PART 7

STORIES

Gabe loved to read books. His fiction collection included a wide range of books by J.R.R. Tolkien, C.S. Lewis, Ted Dekker, Frank Peretti, Victor Hugo, Alexandre Dumas, and others. He also read books on US history, war theory, soldier autobiographies, survival, leadership, anatomy, and less intense prose works. He enjoyed action movies and animations with engaging story lines. As a child, he pieced together thumbnail stories into a juvenile saga of adventure titled, "Chronicles of the Gabe," which featured the main character (himself) performing heroic acts of valor. The imaginative vignettes provided cognitive source material for his "Creature" series. An example he wrote on May 14, 2010, is included below.

The snaking coil hissed over the hero's head. And with a quick flick, it exploded into a deafening snap. It recoiled from the blast, and with the remaining energy, swung itself in a large backward arc, just before being yanked to create another explosion of sound.

The whip was a newly-discovered weapon for the creature. One of the many technological feats of human beings during the short time they would spend on earth. It was ingenious really. A few twirls builds up potential energy as well as centrifugal force, then a slight jerk in the wrist sends out a wave along a leather cord which transfers most of its energy into sound when it reaches a frayed end. It could be used to humiliate, trip, annoy, and even slice open an enemy. But for the creature, it was just fun to use around the mansion. Kill a fly here, knock down a spider web there, and even blow out candles. The miniaturized sonic booms were enough to annoy pretty much the entire household, but somehow, it was like a symphony to the creature. A major phenomenon bent to his whim and will. Thus, he rather enjoyed the noise.

From the Chronicles of the Gabe. Exaggerated for reader entertainment.

Given more time on this planet, he likely would have developed additional fiction works. Some of his ideas for new characters and plot lines were sketched in his notebooks and journals.

Wearing his trademark duster and cowboy hat, August 2014

The Creature: An American Hero

Short stories written between 2012 and 2016

American Hero: The Origin

The Creature, as he is known by the people of his many homes, is a being of immense power and strength descended from the fallen angels that took for themselves wives upon the earth. The original offspring of these celestial beings were giants. Not human, not angel, but something beyond. Originally they measured over a hundred feet tall, purely evil, and they fed on humans. For centuries they tormented the earth and corrupted its population with wicked acts of murder and sexual immorality. The offspring of these giants grew taller, near three hundred feet of terror and vileness. The Creator deemed their race unfit for the earth and destroyed them. However, some of the original giants utilized sorcery to take on human form and breed with humans again. Those descendants were able to live amongst humans though still being twice their height. Each consecutive generation since was just a little shorter than before as the giants continued to take human brides. It was among the first of the short giants though, that the Creature finds his beginnings.

The earth consists of a giant sea, filled with islands and one enormous continent. The technological advancement of the civilizations is growing quickly after having knowledge bestowed from the fallen angels, and it is also growing corrupt. A young woman, recently raped by a giant in human form, has fled to a far western wilderness and given birth to a son. She died in the process. The infant survived, though starved, and grew to be only eight and half feet tall, despite being the son of one of the first giants. No one knows how it was he survived, but it was later discovered that at some point during his time in the wilderness his DNA was spliced with another species of alien origin.

Once he could hunt, he gorged himself on the bounties of the earth and grew strong. Returning to civilization, he was feared and tormented by humans, and he was bullied by the other giants for his small size. Bitterness filled his heart, and the evil that dwelled within him was consummated in the desolation of each human town the giant visited. In all, his anger wrought four counts of mass murder along with the destruction of six of his larger giant brothers.

Then the flood came. Out of nowhere the earth was enveloped in water for what seemed eons. Again, the giant survived through some alien power. As the waters faded, and the earth returned, the giant found that more of his race had survived as well, though not as easily as he had. At this point in history, all record of him on earth drops for several thousand years. During this time, he lived with the aliens who had originally saved his life. They were an advanced race, capable of intergalactic travel and genetic modification post-birth. However, they too were filled with evil, and in time, the Creator destroyed them as well. The giant only barely managed to escape and return to earth, to be an alien on his home planet. In his absence, the giants of the earth had all but vanished, and their height had dwindled closer to that of the alien. They had grown irksome, slow, and lethargic; despite being hailed as heroes, and they wasted their strength on show. So the alien lived alone, scraping by on odd jobs. He was a conqueror one day, and a pack mule the next. Still, hate filled his heart.

One day, shortly after the resurrection of the Christ, the alien found himself in battle. He loved battle. Human after petty human fell before his blade as an invading army rushed behind him, cheering him on. The swords and spears wielded by the nearly defenseless country were of no consequence, and the alien ignored the pricks and stings as they tugged at his thick skin. The battlefield was almost cleared when he saw a child amidst the chaos. A human child had somehow survived the onslaught and was lost from its deceased parents. The alien felt no remorse as he walked toward the kid, sword drawn and dripping with blood. The child looked up, into his eyes, as he swung the blade. Time seemed to freeze as the alien-giant felt his soulless spirit pierced by those deep, innocent eyes. But the blade had already made contact, and the young one's head rolled to the ground as its body toppled back. The giant didn't move, stricken by a feeling similar to guilt. As he stared down at the body of the child, a lone arrow found a weak spot in his armor, slid through his ribs, and stopped his five-sectioned heart. He could feel his life fading as he fell to his knees, yet still his eyes were locked on the child's body. So there he died, eyes open and head down, in front of his fifth, and final, mortal sin.

The world seemed to spin as the spirit of the giant left his body and hurled through space. There was no control, no rest, just agony. And then he landed. Crawling to his feet, the giant looked up, and there before him stood gates a thousand feet high, rimmed in blazing red fire. Screams of horror and pain came from the other side, and the once fearless giant was immobilized by an overwhelming terror. His eyes could not blink, and they could not move as they burned from the heat. Stench filled his nostrils, his body went limp, and all manner of worms and parasites began to leech from the ground and cover the alien. For there before him stood the son of debauchery, the prince of doom, the first fallen angel: Lucifer. The alien tried to move, to run, to shout, but he could not. The monstrous king of demons leaned toward the alien's face. "Welcome home," he said.

The alien was silent.

"What, no warm greeting for me?" Lucifer mocked.

The giant's tongue grew dry and hot as the screaming behind the gates grew louder.

"Nothing? Ah well, I don't always greet my guests at the gates, but you were a special case," he continued. "You see, you are not fully any one species so I cannot take you just yet. You should have another option coming soon, but in the meantime I do enjoy terrorizing my possible clients. Let's see, the list does say you're a mix of all the races I love: the giants, the humans, this strange and small alien group, and even part angel, how quaint. You were no doubt bred to do my bidding, as we can see by the manner of your death." The scene of the murdered child the alien had slain began to play in a loop all around him. "Yes my son, you were born to do my good work. How I wish we could spend more time together. You'd make an excellent right hand servant. Yet even in our spiritual realm there are laws governing existence which even I must follow. Those laws say I can't take you until you've had the chance to pay penance. A stupid technicality really. I recommend against it. Only the weak and petty succumb to the idea that they could actually be forgiven for their twisted, disgusting deeds. But alas, after being betrayed so cruelly by the Son of our most high creator I have not the means or the power to invite you into your true home." Satan pointed at the gates behind him. "Well hopefully you'll see the folly in your second option and return to me. Ah, here is your technicality option now." With each word the devil spoke, the alien felt a new level of fear and pain, as if the very sound of his voice was the carrier of torment. Suddenly from behind him there was a brilliant flash of light. The alien's pain was lessened, and Lucifer shrouded his twisted face. "Hurry up and take him before I take you both!" he screamed.

"You know you couldn't right now if you tried," said a calm voice of power from behind the alien. "Come now, do not be afraid," it said to him once the devil had fled.

The next journey was fast, still spinning and out of the alien's control, but not nearly as terrifying. He was being carried by enormous heavenly beings. Angels. They flew past galaxies and nebulas, worlds upon worlds, through time and space until, in what seemed like just moments, they arrived at another landing.

Blinding white light filled the giant's eyes. He strained to see but could not. A new terror gripped him now. A holy and righteous terror in the face of judgement. Finally his eyes adjusted and he saw a man standing before him. The man was rugged and strong, but gentle. Scars marked his hands and feet, along with his forehead. The giant was stunned, for he recognized the man. He fell to his knees in silence. "Eramathandor," said the King, "I have been waiting for you." The peace which washed over the alien then was indescribable. "You are not human, so I did not die for you, yet you have sins which need reconciling. Your spirit as well as your body is mixed between races, so you have been granted a choice. Be punished in hell, where you just had your little visit, or pay the price yourself with your own life, five times over." The alien could not move, this time out of shame. The Creator continued, "I hope, because I love you, that you choose the latter." Looking up, the alien spoke without knowing the meaning of his words, "I do. I choose to pay with my own life." Peace filled his heart, and angelic power filled his body. Evil was flushed from him and replaced by a blazing sense of justice. His eyes faded as he stared at the King, thankful beyond words.

⁘

In a swirl of flashing light and color, the giant suddenly found himself in stasis sleep on one of his old alien spacecrafts. He was careening toward the earth, nearly two millennia since leaving it. The image of the young child he had slain lay burned in his mind as he broke the upper atmosphere, replaying over and over, the look in the child's eyes as he had murdered it. The ship crashed into the North American Rocky Mountains in the year 1774 AD. The Alien emerged from stasis with a violent roar, and broke from the wreckage with an explosion of light. He could feel the power of the saints burning inside him as he set forth on his mission – as he began his journey to settle his debt, and become truly known as the Creature.

The Creature: An American Hero

Far west of Civilization, in the American Rocky Mountains, a spacecraft careened into the side of a mountain, harboring an unknown power. The year was 1774 and things were heating up in the British Colonies far to the east of the crash site. Troops were being quartered in civilian homes. Oppressive taxation and legislation were increasingly common. War loomed on the horizon.

The great alien emerged from stasis with a violent roar. He exploded from the craft in a flash of blinding light. The earth around the alien was charred and trees were uprooted and laid flat. The only witness to this display of power was a lone French mountain-man, a trapper and trader of furs. He was a sensible man, and not easily surprised. In calm resignation, he accepted the phenomenon as a freak accident, a hallucination, and he continued on his way, slightly more hurried than before. The alien looked at his demolished transport pod and ruled efforts to fix it as futile. It seemed he would be spending a long time on this planet once again. With a massive leap he left the crash site and traveled east, for some invisible force called him there.

As the alien ran, he scanned every living creature he saw. To survive without being hunted on this planet, at least for now, he would need the form of an earth creature. A human form was an ideal disguise since it had similar chemistry and proportions to his own alien body. He took on the anatomy of the *homo sapiens*. The human body was large and well built, but only barely capable of containing the alien's great power.

When he reached the east coast he found a set cheap clothes and swindled a drunken British officer out of a knife and a flintlock pistol. All the while he observed his diverse, new surroundings. The streets were often unpaved, unless it was with large stones. The buildings were strikingly different than the ones he had seen in his past. The clothing style was simple and drab for the lower classes and obscenely useless and extravagant for the rich. The world was a different place than he had left it. Everyone in these colonies seemed on edge. Ten years of oppression was about to be contested.

One night, nearly a year after arriving at the colonies, the alien strode through the streets waiting for a war to start. Suddenly, he heard a shrill scream filled with panic and fear. The sound was unmistakably the cry of a woman in pain. Out of instinct, the alien sprinted to the source of the alarm. There he found a scene far too familiar to him from his past. Two males, full of scorn and desire, were forcing themselves onto a helpless woman. One man was holding her down from the back, while the other had his pants around his knees and was forcing her legs apart. The sickening act was cut short when the alien reacted without thinking; the first man fell back and hit the ground dead from a bullet through the heart. Spinning around, the second man rushed to pull up his pants as the alien drew his knife. The woman collapsed to the ground and huddled behind a barrel as the alien pinned the man to the wall with one hand. Rapists were always loud and obnoxious once they were caught, so the alien cut his yelling short first with a knife to the manhood and then to the throat. The benevolent alien looked down at the woman in pity and watched as she stumbled from behind the barrel and ran into the fog of the night.

Turning to leave the alley, he was caught off-guard by a gang of men who happened to be friends of the ones he had slaughtered. "You piece of scum!" they yelled. The group immediately started to attack the alien, angered by the death of their worthless friends. Bullets from flintlock pistols ripped into his body, and knives scraped and tugged deep into his thick skin. In his human form, the alien did not want to hold them off with brute force, as he did not yet know the limits of what this body could endure. The outlook of this fight was grim, and there was only one way out that did not risk further damage to his new body. He clenched his jaw and let loose an explosion of light similar to the one he had used to break out of his space-vessel. The burst did not harm him apart from causing extreme exhaustion, but the men close to him were vaporized, and the ones farther back suffered severe burns. The alien quickly jogged away from the site to seek medical aid. His vision was cloudy and his head spun from loss of blood. Disturbed by the weakness of this form, he determined that he would have to use extreme will power and efficient fighting skills to survive the fights he would later have in this world.

At the hospital, he was met with a depressing sight. Scores of wounded men were laid on cots, many groaning in pain. They had just returned home from service in the continental army. No war had yet been declared, but the fighting had already begun on many fronts. Over half of the colonists refused to suffer the tyranny of the British crown any longer. The alien understood the desire, the need for freedom, and he supported it. Finding a nurse to dress his wounds he gained as much information of the war as he could, and then he left, determined to seek a side in this war and to bring that side to victory.

The alien healed quickly and eventually did find a side. He joined the colonists against the British army. He fought and lived through many of the bloodiest battles of the Revolution. People saw how he fought and plowed through enemy lines with the rage of a saint and the speed of a lion; they saw how he barely winced as his body was riddled with lead, and as he saved the lives of many of the men with whom he fought. Reporters followed his escapades and recorded his heroism and burning passion in battle, so the public could learn of this brave soldier. The alien did not talk with the humans often, and no human attempted to make conversation with him. His deep brooding and silent strength earned him respect and honor without words. As he continued remorselessly to demolish British troops in battle, he started to gain a name for himself. Reporters called him "a force of nature," "a beast," and "a hero." However, only one name would remain for him on this planet. For the rest of his life, the alien would be known to the humans as "The Creature."

Years later, after the war was won and while peace ruled the Americas for a short time, the Creature stood atop a high peak in the Appalachian mountains of Kentucky. Some invisible, inevitable force pulled at him again. The untamed west, the epitome of freedom, called his alien conscience to await his next purpose. The Creature followed. He travelled the wilderness in his human form seeking out adventure, fights of justice, and redemption. Unfortunately, the deal he had struck before returning to the earth required his life to be given before payment could be accepted. An old evil poked at him, as though to say "Don't you feel slighted? After all you've done? Take me back and make them pay." The Creature did his best to shake the feeling, but it continued to pry at him, and he grew weak.

As he sat beside a fire one night, an eerie quietness filled the woods around him. He immediately was on guard. Heavy breathing and heavy footsteps plodded through the woods behind him. The Creature waited, unafraid, but wary. He turned his attention again to the bacon over the fire in front of him. It was an unfortunate inconvenience that his human body required constant sustenance to function properly. Suddenly, an impact like a cannonball flung the Creature into his own fire pit. The hot coals burned into his flesh, and the mysterious attacker held him down. Enraged, the Creature struggled to escape the iron weight that was forcing him to burn. Using an explosion of brute force he tossed his attacker off and spun around to fight, melted skin dripping from his face and black coals sparkling orange in his chest and arms. The animal was unlike anything the Creature had seen on this planet. Large and brutish, covered in long brown fur and boasting shining teeth and powerful claws, it was none other than the great North American grizzly bear, but being driven by a holy power that struck fear into the Creature. The bear, infuriated that at the Creature's intrusion to his dominion, battered him without mercy, biting and clawing at the virtually defenseless alien. The Creature, unwilling to quit, fought back for what seemed hours, countering the long claws with hard punches until he was too weak to swing. When the moment presented itself, he caught one of the grizzly's blows with his forearm and drew a large knife, only for it to be knocked from his hand by yet another impact of claw and bone. The Creature was losing strength fast from loss of blood and sheer exhaustion. Still he refused to quit. The bear began to bite him and dig into his ribs with skewering claws. The night was exploding with red and orange in the Creature's vision. He could feel his human body dying as his alien soul began to drift. With a final defiant effort the creature drew his pistol and shot aimlessly. The bear, startled by the noise, lumbered away, satisfied that it had killed the intruder and leaving him to bleed into the dirt and pine needles.

The Creature gasped for air. Blood filled his lungs. Broken ribs dug and cut into his organs. Chunks of his own skin and muscle littered the ground around him in pools of mixed bear and alien blood. As the alien's spirit left the broken human body, the world grew bright, the trees vanished, and he felt weightless. A figure floated towards his dimming eyes. "You aren't finished yet," it said. The Creature's vision went black.

◆◆◆◆◆◆

The body of the Creature was discovered years later by the renown explorers Lewis and Clark. They gave it a proper human burial. The alien was there for it, and he nearly shed a human tear as he watched his former, now dead, mortal body being lowered into the ground. He looked down at his new arms. They were very much the same as before, but with a few more veins. As the company left the area, the alien—the Creature reincarnate—walked to his grave and placed there his old knife and pistol. He muttered thoughtful words in a gravelly alien dialect, reminiscent of the lesson he had learned there, and ran to catch up with his group of explorers. He did not look back.

The Creature: An American Hero of the Civil War

The year is 1860. The nation of the United States of America is on the brink of tearing itself apart in a bloody war. An alien roams the country, serving justice, and upholding morality.

A scream. Distinctly African in nature. The creature of legend arrives on scene. Flames whip loudly about a tall wooden cross. Ropes bind several black men as they are being beaten by cowards cloaked in white. The veins upon the alien's humanoid form bulge as his muscles tense. "You sickening, vile scum! You bigoted bastards!" The clearing goes silent. All shrouded eyes turn to the creature. The power in his voice is palpable. "You dare to think yourself above them? How can you walk around as normal people when your minds are possessed by a demon so foul?"

A reply: "Conspirator!" They rush to attack the intruder. The alien utters a few barely audible words that will make their way through history: "And Evil shall be vanquished."

A melee ensues. The alien creature fights with immense speed and force. After a short time, thirty white-cloaked men lay bleeding on the ground. The creature sheaths his knife and holsters his pistol.

••••••••

The hero, cloaked not in white, but in blood red and black strode to the men saved from the lynch. "Who ... What are you?" one asked. "A friend," was the only reply. The creature cut their bonds and sent them north, along a more secluded path. He followed at a distance for two days to ensure their passage into safer territory, then he ventured south again.

He was passing through a field, thick with cotton, when he heard a shriek. A woman's voice. Young by the pitch of it. The creature was instantly at the door to one of the rundown shanties that housed the slave labor. A slave master had his back to the window as he beat a young servant girl. The creature waited momentarily. He heard a smack, and then a pair of pants slide down. With ease, the alien smashed through the bolted door. The rapist was dead, a bullet through his brain, before his belt buckle clanked on the ground. The creature whispered to the girl: "Get your family and come with me if you want to live." She complied. The creature led them north, again returning to the south once the family was out of harm's way.

It was on his fifth journey south that the creature caught wind of a rebellion. Firefights had already broken out in some of the border states. Three states had already joined in agreement for secession from the nation. The creature was deeply disturbed by the course the country had taken. It should be a state's right to decide for itself whether or not to leave an oppressive federal government, but the cause of abolition of slavery could not be delayed. The creature refused to join a side, and instead chose to defend the weak and helpless in all the states. He protected the homes and crops of innocent homesteaders in the south. He saved the lives of many slaves, protecting the south from itself. He fought with the north to overpower the south in pivotal battles, and he always uttered five simple words before fighting. The people he fought for and with, held him in awe. He was dubbed the immortal and the liberator, but for those who actually saw him fight, witnessed how easily and remorselessly he took the lives of countless men and rip entrails from rapists and murderers—to them he was known simply as: a creature.

Knowledge of his legendary skill made its way through the young nation, eventually reaching the White House. The president welcomed the war hero in for dinner one night. The creature was honored deeply, especially when Lincoln humbled himself before the alien and before God and begged for advice in this war. "How do you save the most people? How can one make the right choice in such a controversial war?" The creature sat for a few minutes, puffing a cigar. "Pray," he finally muttered. "Pray for wisdom to see a clear path, and then pray for safe passage along said path." A few parting words were said, sealing a friendship that would last but a few years.

A couple of years of fighting later, the creature found himself atop a hill overlooking a small Pennsylvania town. He could smell conflict floating in on the warm summer's breeze. Union forces were massing on the northwest side of town, with confederate soldiers barely two miles out. The creature knew this would be a pivotal battle. The Confederate advances northward would stop here.

The initial attack was heavy. Union forces lost many men as they were peppered with artillery and rifle fire. The creature set up his long gun on top of the hill. There were more union troops just below him. He looked through the narrow scope atop his rifle and fired. Four seconds later, a confederate artillery gunner dropped dead. With the north side of Union defenses taking painful hits, the creature picked off as many attackers as he could. After a day of taking out confederate soldiers from the hilltop, he was out of powder.

The creature ran down the back side of the hill and to the northeast under the cover of night. Shots were still going off, as were artillery shells, so the creature had no problem shooting any night watchmen he saw without being noticed. He had twin 45 caliber revolvers. He used one at a time normally, but once he reached a confederate camp, he decided to pull out both. The creature made sure his speed reloaders were full, and the guns were loaded. After slitting the throat of a man who had left camp to piss, he waltzed into the middle of the campfire circle and started shooting.

The entire camp was decimated within minutes. Most of the men were shot through the head. The rest were cut nearly in half. The creature mumbled a short prayer for the men he had killed and started to move toward the next camp.

Suddenly there was a sharp pain in the creature's side. A knife had been plunged into his ribs. A bullet ripped through his right shoulder. Help had come too late from another camp, and now they were out for revenge. The creature shot into the dark, easily hitting a person with each bullet. He ran through the camp to seek cover. Two more bullets hit his leg and then his side. He slid to a stop behind a large rock heaving for breath. He reloaded, popped up and shot down twelve more men. A bullet ricocheted of the rock and hit him in the chest, stopping at the ribs. He dropped down, winced in pain, and reloaded. These paper cartridges were the last of his ammunition. He shot fiercely with twelve more rounds, knocking down twelve more men. But there were at least fifty left that had been advancing to the hill in the night. The alien charged out from behind the rock, pummeling, cutting, and slicing anyone in his path. He took seven more hits from bullets and three more knife wounds by the end of the night.

In the morning, as confederate troops marched through to flank the union forces on the hill, they did not notice the bleeding alien on the ground amongst the other dead. Clinging to life the rest of that day and into the night, the creature passed on when the church bells of the town chimed midnight.

++++++

It was several months later that the creature found his way back to the battle grounds. He was the same as before, but a little smarter and faster. He found the unmarked grave that housed his former mortal form and laid a rare alien flower at the sight to signify his growth in that life. There was a speech being given by an old friend of the alien, commemorating those who had died in this bloody war.

The creature shook off the slight November chill, and walked westward. A cold and harsh winter was coming. Business would boom, lower classes would gloom, and another war would come. There will always be another fight and another battle to be won. From then until eternity passes. All because of five simple words: And evil shall be vanquished.

The Creature: Hero of America's Working Man

An ear-splitting boom and a blinding flash startle people all across the western states. The creature has awoken. The year is 1914. The wars of Teddy Roosevelt are over, and now a war between the superpowers of the world is looming. The United States is not yet involved, but it is only a matter of time before they are.

The creature emerged from stasis with a deafening explosion. He had entered stasis for a ten year period to obtain a needed respite from the human world. He left the mountains in his alien form and traveled east to seek out a moral fight. As he ran, he felt electricity in the ground. An odd phenomenon resulting from the experiments of an eccentric scientist a few miles south.

The creature re-donned his familiar mortal human form and entered a large city. As is classic with this hero, he was drawn to a place where he heard screaming. A man and wife were being beaten mercilessly by mobsters. They yelled at the creature to mind his own business. He merely chuckled. All eight mobsters were shot through the head seconds later. The creature had lost no speed off his trigger fingers during his ten year snooze. He left the alleyway and walked down the cobblestone street. The recently invented motorized buggy was prevalent on the roads. One puttered past the creature as he walked. Everyone he saw avoided him and gave him questionable looks. The creature's garb and manner were well outdated after his reclusion from society. After ducking into a clothing shop and stealing a suit, he rigged a harness to conceal his knife and pistols.

He tracked down a wealthy mobster and stole one thousand dollars. With this money, he repaid the store from which he had stolen the suit, and he bought new pistols. These new guns were of the same caliber as his last ones, but they held nine rounds and were semi-automatic.

Later, as the creature was wandering through the streets of Chicago, his attention was caught by an open bar. Music and laughter wafted into the streets. The creature entered out of curiosity. It was crowded and loud, but the crowd grew quiet soon after the creature entered. He walked slowly to the bar as they stared at him. Three men approached him from behind. "Ye can't be in here unless you've paid yer dues to mister Morgan. And ye don't look like you've been here before. Get out stranger." The creature drank a shot and turned around. "Unless you've got a mind to get rid of me yourselves, I'm not going anywhere." One man hit him in the face. The creature easily tossed all three back with one push. He instinctively ran for the stairs, smelling corruption and abuse coming from the upper floor. The men chased him and shot twice. The creature spun around and drew his pistols. Three bullets hit their marks and he ran up the rest of the stairs. Smoothly smashing down the door at the top, he entered a large, luxurious office. A man looked up in surprise from behind a naked prostitute and drew a small derringer from his pocket. The creature just chuckled. The two tiny bullets barely broke his skin. Tossing his jacket to the whore, he walked up to the man. "I've heard you've been extorting the business owners in this area of town. Making them pay you so they can stay open. I've also heard you have large holdings in the steel industry. If it consoles you, after you die, I will ensure your stocks and shares are divided amongst the people you have abused. Any thoughts?" The man replied: "Go f*** yourself." The creature muttered: "And evil shall be vanquished." The prostitute screamed as the wall next to her was splattered with the man's blood. The creature smashed open the dead man's desk and pulled out a bundle of cash and threw it to the whore. "Keep the jacket." He pulled out another bundle and walked down the stairs. The bar was hectic. The creature silenced the room by firing four shots into the air. "The next round of drinks is on me!" he yelled. He tossed some money to the bartender and left the building.

The creature awoke the next morning in a gutter. Some men had jumped him after leaving the bar. He was shot in three places, cut in two, and his head was quite concussed. Groaning, he heaved himself to his feet and stumbled to a nearby restaurant. Breakfast was nothing to be proud of—powdered eggs, sausage made from cats, and four day old bread—but it would suffice. The creature left a generous tip.

Good medical care was difficult to find. The hero eventually managed to convince a doctor to treat his wounds, assuring him there was no gang affiliation. The creature healed at an accelerated rate, and was back to full functioning by the end of a month.

It was during a cold winter that the creature heard of a major workers' strike in the steel industry. He travelled many miles to the location. The union members threatened his life if he were there for a job. The creature was perplexed. They refused to work, yet they would kill to keep their jobs. Entering a large factory, the creature made his way to the top floor where the overseer was chattering busily on the phone, trying to convince the president to bring in military force. "Then it is agreed!" He turned to the creature. "What the hell do you want? If you're here for a job it's yours, if you're here on behalf of the workers, get out."

"Why are they striking?

"The regular bullshit. Low pay, bad conditions, low pay. A bunch of lazy complainers if you ask me."

"Is it true?"

"What?"

"About the conditions."

"Do I look like I give a shit?"

"And evil shall be vanquished."

"What?"

Bang.

As he left the room, the creature muttered a prayer for the man's soul.

The workers were getting loud and physically violent outside. The creature left the area. He had no desire to help these men any further.

———————— ·+·◆◆◆·· ————————

The First World War took its toll on America and the creature lived through the entire thing. The men he fought in the trenches alongside admired him. Wherever the creature was stationed, he inspired and lead the men around him, even the high ranking officers. A sawed-off shotgun was strapped to his leg, a pistol on each hip, a knife across his chest, and a rifle in his hands with a bayonet. The creature was known for clearing out enemy trenches single handedly. Also, though, he was known for his mercy. Many enemy soldiers did not want to be there, in the filth, any more than the allied troops. Often the creature would spare as many men as he could. Some deep alien instinct told him that the enemy countries, especially Germany, would need as many of their men as possible to survive after the war.

It was several years after the war that the creature found himself on the east coast looking out over the Atlantic. Since landing on this tiny rock of a planet, he had spent all his time on one continent, and yet he was somehow content. He turned his back to the east and strode to a house that overlooked the bay. Having been informed that there was a meeting of high level politicians and mobsters in this house, he skirted the edge of the shrubs to the back door. The door was locked, but the knob broke easily in the creature's grip and the door swung silently open. The creature strolled to the large sunroom and stood at the end of the long table. Stunned men looked at him in confusion. "Gentlemen! It has come to my attention that you and your kind have pushed down the common man in order to further your own well-being. Now I am a capitalist, but I cannot allow these slights to go unnoticed. The survival of an economy requires a free market and a common moral backbone. You, my power hungry friends, are lacking in more ways than one." One replied: "You can't do this. You don't know the hell storm you would unleash. Our economy would fall without us." The creature was unphased: "I'm willing to face that fate." He drew the twin pistols and pointed them at the first two men. "If you have last words, speak them now." They all whispered in unison: "God, please no!"

And evil shall be vanquished.

◆◆◆◆◆

Five seconds later, they were all dead, gone to heaven or hell or some place in between. The creature stood for a moment, taking in the gravity of what he had done, then turned and walked out the open back door. In less than four years, the economy would tank in the worst depression the world had yet seen. But this sacrifice was a necessary one. The creature walked westward, not even wincing when a bullet, from the gun of a private guard who had run to the back of the house, ripped through his skull and brain. His eyes snapped open and he was looking at the inside of his old spacecraft. He grinned, then mumbled to himself: "The bell rings for round number four...."

The Creature: Hero to the Weak and Helpless

The alien took hit after hit from the large man in front of him. Arms tightened, hands up, and abs clenched, the creature let the blows come. The man, getting tired, paused the onslaught. The creature swung out hard and fast, smashing the man's face into the ground with one powerful blow. The bell rung to signal the end of the match by knockout.

The year was 1961 and the alien was occupying a small town just east of the Rocky Mountains. The town drew income and entertainment from weekly cage fights. So far, the creature was a town favorite and completely undefeated.

There were spreading rumors of a military draft and many of the men were eager. The creature was not. He could sense the disillusionment and horrifying acts of hate that would ensue as a result of the coming war. Nonetheless, the creature did not hesitate to board the plane when he was called overseas.

The country of Vietnam was a hell hole. Festering swamps covered the majority of the land, and dense, bug-infested forests covered the rest. The creature arrived at the camp of his new platoon and organized his gear. He had barely been there a day when the platoon was called out on its first mission.

It was a short helicopter ride to the town they were supposed to demolish. The creature leaped out before the bird hit the ground and began shooting at the multitudes of swamp rats that had crawled out of the forest. The massive machine gun the creature wielded quickly cleared a path. After several hours of intense battle, the Vietcong was routed and the creature's platoon took the village. A few of the men began to question and interrogate the adults in the town.

Many of the soldiers the creature was with had been there for several months already and were exceedingly pessimistic, vulgar, and heartless. The officers interrogating the village leader began to beat him mercilessly. The creature ran up and caught the next blow with his hand. "What the f*** do you think you're doing private?" screamed the sergeant. The creature coolly replied: "He doesn't know anything." The sergeant relented and stormed off.

At the next village they raided, four men decided to relieve an abundance of pent up sexual tension. The young Vietnamese woman stood no chance. She kicked and screamed as she was hauled into the woods. Hearing the cries, the creature left his post and sprinted to the location. The first man was making his move just as the creature arrived on scene. The tactical tomahawk flew from his hand, smashing into the tree directly in front of the man's face. "Let her go scumbag," the creature snarled. Scrambling to his feet the man pulled his pistol on the creature: "Why the f*** would you care? Get the f*** out of here!" The creature spoke louder this time: "LET HER GO." The four men stepped back at the power in his voice. The first man mumbled about a waste of time and stormed off, closely followed by the other men. The creature watched with sad eyes as the woman ran back to her demolished village and her terrified family.

Sleep served to be elusive to the creature for many nights during his deployment. Aimlessly, he would wander around and outside of camp, even when it was not his watch. In the midst of one of these sleepless nights, the creature found himself several miles from camp in the middle of the forest. He could hear and smell swamp rats surrounding him. His growl at the stench of communism rumbled low through the trees. The men attacked.

The creature had only a pistol and his knife. The gun was empty in a matter of seconds. The knife blade snapped when it twisted in someone's spine. The creature fought with his bare hands for a few more minutes. Bodies strewn about him, the alien stood to admire his work. He didn't have to look to realize his arms were soaked in blood. On the way back to camp there was a river. He would stop there to wash off.

Several weeks later, the creature was again drawn out at night. His platoon had chosen to stay the night at the village they had just raided. He heard shuffling and muffled yelling. A few of the men were again forcing themselves onto a woman of the town. The creature arrived on scene with a fire in his eyes. "I already warned you once," he growled.

"Just back the f*** off man!"

"Three, two, ..."

"I'll f***ing kill you!"

"And evil shall be vanquished."

The tomahawk jutted out awkwardly from one man's skull. Two other men were riddled with bullets. The leader's throat was slit, and his manhood severed. The creature walked heavily back to camp.

Several months later, the creature's unit was withdrawn from Vietnam, returning home to abandonment and hatred from many of their previous supporters. All the men, no matter how they had fared or acted in 'Nam, now stayed close packed as they left the airport. The walk to their bus was a gauntlet of disgust. The soldiers took the branding, name-calling, protesting, and abuse in stride. It was almost a nice experience compared to what they had gone through already.

The creature got off the bus in the middle of Colorado, and began to trek towards the town he had occupied before the war. He was in the slums of Denver walking north when he sensed a pending assault. He stopped and waited for the rest of the men to surround him. Coolly, he laid one hand on his 1911 and another on his tomahawk.

"Give us what you got and you can go," one said

"Back off," was the creature's reply.

"Hey this is one of those little soldier f***s from that stupid war overseas!"

"Last chance."

"Let's kick his ass!"

With a heavy heart the creature muttered, "And evil shall be vanquished."

The tomahawk split through the collarbone of one man and the jaw bone of another. Eight bullets flew from the .45 into eight men's hearts. The creature caught an assailant that had jumped on his back, and threw him across the alleyway. Another gangster had shoved a knife into the creature's ribs. The alien easily pulled it out and sunk it deeply into the man's back. With muscles as fast as lightning, the creature dodged four bullets and smashed two skulls in with his bare fists. The last assailant was running down the alley in a desperate effort to escape. The tomahawk whistled mercilessly through the air and met the escaping gangster's head with a bone crushing force.

Leaving the area quickly, the creature retrieved the axe and picked up the eight shell casings he had spent. He was stopped in his tracks when his ears heard the far off cry of a small child. Not a playful cry, but a distraught one. The alien ran across the street to the next alley and scrambled to the rooftops. He quickly found the source of the cry. A domestic disturbance. Inside a rundown apartment, a man was being loud and abusive to a defiant wife, and two children were watching with expectant fear. The creature could see this had happened before. The woman shouted something, and the man clobbered her in the face. The smaller of the two children screamed. The man shouted something and walked toward the children. He didn't have a chance to carry out his intent. The creature stood like a looming force at the open window of the fire escape he had opened. "STOP!" he boomed. The man turned around, startled. "Who the f*** are you and what the f*** do you think you're doing there?" the man screamed. The creature's movements were swift and firm as he stepped through the window, clenched the man by the shoulder muscle, and pulled him out onto the roof, closing the window behind him. The family waited in shock.

On the roof the creature smashed the man's face into the concrete. "HOW DARE YOU THINK YOU CAN TREAT A FAMILY THAT WAY! YOU SICKENING PIECE OF SCUM!" the creature bellowed. The man was pissing himself out of fear. The creature threw him against an air duct and caught him on a clenched fist in the stomach. "NEVER GO NEAR THEM AGAIN!" the creature roared. He picked the man up by the belt with one hand and walked to the edge of the roof, extending the man out over the precipice. "It's what you deserve," the creature muttered, "but it's not what you get." The creature jumped off the roof, abusive husband in tow, and landed in the alley, cracking the pavement under him. He walked to the main road and threw the unconscious man into the gutter. After climbing back to the window, he stepped inside and pulled out an old, tattered wallet. "Take this," he said to the woman, handing her a wad of civil war era money. "It's worth a lot more than it looks. Oh, and that man won't be bothering you again. No, he's not dead. Just been taught a lesson in respect is all. Good evening." With that, the creature excused himself and continued his journey northward, reaching his old town a few days later.

As he walked down the short main street of the little town, the creature was stopped when he saw a woman and she made eye contact with him. It wasn't the usual greeting eye contact. She knew something about him. The creature sensed that she knew what he was. The woman walked up to the alien and put a hand on his chest. The creature watched. "Your heart beats very slow. And there are three thumps instead of the regular two," she began.

"Who are you?" demanded the creature.

"You run a surprisingly high temperature and yet do not sweat."

"Tell me who you are!"

"And despite your power, prowess, and agelessness you can still die."

"How do you know me?"

"I always do research on my targets."

"Wha-"

The blade, made of an alloy from the creature's home planet, slid easily through his chest, and into his heart. The impalement alone wouldn't have killed him, but the metal released a toxin into his blood. The creature pulled the blade from his chest and pinned the woman to a wall with it. "No more targets for you," he muttered. In the five minutes he had to live, the creature stumbled to the outskirts of town. There were protesters at the grave site of soldiers where families were mourning. The creature collapsed in the middle of the ring of hippies and abusive hypocrites and let himself die. As the toxin finished its work, the creature's body began to glow, and then burn, eventually exploding in a massive flash of light that blinded and wounded all of the protesters. Evil shall be vanquished.

The alien stared at the stars above the wreckage of his ship in the Rocky Mountains. He was content to stay in these hills, no longer concerning himself with the trials of man. However he would not be granted this privilege just yet. Walking through the darkness, he sang a few words of an old alien hymn. Roughly translated, he sang:

"No rest, no sleep, no respite
till every wrong be made right.
This life of mine
I give to you.
Eternal service,
I will stay true.
On the world stage,
This war must rage,
And for you I stay
To save a few
To die for you
To follow through."

And so began the next, and greatest chapter of the great hero's life. He would be a killer, a savior, a saint, a soldier, an angel, a martyr. His actions would be legendary, making their way into stories and songs. The entire world would know his presence, and mourn his final passing.

The Creature: A New Year's Love Story

The date was December 31, 1979. It was 10:07 pm. The creature sat in a bar watching the people around him sing, drink, and carry on about the ending decade and the beginning one. He sat alone. It had been a few years since he had re-awoken at his abandoned spaceship after being murdered in the year following the Vietnam war. A new purpose called to him, something would happen soon. He may live through it, he may not, but it mattered not to him. For now he sat and watched, waiting for the signal to begin his next mission. The people in the bar were growing rowdy, and the bouncer was kicking people out. Spying a distressed female at the bar, the creature rose from his seat in the corner and stepped behind the man that seemed to believe the girl before him was a trophy to be nailed and mounted. She did not feel the same, and the creature could sense it. The man made a play for her waist to pull her close, she shied back, and the man, beer on his breath, forced his want as the girl cringed and pushed away. Seeing enough, the creature tapped the man on the shoulder. He turned around, ready to pick a fight for the distraction. His eyes locked on the creature's. Suddenly, the world stopped for the man as fear filled his heart. The eyes of the creature contained a power that is rare on the earth. They burned a fiery green, and pierced the soul. They held no fear, no pain, no caution. They were the eyes of an animal. Men have always feared animals, thus feeling the need to control them. But the creature would not be controlled, and the man left without another gesture or word. Shocked by what she had witnessed, the woman who the man had been hitting on slid down the bar and looked into the creature's eyes. She was struck with fear as well, but it intrigued her more than anything else. Looking away she said, "Thank you, I guess I owe you a drink." The creature replied, "No, you don't owe me anything. Just stay safe and have a merry new year." She laughed at him, "It's happy new year silly, and merry Christmas." The creature smiled, "I'll try to remember that."

The creature spent almost two hours sitting at the bar talking with the girl. She seemed to enjoy his company, which was something the creature had not experienced yet in his long life. It was satisfying. Gradually, something awoke in the creature. It could be called joy by some, love by others, but deep in the creature's alien heart, he knew it to be something more. It was a feeling of true care for another person. Throughout his life, his serving justice and protecting the weak had been due to his passion, benevolence, and mission. This feeling of care, the power it held, it was addictive. As midnight neared, the woman seemed completely comfortable in the creature's presence even as the other men and women in the bar avoided him and his gaze. The countdown came and the creature joined with a smile counting the seconds to the new year with the humans. Everyone cheered as the clock struck midnight, but the creature's yell was cut short by the lips of the woman. He was frozen in shock for what felt like an hour as time froze with him. Gradually his eyes relaxed and closed, accepting the gift from the human girl. Time resumed regular speed as she pressed into him. They spent the rest of the night together, exploring the city, talking of the things they wished to do within the next year, and talking of their pasts. The creature revealed much to that girl, and he could not tell if she believed all of it or not, but she seemed happy anyway. As dawn neared, they found themselves at the woman's home: a small apartment toward the edge of the city. They both slept soundly, exhausted from the night. As the creature awoke late in the morning, he studied the girl that had slept at his side. She was tall, strongly built, beautiful in every way the creature could imagine. He rose from the bed silently, so as not to disturb her rest. His mortal form required sustenance so he began to prepare a breakfast. It was crude and simple, using the few cooking skills he had learned on the dull days between battles in war. The woman awoke as he was struggling not to burn the eggs. She spoke with a tired, but somehow flirtatious voice, "Hey." The creature turned around with the pan of eggs, eyes wide, "I hope you didn't mind if I..." "You're fine," she laughed, "I hope you made some for me." "Of course," the creature replied, "It would have been rude not to do so." She smiled, humored by the creatures palpable sense of right and wrong, good and bad, of justice, even in things as small as breakfast. She was growing to love that about him, and it had only been 12 hours she'd known him.

The woman and the creature stayed together for some time after that. They never grew physically intimate beyond kissing, but the relationship was something the creature had desperately needed, and gave him confidence in the next phase of his life. Then one early spring morning in 1982, she vanished. The creature came to her door that day with flowers. He knocked, but with no answer, so he let himself quietly in as she had explicitly stated was fine with her. He placed the flowers in a vase on the table, and left a card beside them. Looking all over the small apartment, the creature could find no sign of her. Everything was as it had been just the day before, but she was gone. As he returned to the table, he saw a piece of paper sitting on the edge of a chair underneath, blown there by wind from the open window. He picked it up, and read the last note from the girl to himself that he would ever receive.

"Eramath... I'm sorry to leave this way, but fate has called me elsewhere. I say fate, but really it is your Creator, though I call Him by a name even you could not pronounce. I loved our time together, and I will cherish it for eternity as I hope you will. If by chance, we meet again on earth, in heaven, or elsewhere, I hope you will remember me as I will you. As for now, I have been called to fight with the archangel Michael in a distant part of the world. Finish your reconciling, my dear creature, and gain your salvation."

The creature stood for quite a while, silently reading the note over and over. And then, leaving the flowers and card on the table, he left, oddly at peace with what had happened. He smiled to himself and whispered, "An angel."

✦ ✦ ✦ ✦ ✦ ✦ ✦

The card was discovered some time later by the land owner clearing out the apartment. It caused the man to pause as he read the heartfelt words, from an alien to an angel:

> "Beyond the sun and moon
> your beauty reaches far
> Causing my head to swoon
> I wish you to know my heart
> I am bound unto this earth
> until a quest is done

and I wish not to cause you hurt
should I need to run
You are a light in this world
of dark and deep despair
I will always wish the best for you
no matter when, no matter where
So remember me, when I'm gone
As I will your eyes of hazel
And forgive me, when I go,
For I'll miss you my angel."

The Creature: An Epilogue

The creature, a hero among angels and mortals, knelt beneath the willow tree. There lay five tombs, unmarked but for a small insignia at the apex of each. It was the three pointed symbol of infinity, and it was the symbol of his existence. As he walked slowly backwards from the five forgotten graves, he saw the archway that marked the entrance to the monument. It was marked with the same symbol and the simple words "Here lies a hero." Thousands of people were surrounding the area, walking to and from the tombs, all of them grieving. The hero recognized every face, remembered every name, and looked on as they drifted past him to pay their respects to the mighty alien that had saved their lives. The creature paused in the archway as people walked unknowingly through his now immortal form. He looked up, through the sky, through the galaxy, and into Heaven. "May I come now? Have I reconciled my sins?" The Creator looked upon the alien whom He had allowed to serve the beloved people of earth, and He was pleased. "Eramathandor, son of the ancient Nephilim, your seat has been prepared." The voice of the Creator was beautiful, clear, and overpowering on such a level that even the mortals around the creature who did not hear it were taken aback by a sudden inner peace. Eramathandor, the creature, took one final leap. He rocketed over the trees, and the throngs of grievers, over the clouds, past the moon, beyond the solar system, past galaxies, through nebulas, in and out of black holes, and finally, to the enormous white gates. He slowed to a stop. Peter greeted his old friend heartily, "Eramath! Good to see you! I see earth has treated you as it has the rest of us here. Hahaha my how you look the same, but I suppose certain races don't require as much change to fit into their immortal bodies. Now tell me, after He sent you back the first time, and your ship crashed on the opposite side of the world from where you had lived, what was your first reaction? No doubt you were shocked at the progress humanity had made?"

Eramathandor laughed deeply, fully renewed, and for the first time in an eternity, happy. "Oh Simon-Peter, you have always been curious. I was indeed surprised, especially to see a human wearing animal skin for clothes on such a distant continent. But I am more surprised to see you tending to the gates still! Hasn't the Christ forgiven that little incident where you pretended not to know him?" Peter chuckled, "Aye, that was a sin long forgiven. I stay here by my own choosing." Eramathandor, still clothed as he had died, asked, "So then, where do I hang my guns?"

⁘ ✦✦✦ ⁘

Mere months before the creature returned to the presence of the Creator, he had been in the northwest, defending his chosen country from invasion. Hundreds of thousands of Chinese and Russian soldiers were pouring over the Canadian border into the rather dis-United States. The creature, openly showing his alien form, lead a band of just 1000 soldiers against the onslaught. Armed like farmers in comparison to the infantry of the invaders, the tiny resistance stood no chance. The creature fought powerfully through the enemy ranks, inspiring and picking up the resistance fighters around him. However, the battle was horrendous, lasting over twenty-four hours before the final man of the resistance fell with praise on his lips and patriotism on his heart. The creature, surrounded by thousands of enemy troops, summoned an explosion of light such as he had used to save a girl from being raped over two hundred years before. He clenched his jaw and set his stance as bullets ripped past his thick skin. Releasing the explosion he collapsed to the ground and watched as over half of the invading army was obliterated by the shock wave and incinerating light. In a burst of strength, he hauled his bullet-riddled body to his feet and sprinted away from the battlegrounds to desperately try and find more resistance fighters.

He slowed his pace to a walk when he entered a small Montana town. The streets were empty, windows closed, almost ghostlike in appearance.

The creature spied a few faces peeking out from behind curtains, and a gun barrel or two behind doors. The alien spoked, "Americans! Why do you not defend your country or at least flee to a safer area so that you do not suffer loss in the attack?" A solitary voice replied, "We were told to stay. They have to space for us south of here." The creature, worried for the safety of the people in the town replied, "Get up and out and start moving, to the woods if necessary. The invading army will be sweeping this very town before morning!" The authority in his voice compelled the town to obey. As they were leaving, the creature looked to the north. To his horror he saw that the invaders had already reached the far hill. They would arrive in an hour or less. He shouted, "Move faster! I'll do my best to hold them back, just get to safety!" The people of the town immediately obeyed and were in awe of the great alien, dripping orange blood from multiple bullet wounds and yet standing like a mountain to face the coming storm, as he willingly sacrificed himself for their safety. He did not see it the same way, though. Along the Canadian border, the US Army was holding back the invasion, but there was no one to protect the people in the path of this particular unit. It was the creature's duty and great desire to protect these people. Sins of his past had yet to be reconciled even after two centuries of vanquishing evil wherever he found it. And what better sacrifice than to lay down his life for the innocent?

The town was empty when the huge platoon arrived. One of the generals screamed at the creature in Russian and started shooting. Dodging most of the bullets, the creature slid through the dirt, coming to a stop behind an old shed. He assumed his old human guise to be a smaller target and readied his legendary pistols and knife. When he emerged and the firefight began, the enemy was almost more terrified to see the alien fighting them with a body like their own yet ignoring the pain from his hits. From a distant tree-covered knoll, the citizens of the town watched the creature rip through the enemy forces. The pistols were out of ammo within a few minutes, and the knife work started. The agility, brutality, and rage with which the creature demolished the rest of the platoon is still spoken of to this day in that small town. After two hours of intense warfare, the creature ripped off the head of the final invader with his bare hands as his body returned to its large alien form. The dirt roads upon which the fighting took place had transformed into dark red mud from the blood of the dead intruders. The creature, by certain divine purpose, was still alive and walking.

The hero walked slowly away from the small town, moving west. Detected by some seventh sense, battle and injustice beckoned him. In the following month, he helped bring the United states to victory over the invading communists, spilling their blood over the mountains and back. His picture and nickname were displayed in the news, in magazines, on posters, to such an extent that the entire nation knew who he was. Many people were terrified of the previously unknown alien. They wanted answers. Those who the creature had saved personally vouched for him publically, but the confusion and chaos from the month long war had resulted in an even more disturbed American government. They arrested the creature and tortured him, physically and mentally, with questions about aliens and threats and his view of America. They did not realize the mistake they had made until it was too late.

After three weeks in custody, the creature heard the Russians were mounting a nuclear attack on his country of choice. There would be no stopping it unless the creature could be involved. Neglecting his oath to protect all innocent human lives, he blew up the building in which he was caged with an explosion of light. There was less than a day before the first nuke would touch down. He sprinted across the country and did not stop. Miraculously, his feet moved increasingly faster, and even on the ocean, he maintained speed and stamina. His flesh barely stood up to the breakneck pace at which he ran across the Pacific to the country of Russia. News of his escape had travelled and the entire nation watched his progress, all of them hoping he was going to do what they thought. The creature found the Russian missile silos within hours of arriving. He disarmed as many as he could, but he was almost too late. Three warheads launched from their holes. The creature leapt mightily through the air and caught the fin of one of the rockets. He crawled up the nuke as it soared through the sky, growing further apart from its two companions. Flesh and hair was being stretched from his body as he drew one of his large pistols and shot into the rocket. It exploded midair and launched him through the sky. By chance, luck, or predestination, he caught one of the other rockets with his drawn knife. Three shots and that one too exploded with a blinding flash. Somehow, the creature maintained consciousness as he was hurled into the third rocket from the second nuclear explosion. His skin was burnt, nearly falling off. His alien form could take abuse, but was dying quickly. The creature had no choice. His life for the humans. That would be the final price. Weakly, he pulled up the pistol and shot three more times. The final bomb exploded over California, sending debris to the ground, but keeping the nuclear devastation far away from human lives.

The creature flew through the air from the final explosion, unconscious, but alive. Never in the history of humanity had a solitary being survived three nuclear explosions and lived to tell the tale. The creature would be no different, for although he had survived the nuclear blasts by a bizarre alien miracle, his destiny on the earth was fulfilled. His hearing was gone, eyes blinded, clothes burnt off, skin blackened and cracked, and yet he was at peace as he plowed into the ground in western Nevada. And so the creature left his world for the final time in much the way had entered it. A brilliant explosion of light signaled the departure of his spirit from that final mortal form. The news captured footage of the alien as he fell to the ground after his final sacrifice. He had saved over a hundred million lives that day, and the government of the United States, acknowledging their mistake, bestowed upon him the greatest post mortem honor that could be awarded.

A national funeral was held. The body of the hero in his alien form laid in an oversized coffin next to his old human bodies from the centuries past. The first, with a pistol and a knife from the Revolution. The second held a long rifle, and twin revolvers from the Civil war. The third was wrapped in an American flag with dual 1911s in his grip and an account of a veteran who had fought alongside the creature in the first world war. The fourth carried a pistol and a tomahawk from the Vietnam war, and was rested with a memoir from a family who had encountered the noble creature. The final body, his eight and a half foot tall alien form, was laid beside the other four, buried with a medal of honor, and a note that described who and what he was. The final resting place of the five bodies of the creature is a national monument to this day, surrounded by the wreckage of his old spaceship, and marked with a stone arch. It serves as a reminder that one single life, if lived to the fullest, will have an effect so profound it will never be forgotten.

The creature was at the funeral, in the back, listening to the speakers and testimonies of the people he had saved. When the crowd was allowed to pay their respects, he walked up to the five headstones and stared at them, remembering over two hundred years of servitude that had been the best ones of his life. Five sacrifices to equal five evil deeds from over two thousand years before when his race of giants had been more prevalent in the world. He was the last one. The second chance at redemption was owed to the Creator who had heard his pleas for forgiveness at the gates of hell. Being a divine creation, but not human, the creature was allowed a second chance to reconcile his sins, paying the full price for his former life. Upon being sent back to earth, the Creator had spoken over Eramathandor's new life as a servant of justice, ensuring His will be done and the creature's purpose be completed.

> "Though he falter,
> though he fall,
> he will remain,
> through it all.
> And fight evil,
> wherever birthed
> to redeem his soul
> upon the earth.
> Cursed to live with numerous lives
> Blessed to die on number five
> Five sacrifices, for five mortal sins
> Before his earthly pain shall end."

The Creature: New Worlds (2016)

"The year is 3550 A.D. according to the old earth system. It has been nearly two centuries since the great devastation that ended the world that the alien had called his home for so long. His sins are long paid for, but he thirsts for adventure and battle. For such is the nature of descendants of the Nephilim, to crave a fight. With screaming engines, the old spacecraft burned through the outer atmosphere of a strange new planet with quickly growing civilizations. The autopilot was still defective and the ship crashed violently into the side of a mountain on the planet's largest continent. The alien emerged from stasis, not with a roar this time, but with a grin. Bursting from his broken ship with an explosion of light, he stepped into the gleaming new world, yet untouched by the grave evils that tore apart the alien's old home.

The population of this planet was small, but growing. Large cities were beginning to discover more efficient sources of energy to light their streets and power their tools, and with their metal forging skill and knowledge of mathematics already extremely high, fueled transportation was just years away. The gravity was a rich 1.6 times that of the earth's, and the air was similarly fractioned to what was compatible for humans, which meant plenty of nitrogen for the alien. The people here grew tall, thanks to the greater gravity. On average, the height of the male humanoid residents was just under 10 feet, and the females were close to 8, making the hero feel rather short. Their body types ranged from cat-like with lean and powerful muscle, to the familiar soft form of most humans the alien had seen. Their skin was also varied, from a rugged striped green of forest dwellers to the deep, yet bright purple of more city-oriented folks. The alien had not yet contacted any of these inhabitants, but his research on the planet before setting out for deep space travel was thorough. The fourteen months of stasis to dream about it had helped seal the facts in his memory. Unfortunately, there was one thing the alien did not yet know: what language did they speak?

Setting out across the foreign landscape, the hero relied on a deep sense of drive for direction. Something, somewhere on that planet called for help. The hero could feel it, and he followed its call. His body adapted quickly to the new planet's gravity and terrain, a unique ability of his species that made them ideal conquerors, or in this case, an ideal explorer. The miles dragged on, through mountains whose peaks could have been satellites, across rivers a mile wide, through forests with trees taller than the redwoods of North America. The alien was thrilled with each turn and each discovery. Nearly a month after starting his trek across the vast continent, the alien made first contact. A small hunting party armed with what appeared to be gigantic bolt action rifles was crossing a valley below him. There were four men and two women in the group, indicating some level of equality and respect between sexes. They had shimmering green skin with dark green stripes, and they were covered by thin, soft hair. Their build was indeed catlike, though they walked with chests out and upright, and were clothed in tanned red leather. The alien, though slightly shorter than they, took up their form as his guise for this planet, as to best accommodate his immense power. As he began to approach the group, he heard their voices, and was shocked when he understood them. They spoke with calm, deep voices in a language which reflected the human language of Latin. Suddenly they went silent, and the clicks of sliding bolts signaled the time for the hero to emerge from the tall grasses. He rose slowly, their sights trained on his chest. When they saw his naked body they lowered the guns. The leader spoke, "By the sun, man what on earth are you doing in the game fields unarmed? And naked no less?" The alien spoke slowly still growing accustomed to the feel of this new body, "I seem to have quite lost my way, and my clothes along with it. I would be deeply thankful if you could point me to the nearest town." The leader replied, "Someone your size wouldn't last another night out here like that and the nearest town is three days journey toward that mountain," He paused, "Stay with us for the next week and help us hunt, and we'll take you back." The alien replied, "I am in your debt." One of the females walked up and tossed the alien a pair of leather pants, "Those are my extras," she said, "but they should fit you. Just don't tear them up too bad." She winked and smiled as she turned back around. The alien wondered if a wink meant the same on this planet as it had nearly five hundred years ago on earth. When his sharp ears picked up one of the males saying to her "You already like him, don't you?" the alien's suspicion was confirmed.

The hero traveled the next week with the hunting party, observant of their cultural interactions and linguistic intricacies. They too, seemed observant of him, for they had never seen a short, yet thickly built one of their people take down a mammoth beast (as they called their primary meat source) without so much as a knife. He quickly earned a reputation when they returned to the town and the hunters told their stories. They begin to know him as a beast, a warrior, and a savage, but the name that really stuck, the name that he came to be known by on that planet, was once again, a creature.

The alien lived amongst the forest dwellers for nearly three earth months, which translated into approximately three weeks on that planet.

They too used a seven day system oddly enough, but each day was much longer due to the size and orbital radius of the planet. The sun of this planet was a deep red that somehow put out a brilliant white light that made the entirety of the planet appear as though it were a photograph, or an artist's dream. The hero was eerily comfortable with it.

As time passed, the alien became aware of a looming threat to the land and population of this world. The news system, which was surprisingly advanced and accurate for an underdeveloped planet, carried word of a great army, advancing from the far eastern sea across the desert. The army was said to be bent on conquering the world, and many city states had already fallen in their path. The forest dwellers began to prepare for conflict. The hero began to seek out a side, a side which he would bring to victory.

After many weeks of gathering intel, researching the planet based on the population's records, and examining the histories of the different races, the Creature chose his path. The forest and mountain dwellers were kind, good hearted, and moral. The desert and grassland folk were rough and abrasive, but fiercely loyal and honest. The more advanced city inhabitants were calm and collected, very intelligent, but lacking in certain survival instincts. The invading race however, the army from the volcanic islands of the eastern sea, their history was splattered in blood. Since the birth of that world, the volcanic people had stopped at nothing to bend the will of others. Now it seemed they had harnessed geothermal energy and the ability to store it, and were prepared to take on all the other races in a fight for domination. The hero knew what must be done.

On this planet, the inhabitants used mainly canons and other smaller caliber firearms for defense. In that sense they were very advanced since fully automatic rifles, though expensive, were not uncommon. Also, veins of metal ran thick through the crust, allowing for simple electronic communications similar to the human telegraph. However, transportation was still mainly horse-like animals and wagons. Though both were very efficient and advanced in their own right, from greased ball bearings and light metal alloy wagon parts, to the selective breeding of faster, more powerful horse-like beasts. The alien, when being completely honest with himself, actually loved the current time period of this planet. It was not as advanced and overpopulated as the earth had been, yet not at all new to civilization and technology.

The hero met with the female from the hunting party which had originally found him, to return the pants, since he had managed to buy himself his own tan leather clothes. When she saw him holding out the article of clothing, she laughed, "Keep them, I don't need them anymore either."

The Creature replied, "Well then how about I pay you back with a meal, or a knew dagger, your choice."

She grinned, "The blade it is then."

As they browsed the selection of knives at a nearby store cut into the side of a gargantuan tree, the alien asked, "Are you prepared for what is to come? The war with the volcanics?"

She seemed hesitant, "Yes... I suppose it can't be worse than the last war we had with them...."

"Well, if it consoles you at all, I'll be helping in this one," the alien teased.

"With just your body, like with those beasts? I'll believe it when I see it," she retorted.

"Not exactly," he replied, "Do you know where I can find a proper set of guns around here?"

He had asked the right person. By that afternoon, the hero felt like himself again. A belt wrapped around his waist, lined with clips of ammunition and two enormous pistols. Another belt slung over his shoulder with two sheaths on his back: one for a long rifle, and the other for a sword with a blade nearly six feet long. A set of an armored vest and gauntlets later, and the female forest dweller couldn't help but smile at the powerful looking Creature. "You look like you were born for it," she said. The alien smiled and thought to himself, she has no idea how right she is.

That night, the hero could sense the impending danger. It invigorated him. Since he was young he had longed for battle, longed for a fight. However, it was not until just over a millennia and a half ago that the drive for combat took on a righteous form. The evil that had once dwelled within him was extinguished by a bear in the rocky mountains of earth, a bear no doubt sent by the Creator and given the power to overcome the alien so that he might learn the lesson he needed. Since that day, each new body, each new fight, was one with a goal of defending justice and vanquishing the evil he once served. So as the alien lay there, in the lengthy night of this new world, he dreamt of the battle to come and the glory of fighting for the underdog once again. The day dawned, and the hero was awakened by the female. "Hurry!" she shouted through the cracks in the shanty the alien had built, "Get your green ass out of bed or you'll miss the warpath convoy." The Creature chuckled as he readied his gear, "So it begins."

The convoy was aptly named. A train of great horse-like beasts clad in green-colored metal mesh pulling large armored wagons stretched down the main cobblestone highway through the giant trees for over two miles. The might of the forest dwellers' army was impressive, but the hero knew it would be dwarfed by the volcanics' horde. The armored wagons clunked along at a surprisingly quick pace, requiring the hero to run just to climb aboard one of the soldier transport pods. He sat next to the female without noticing at first. She spoke:

"For being so intense, I'm surprised you almost missed departure."

He turned to her somewhat startled, "Wouldn't miss a fight like this for the world! But why are you here?"

"Sniper," she gestured to the proverbial canon leaned against her shoulder. The scope was four inches around at the eyepiece and 6 at the end. The barrel was over four feet long, making the entire gun as tall as she was, with shells that could have been considered heavy artillery on earth. The hero nodded, impressed.

The majority of the trip was spent in silence. The 48 hours of daylight passed slowly as the giant trees gave way to rolling hills and plateaus, and the wide, rushing rivers turned to small creeks and gullies. They stopped to camp for the night. Laying sleepless on the ground, the Creature could feel the tremors of the approaching horde. They were powerful in a way that the alien had only experienced one other time in his long life. He rose from his place and began to walk aimlessly through camp, conversing with the Creator. The coming fight seemed impossible, even with the hero's great power, but the Creator confirmed His blessing, strengthening the alien with a new prophecy:

> "Fight until the battle's end
> fighting for those fallen friends
> Life given unto what's right
> bring the darkened day to light

Finish the deed, stay your course
upon giant steed, settle the score
Fight for them, with all your might
before the jaws of death shall bite."

The alien thanked the Creator and turned to return to bed, when the female appeared suddenly from behind a tent.

"You know Him too?" she asked.

"Yes," the alien replied.

"But you aren't actually one of us?" she continued.

"No," he said.

"So… then what?"

The Creature shifted slowly form, green skin turning to deep tan, cat-like body turning more human-like, height remaining the same. The female stood in awe.

"Son of the Nephilim…" she muttered.

"You know of us?" he asked.

"It's an old prophecy from our own holy scripts. '…and the son of the Nephilim will bring terror to thine enemies…' That's all it says, and no one knew what it meant… until now."

The alien could not help but beam with joy, "Yet another sign it is right for me to be here. The fighting will start tomorrow, stay alive for me." He shifted back into his forest dweller form, and smiled as he walked back to bed. The female laughed to herself and returned to her quarters as well.

The alien was right, for the following morn, the trumpets of war were sounded. Each regiment and battalion fell into place according to strategy, and the hero stood like a figure of stone on the apex of the front line. The forest dwellers to his left and right had heard the rumor, and he could hear them speaking of the prophecy, for it gave them hope. The black shadow of the volcanic horde could be seen coming from the east; it seemed to cover the entire horizon. From the north, the city and grassland dwellers came with their armies, and from the south, remnants of the defeated desert folk trailed in. The line of armies stretched nearly as far as the approaching horde, but it was not nearly as thick. Still, they had to hold this line or face the annihilation of their homes and families. The battlefield, covered in shrubs, short trees, and creek cut gullies and hills, was silent. Not even a breeze to sway the grass. A voice echoed out from the distant volcanic people's army.

"Join with us, relinquish your property, and be granted riches and positions of power. Oppose us and be destroyed. We care not either way."

The united armies facing them responded with resounding defiance and bravery, each in their native tongue saying, "Born free. Live free. Die free..., Born free. Live free. Fight free..., Born free. Live free. Die free."

The battle cry repeated and rose in volume until the entire world seemed immersed in the simple chant that united different races against an undefeated evil: an evil that had devastated lands of the far east and travelled through monster infested seas; an evil that had conquered nations, races, and continents; an evil that seemed invincible; an evil that they would fight to the death.

When the chant halted, the volcanic people responded with anger. Their cries and screams sounded like the pit of hell had spewed forth its tormented souls to walk the earth in terror. The ranks of the opposing armies shuffled, nervous at the sound of a fear that feared nothing, a terrorized army born to terrorize. As the volcanic clamoring raged on, the hero spoke with a sharp and piercing tone to the troops among whom he stood.

"Free people of this planet. You stand here today to face a force that would have you bow and be enslaved. You stand here today in faith that your races shall not end, but survive and flourish. You stand here today to fight. So fight with me. I no longer have reason to hide what many of you already know. I am not of this world. I am an alien to this place, but an alien that was treated with compassion and welcome. So I fight for you. I fight for your homes and your land, and I will do so until my death. SO FINISH IT NOW. FIGHT WITH ME. DIE WITH ME. IN FREEDOM. AND IN VICTORY."

The allied troops rushed forward with a roar of power. Canons in the back launched explosive projectiles into the enemy ranks in front of them, snipers dropped the most powerful looking volcanic soldiers they could see. The apex of the infantry front line plowed into the volcanic horde with immense force as the mounted cavalry units hacked their way into the flanks of the black mass. The hero finally got a close look at those he would be fighting in this battle. They were hideous, borne from magma and shaped by the whip. Their skin was grey and ashy, flaking as though burnt, with stripes of red that seemed to ebb and flow like the molten rock whence they were hewn. Yet despite this they were still flesh and blood, and the hero's powerful handguns dropped one after another with consecutive headshots. The fighting was going well, the horde seemed to collapse before the allied forces as green and black blood alike was spilled upon the ground. The alien fought as he had once before, without mercy, hesitation or remorse. He did not feel the nicks from the blades, nor the gashes from the bullets that tore into his thick skin. He only felt alive. This first onslaught lasted the entire day and into the night before the volcanic horde began to fall back. In camp later, the Creature could feel the excitement and hope that came with a first battle win – a win that would dim soon if the war progressed how the hero thought it would. Small scouting squadrons were still in conflict on the edges of enemy territory for the next few days as both sides licked their wounds. The alien joined a party that was aiming to get intel on the invading army's strategy.

The scouts were armed with short rifles and knives only, to travel as quickly and as light as possible, which made them vulnerable if they were to be surrounded or cornered. The hero was wary as they approached the southern outskirts of the charred earth that signified the volcanic horde's presence. Four of the forest dwellers covered themselves in the black ash and began to creep toward the enemy camp on the next hill. The other four trekked farther east, hoping to gain view of the artillery being used. Setting up his long gun on the edge of a short cliff, the Creature watched and waited. A tank status soldier, just in front of the first four scouts, fell dead with a bullet in the heart. Empty shells sung as the hero reloaded. Three more enemy infantry dead before the scouts could be seen. The hero could hear gunfire from the scouts that had continued east, but he could not see their group to provide backup. Then he heard two shots nearby and the far off gunfire stopped. He scanned to make sure the four scouts ahead of him were safely moving, when he turned to the right and saw the female on a short hilltop half a mile south of him. She turned at the same time and winked. The hero shook his head, praying for her safety. When he looked back through his own scope he froze. Within those three seconds he had looked away, all four scouts had died. Two were held in each hand of a 15 foot tall monster of a volcanic. The burning yellow eyes seemed to stare straight into the alien's as it dropped the four dead scouts and began walking toward the cliffs.

The Creature whispered a prayer and begged forgiveness for the four lives he had failed. "For those fallen friends." Leaving his long gun where it lay, he shouted to the female to leave the area. She heard the tone in his voice and obeyed. The Creature ran toward the giant among giants, barely dodging the bullets from the beast's hand cannon. The alien was barely more than half the height of the monster, but his passion drove him forward. The beast dropped its gun and drew an enormous sword, taller than the alien. The hero fired the remaining bullets in his handguns, peppering the beasts arms, and drew his own sword. He did not slow pace as he blocked the monster's first swing and slid between its legs. Spinning back around he nearly missed being beheaded by a lightning fast swing. Block, parry, spin, attack, miss, block, parry.... The hero could barely keep up with the brutally-fast monster. He began to grow tired, and the great monster's blade made contact: in a clean, powerful swipe the alien's leg was torn from his body and he fell to the ground. In a last ditch effort he drew a pistol and placed a bullet between the beasts eyes, just enough to stun it. He dragged his body out of sword range and clenched his teeth. An explosion of heat and light shot forth from his heart, cauterizing his wound and knocking the giant back nearly fifty yards with severe burns. The hero, faint from the effort, stood slowly to balance on his remaining leg. He walked up to the unconscious giant and lifted its sword from its hand. With a painful yell the hero swung the blade over his head and decapitated the monster. Immediately afterward he collapsed to the ground, unable to move.

He lay there for three days of that planet's time. Two more battles had been fought by the time he regained consciousness. "Finish the deed, stay the course." His sharp ears picked up the sound of a nearby fight. More giants. The volcanics had released an army of giants. Crawling to the top of a hill, the Creature squinted through his bloodied hair and saw a dismaying sight. Sixteen, eighteen, twenty-foot tall monsters were tearing apart the allied ranks. Battle tanks, powered by the planet's heat, shot down and crushed those on the front lines while pouring black, sulfuric smoke into the air. The allied cavalry's attempt to respond was futile as the giant volcanics threw their steeds into the air with swift, well aimed kicks.

Sorrowful and rage filled, the creature on his remaining leg and let out a roar that shook the earth. The fighting seemed to still as troops from both sides looked at the small hero, a shadow of a figure standing on a hill with the sun creating a wreath of fire around him. Out of nowhere a mammoth deer-like animal appeared next to him. Struggling to stay balanced, the Creature swung himself to the animal's back and set his hands on the metallic horns. "Upon giant steed."

The strength of the animal on which he rode was palpable to the alien. As he barreled towards the battle, he could feel surges of energy entering him from the animal. It was an unnatural, immortal energy that could only be from the Creator. Refreshed and invigorated, the hero drew his giant pistols and loaded them, holding onto the animal with one hand at a time. Once he got close, he started shooting. It took an entire clip of bullets unloaded to a giant's head to kill it. The Creature had to work fast. Releasing both hands from the horns of the animal, he dual wielded the guns taking down the sixteen and eighteen-foot giants one by one, roaring a deep alien battle cry the entire time. The allied troops looked in awe and the volcanics looked in fear. "The son of the Nephilim..." they all muttered. The mammoth deer upon which the hero rode trampled over the corpses of the fallen giants, and gored the ones still living with six foot long horns. It was quick and agile for its size, keeping the alien safe by dodging shots from the battle tanks and leaping over the shorter soldiers. The hero was running low on ammo, but kept shooting. A sword was swinging toward his neck when the last bullet flew into a giant's head. It didn't work. The hero watched in slow motion, as the blade neared his throat. Suddenly a bullet the size of a football blew the giant's head clean off and the sword just nicked the hero's shoulder. He looked back across the battlefield. The female stood there, rifle smoking, and nodded to the Creature. He smiled. "And evil shall be vanquished," he said.

Leaping from the giant steed, the hero drew his sword.
With a strength not his own, he kept unto his word.
With fire from the heavens, he cut into the horde,
Fighting on just one leg, as we all have heard.
He did not feel the bullets, as they tore his flesh
He did not feel the sword, lodged deep into his chest

One by one the giants fell, like bloodied cotton mesh
Before the Hero and his sword, and you all know the rest.
   As he slew the final beast, and ended our great war
   He let go a flash of light, and left our planet's floor
Though we all did mourn, and though he had died
We had always felt, he still walked by our side
And return one day he would, to see what he had bought
To see the peaceful world, that his death had wrought."

"And that's the story of the son of the Nephilim, Children," said the female as she finished the poem from the history book and set it down. The kids, her kids, at her feet clapped and spoke to each other in awe. Running off, she could hear them acting out the story they had just heard. "You be the female, I'll be the hero, and he can be the monster!" one said. "Why do I have to be the monster again?" whined the larger of the three. The female smiled to herself. They were beautiful children and she was proud. They were shorter than most of the kids their age, but built strong like their father. Her husband walked in and set down his rifle, dinner slung over his shoulder. He smiled as he kissed her. And laughed as his children welcomed him with a great bear hug. "Yes children," the female thought to herself, "that's the story of the Son of the Nephilim, the hero, the alien, the Creature. That's the story of how our world defeated evil and found peace. That's the story of your father, my husband."

That night the alien lay awake beside the female. He was glad, for he had found a happiness that he had never known. Yet something still called to him. There were still wars to fight, and evil to vanquish. Soon his sons and daughter would be old enough to fight alongside him. Soon could still be too late though. He could feel it. Another war was coming.

The Bears

Short story, Berthoud, Colorado
06 January 2014

Walking through the mountains next to a creek one afternoon in early spring, I noticed a change in the air around me. I had been camping for several days, and had grown accustomed to the regular smell of pine and dirt and water, and even that of many animals. But this was something new that sent shivers down my spine. Laying a hand on my .357, I stopped walking. I slowly drew the powerful revolver and brought it up next to my ear, at the same time unsheathing my long bowie knife. The change in the air was more potent, as if the source was drawing nearer. I stepped in slow circles, scanning the forest around me. This was an extremely un-ideal spot to be cornered. Steep grades dropped on either side and dense, brookside forest loomed in front and back. My head snapped to the left when I heard a tree branch crack as if under foot. I scrambled up the opposite finger about half way and peered through the trees. Nothing seemed to be moving, but I could sense the presence of a very large animal. The snort behind me caught me fully off guard, and, leaping several feet into the air, I spun around with my revolver braced and readied. The next series of events are blurred together in my mind. I remember running frantically through the forest, yelling, shooting, stopping only when the ground beneath me gave way in a sudden cliff. I remember waking up in a ravine with blood pouring from my leg. Somehow, I managed to bandage the gash while drifting in and out of consciousness. It was deep, but not so deep as to remove the use of my leg. Standing with the boulder that broke my fall as a brace, I squinted at the top of the gorge. There would be no climbing out. Looking around my feet, I found my revolver, scratched, but functional. My bowie knife was nearby as well. Covered in my own blood from when it hit my leg during my fall. I could still smell the presence of the massive beast that drove me there, and I vowed that evening to bring its life to an end. With renewed energy and rage, I drag-limped back to my camp, taking the high paths and ridges to avoid the dense forest. The cold light of the moon and stars was an hour through its course before I reached my tent and truck. By firelight, I rebandaged my leg in a more sanitary manner, and prepared for the next morning. When I awoke, the sun was well in the sky, the smell of the beast still lingered. I limped out of my tent and ate a small breakfast of cold bacon and tortillas. The fire had burned low, so I splashed water on it to finish it off before I set out on my hunt. I double checked my revolver, ensuring I had the high grain loads and a full cylinder. I retrieved the rifle from behind the seat of my truck and loaded it with high powered rounds. I chambered a bullet and decocked the bolt. Driving from my camp, I could still smell the beast. Miles went by on the winding dirt roads before I reached my destination. The path ended at a high, grassy knoll overlooking miles of rolling mountains. I could see with keen eyes, my camp in the far distance. I peered through binoculars to search out the beast that had tormented me. When I laid eyes on the monster, it took me nigh on five minutes to convince myself I wasn't hallucinating. It was a bear, but not a normal one. It was not a grizzly or a black bear, or even a lost polar bear. The beast walked on its hind legs like a human, and held a massive staff-like war hammer in its right paw. In a bizarre sense of civility, it was wearing a deerskin loincloth and hood. Despite its humanish behavior, it was obviously bear. Long claws were borne on each extremity, and a black nose sniffed the air from under the shade of the hood. Long, course gray fur covered all but the animal's chest. I pulled the binoculars from my face, my mouth pursed in deep anxiety. When I looked through the glasses again, the animal was walking down the path that led to my location. I prepared my rifle, and lay flat in the grass, ready for an impossible shot. I looked through the binoculars again, and as if the animal could feel my gaze, I saw it look directly at me and snarl. I immediately dropped the field glasses and aimed my rifle. The first shot was far low and left from the wind. I adjusted, the second shot punctured the hood, but missed the head. The third shot ricocheted off of the huge hammer. All the while the beast ran toward me. As it barreled up the hill, I stood and aimed, waiting. It had covered the miles in impressive time. Now, as it neared the top of my knoll, it would meet its end. I waited till I could see the blood-red eyes and smell the foul breath. I fired. The bullet ripped through the monster's chest, exploding the heart. The beast fell before me, twitching. I fired twice into its head with my revolver. The muscles of the giant animal relaxed as the life drained from them. Its huge stone hammer lay next to it in the grass. I felt relieved, that the deed was done. I felt no remorse or desire to bury the animal as I walked back to my truck. I tossed my rifle on the seat and crossed my arms to rest my head on the steering wheel. I needed to drive to town and get my leg looked at, but I wouldn't have the chance right away. I was shocked out of my rest when my truck jolted sideways with a deafening crunch. I looked around frantically and saw the source of the crash. Another of the giant beasts had come to its brother's aid too late. I leaped from the opposite door and rolled into the long grass, drawing my pistol. Three reports rang over the hills and the second beast collapsed to the ground with three bullets in its chest. I winced, as the jump from my truck had impacted my injured leg. Standing up slowly, I examined the damage to the frame of my truck. I would have to walk back. I reloaded both of my guns and grabbed the half empty water bottle out of my truck seat. Setting off in the late afternoon, I journeyed east. The nearest town was ten miles away in a straight line, but it was nearly twenty with the route I would need to take. I don't remember much of the walk. It took the entire night and most of the next day due to my injury and the terrain. I remember wolves howling around me, rain pouring down my face, and darkness. Although it was daylight when I arrived at the general store, I could barely see due to dehydration and exhaustion. I collapsed into a lump on the floor, fleeting shadows darting above my eyes. When I reawoke, I found myself in a hospital bed. I pulled the hoses and sensors from my skin and limped to my clothes. Once dressed I left the hospital, thanking the nurses on my way out. The fresh mountain air outside was a relief. It smelled natural and clean again. Three days of hitchhiking later, I was home. It would be years before I returned to the fated location of my encounter with the beasts. When I did, I found but a few bones left of the giant animals. And a mere shell of a truck between them. But it was enough. Enough to prove that what happened over those few days was real. That I was not crazy. And that I had survived.

Friday the 13th

Berthoud, Colorado
26 October 2014

Gore and blood, chainsaws rip
Machete's cleave, spine from hip
Misfortune and shame
Are all that is left of a once
      great name…

Friday the 13th is a
      twisted delusion
Of a once great celebration of
      mass confusion.
People would dance, and
      merrily sing
Above roaring fires their voices
      would ring
The night would end with the
      break of dawn,
And the people would return to
      their tents with a yawn.
For it was all in fun,
      goodwill, merriment
It was not till recently that Friday
      the 13th began its descent.

It was a dark and cold night, in
      June of 1874
That young Rosie Smith crept
      'cross the wood floor
Each step was a creak, and each
      breath a whine
When suddenly a squeak, came
      from behind.
Rosie turned to face the source.

Her scream echoed through
      the woods.
It was that fated Thursday
      the 12th
That evil replaced good.

The following day the sheriff
      rode in
The parents sat in shock to
      the side.
The sheriff silently nodded
      his chin
And walked through the door
      in stride.
The scene was brutal, not fit
      for description
For those faint of stomach would
      have a conniption.
Suffice it to say, in a twisted
      display of horrid fates,
There lie the evidence of a
      satanic tradition.

The sheriff was a good man,
      though hardened inside
However this gruesome tribute to
      death made him decide
Too seek out the cult responsible
      for this murder
And bring them to justice with a
      Colt .45

The day of searching was long
and hard.
And the sheriff was tired as he
returned to his yard.
A party of the 13th raged through
the night.
When at about 2 AM he woke
with a fright.

No one knows how he knew,
and no one will forget what
he did.
Stepping into a circle of dancers,
he called out to all that hid
Behind masks to show their face.

The towns people obeyed with
cheers and hollers
And threw their masks up
towards space.
One sole individual did not
follow suit.
The sheriff readied his gun
to shoot.
Six bullets tore a path straight
and true.
The lone masked man his last
breath blew.

The gaping hole in the
murderer's head
Made it impossible to tell who
he was
And the sheriff's sanity
was questioned.

But before any could speak, he
walked to the body
And stilled the
building aggression.

For from the pocket of the
man deceased
The sheriff drew a bloody
knife, with
this came an evident piece
Of the dress belonging to poor
Rosie Smith.
The sheriff was hailed a hero
For killing the murderer at large
But he felt to be worth less
than zero
For letting a killer get that far.

So although the story ends well,
With minimal suspense and gore,
This version doesn't sell.
People beg for more.

Instead of honoring a noble act
They glorify lust and death
Rumors spread and stories stretch
To make one hold his breath.

So there it is, plain and good,
The true story of justice the
public tries to demean.
Remember it, like you should,
The real meaning of the
Friday, thirteen.

The guitarist

Golden, Colorado
27 October 2014

The guitarist sang with eloquence
His twangy strum enthralled.
He played from sheer benevolence
His words were meant for all.

He sat upon his corner
Day after toilsome day,
Bringing joy to those around
When they'd pass his way.

He didn't make much in the way
    of a decent living,
But he did fine and didn't mind,
    he just cared about giving.

As the years dragged on,
He began to grow a little frail.
His voice grew a little softer
His skin began to pale.

Still he played his heart out
To the people of the street,
No matter the time or weather
With a smile he did greet.

He had become a figure
That some barely payed mind,
A symbol of an older time
When people were more kind.

One morning as he played
A group of teens stopped by.

He asked if they'd like to stay
He had a new song to try.

One of them threw an insult
Another a sly retort,
They were only there to pester
They saw it as a sport.

But then the old guitarist
Began his new formed song,
And the group of boys went silent
Stopped and listened long.
For he sung about their histories
Each pain and trial and spill.
He sung about their futures
Each success and failure
    and thrill.

And then he sung about
    them now,
And what they each could be,
If they made one simple change
To open their eyes and see.

The melody swelled with each
    mighty chord,
The solo filled the street.
The boys each saw a younger man
than sat there at their feet.

They saw him as he was,
Deep in his gentle heart.

He had chosen blessing others
As his work and art.

Then he ended his song
With a quiet plucking strum,
A little tap on silenced strings
And a harmonizing hum.

And eyes closed in perfect peace
He left the world then,
The boys that had walked up
    to him
Walked away as men.

They all attended the funeral
Of the old guitarist,
And thanked him for
    the guidance
The wisdom of a simple artist.

As they went on their way,
They seemed to hear the breeze
Whisper of the mountains tall
And of the stormy seas,
Of the past so hard,
And the future yet to be,
Of an old guitarist,
And the things that he had seen.

The fighter

Golden, Colorado
02 December 2014

The fighter stands in
    sacred silence
His mind as quick as his fists
He stands his ground in
    calm defiance
Three dark figures loom in
    the mist
It had been a while since he'd felt
    the crack
of colliding flesh and bone
But he would lose no time in
    the attack
his skills are always honed.
A girl cowered behind him
fearing for her life
The fighter, stanced and ready
heard the click of an
    opening knife.
"Just let us have her for a go"
    they said
"We promise to be ... gentle"
"Don't you dare" the
    fighter replied,
"You bastards are all mental."

The figures walked speedily
through the moonlit shroud
The first one met a grisly fate
As his neck snapped loud
The other two, now cautious
prepared to jump together
The fighter had a fist for each

knuckles clothed in leather.
They leaped to him,
    blades flashing
The fighter stepped back quickly,
They swung again, missing still
The pail moon's light was sickly
The third time they
    made contact,
but the fighter did as well
Two knives jammed into his ribs
Two rapists, straight to hell.

The fighter took a knee,
struggling to breathe
the girl he saved was stunned
and stared in disbelief
"You're hurt," she
    feebly whispered
as she walked up to his side
"Better me than you," said
    the fighter
"It wouldn't matter if I died."

The world began to fade
In the fighter's eyes
The girl begged him to stay
But he couldn't hear her cries
The night disappeared
into a brilliant white
He heard a voice address him
"You did well tonight."

The fighter awoke much later
in a hospital bed.
The girl sat beside him
Her eyes were tired and red.
When she saw his eyes open,
She knelt and grabbed his hand
She smiled at him and he
    smiled back
He mustered the strength
    to stand.

"Why did you do it?
Nearly give your life for
    my safety?
Am I really worth that much?
You could have so easily let them
    take me."

The fighter looked down upon
    her face
Compassion filled his gaze.
"I had a daughter once," he said
"She was the reason I stayed.
Don't you ever think you're not
worth what I was willing to give
I would do it all again
And still die so you could live."

The girl's eyes grew teary
And the two embraced
To this day she visits him
A void in her own heart replaced.
Her stepfather had been one of
    the men that night
who had attacked the
    lonely fighter

And when she had heard his
    neck snap
Her heart had grown lighter.

Fate, some say, had put her in that
    broken home
Her straw was short and her cards
    sorely dealt.
But the fighter had shown her a
    different truth
A truth that caused her heart
    to melt.
She was valuable beyond compare
To a total stranger.
There was someone who would
    give their life
Because she was in danger.

The same holds true for all
the innocent, the lost
There is someone who is willing
to help them bear the cross
They come in many forms
To fit the situation
It just so happens a weary fighter
was her own salvation.

The killer

Golden, Colorado
01 March 2015

The killer stared blankly
at the deed that he had done
twenty men lay bleeding
before the barrel of his gun
He had not desired this
such sad and gruesome fate
"How did it come to be?" you ask
We must turn the years back eight.

A child of just twelve,
stood shocked in his yard
the church across the road
    from him
crumpled, burnt, and charred
Screams from beneath the rubble
pierced his young ears
such horror there befell him
it stuck through the years.

But that's not all you see
for across the street he ran
and began to pull the rubble
off an old, and gentle man
He had barely set him free,
when a finger brushed his knee
so he dug into the pile
setting a young girl free.

So many more to save
he could not do it all,
so many dead beneath the stones
why did the church fall?

In the middle of his work
strong hands yanked him back
three leery men stared at him
ready to attack.

The boy then saw the truth
of what befell that day
three men of twisted mind
    and faith
an entire crowd did slay

They claimed that they
    were better
than those inside the church
so death they did deal
from their high delusioned perch.

They beat the boy that day
to a limp and bloodied mess
ignorant of the mistake they made
in causing such distress.

Two years later, the boy
took his first justified life
A rapist from the city
was ended by a knife.

The following year he did
take three more from the earth
the men that bombed a church
would no more find such mirth.

And so the trend continued
the boy became a man
he hunted down all evil
and slayed it where it stand.

The public was afraid of him
the cops were on his trail
yet still he did his sworn job
leaving a trail of bodies pale.

They did not understand him
and why it was he killed
they did not know his victims
were, in evil ways, skilled

A murderer on Tuesday
a rapist the following night
a child molester Thursday
and a human trafficker beneath a
    city light

Constantly he hunted,
and was hunted the same
for and by the twisted men
who sought to cause pain.

Then on a fateful,
lonely twentieth birthday
the man entered a den
of evil men to slay.

He had predicted five
murders and slavers all
but twenty men instead
stood shocked at his gall

The man did not hesitate
despite his disadvantage
and once the smoke had cleared
his strength chose to vanish.

Sitting there against the wall
blood dripping from his chest
the man remembered eight
    years before
how he wished he could have
    helped the rest.

But now he felt relieved,
his duty finally done
he had rid the earth of evil men
he had killed all killers but one.

If he lived he promised
to change his way of life
to rebuild that sad old church
a new way to end strife.

Unfortunately, the chance
    came not
for in peace he breathed his last
satisfied with his life
and the judgement he had passed.

Some say a killer can never
see the pearly gates
when their sins are unrepented
and blood covers their plate.

But I believe in this case,
a man fulfilled his calling
and so should be forgiven
and saved from final falling

And such it was the killer
a youth of twenty years
found his way to paradise
on a wave of silent tears.

PART 8

POETRY, SONGS, AND LETTERS FROM BASIC TRAINING

Written during US Army Basic Training in Fort Benning, Georgia

August 2015 through November 2015

Letters from basic training – August 2015

06 August 2015
First letter from Gabe to his family

It's not like I thought it would be. As I write this, I am still at in-processing or "reception." To put a long and boring story short, it is terrible. We are getting more sleep than I thought we would so that's nice, and I suppose it is good to have the chance to adjust to Georgia weather and the ways of the Army in terms of handling gear. I just want the real thing to start though. I am trying to be patient and praying often. I can put no value to the amount I miss you all because I have felt nothing like it before. Hopefully by next week I will start Basic for real. Until then I will "soldier" on I guess. I love you all so much.

Love, Gabe 20150806

Please continue to pray. I sorely need comfort and encouragement in this place that seems so dead to God. It is still reception, and though it is not physically or mentally difficult, it is stressful and gives me too much time to think about how long I have before I get to come home. Some things have been said around me that make me doubt certain things I once believed about the army. Again, I miss you all more than I can bear and I love you all with all my heart. Please pray I maintain the strength to see this through to the end.

Love, Gabe 20150807

P.S. I will have an address once basic actually starts. They will send some sort of army letter saying what can be sent. I can't wait to hear from you!! I feel alone here. It is my faith and my love of God and you all keeping me going. And it's only the third day!

Dad, some things you have said before I left are beginning to appear true. I have only met one or two guys here of my like mind. It seems I recognize the truth to things you say after you tell me, and I am sorry for arguing so often.

Mom, I am so sorry I was contrary on the day I left. I love you so much and it pains me to know my being gone is hurting you.

Girls, I love you both. Olivia, the song you wrote is comforting to me when my mind begins to wander to dark places. Thank you for it. Prill, enjoy CAP [Civil Air Patrol] but don't become infatuated until I can tell you what basic is like! ;)

08 August 2015
Second letter from Gabe to his family

I still miss you all desperately. The sprit over this place is stifling. The attacks are frequent but the comfort of the Lord always pulls through eventually. I can't wait to get past the dumb stuff and start gaining the more useful training, though I don't deny I am learning much about patience and what it is like to literally be bored to tears.

Thank you for continuing to pray. Processing may take a total of ten days which puts my true BCT ship day on Friday the 14th. I have been told it will take 16 weeks total to get through basic and AIT. I am hoping the Palmers can come down for the family days we get for those graduations. Christmas "exodus" is 16 days starting mid-December so I will most likely have finished airborne school by then even though the army is far less on time and organized than contracts lead you to believe.

Again thank you for praying. It is helping greatly. I am adapting and my mood is lifting even though I can still feel the oppression of how Godless this place is. I love you all and I wish I didn't have to wait until Christmas to see you! Stay well and stay safe :)

Love Gabe 20150808

I'm sure once basic actually starts I won't have as much time to write, but for now I'm glad to be able to communicate somewhat and to get my feelings down on paper. I'm beginning to adjust more. The bunks are almost just like the ones at college but no fitted sheets, so making them is tedious. But it's not bad. The food is a little worse than college though haha…. All the sergeants here are so pessimistic or angry or negative about so many different things, it's crazy. There's no honor, no grand ideals, no drive to fight for righteousness and justice. They don't care. It's really kind of sad. This isn't the army I thought I was joining, but I'll do my best with God's help to make myself and others the soldiers he wants us to be.

I'm sorry if I seem like I'm ranting or complaining, but the principality or power that rules this place has a firm grasp on just about every aspect of lives here.

On the bright side, I got a good word today. I went to Catholic mass just to ride the bus out of the three-building area we've been confined to. It was kinda lame and the pastor or minister (or whatever that dude is called by Catholics) didn't have any passion, but we read an excerpt about Elijah going into the desert and being sustained by God, even though he begged for death. I feel like I may be in or entering a desert of that sort. I could be wrong and I hope I am, but it is encouraging to know God provides every step of my way.

Again I love you all! I will be looking forward to when you are able to reply! :)

Love, Gabe 20150809

I left home to fight a war

10 August 2015 (one week after leaving home)

I left home to fight a war
That doesn't yet exist.
For ancient conflict
And settled score,
Evil I must resist.
This training though,
Seems futile.
My soul is heavy weighed.
I long for family
And friends,
My time with them delayed.
Peace and joy
I hope they have
The time that I am gone.
I must return
Soon as I can
And 'til then be strong.
But worry
Plagues my mind
That sick and aching spirit.
The voice of calm
I long to find
Dear God I long to hear it.
Home now far away,
Part of life behind.
The grief does not
Give in
Eating at my mind.
Save me Lord
From this hell.
Be with me in the desert.
Let me see
My home again.
Be with me in the desert.

Letter from basic training – August 2015

10 August 2015 (Third letter from Gabe to his family)

I'm finally becoming more comfortable here, and by that I mean I'm getting used to the odd hours of sleep and awake, the lower overall average IQ, and the people with no joy or passion in life. Rant end.

On the bright side, I have been getting along with some of the other recruits.

Also, the Lord has been speaking to me more often! It's usually small things like some good wisdom I can glean from a sergeant or a scripture that really hits home (I got to keep my Bible!) or even just a thought that proves to be profound. It has been increasing as far as I can tell, which is awesome!

I had a dream about us last night about our family. I don't remember who was there, specifically. I just remember I was with you all. The location was some large, unfamiliar house in a large suburb-like neighborhood (reminded me of Greeley). The power kept flickering on and off, and it was night. People were going crazy in the street, racing actual race cars with regular cars around the street, people rolling out in the middle of the road with no shirts and screaming and laughing maniacally, fireworks going off in random directions. Jubilee [our dog] was scared and hid under some furniture. I don't remember much else.

It has occurred to me that we have family out here that we will want with us if things go awry. Getting training to help bring them to Colorado now seems like a more likely, and more satisfying, outcome to this journey, now that I've realized how hopeless and cold it is here spiritually. I miss you all, and I love you all!

Keep training Jubilee to be an obedient guardian.

Love, Gabe 20150810

P.S. Despite an overall adaptation I still find myself struggling through waves of sorrow and homesickness. Please pray. I love you :)

———————— ·‧◆◆◆‧· ————————

People here aren't the brightest. Today someone talked in formation and whistled at a female commander as a joke and a sergeant heard it but couldn't find the guy, and now they are threatening to punish all of us. It may just be physical which I don't mind, but one dude threatened our ship day, contract, even careers. I am at peace oddly enough, while tensions are high, but I cannot handle spending more time here at reception. I know this won't reach you before Friday so I'll have to let you know if I shipped on time in a later letter. Honestly, if that happens, I couldn't do much, but just know I would rather ditch the army and come home than spend another week in this infernal place with no training and just sitting all day.

Please continue to pray for me, and that the army will give me the training I need, and if not, that I can come home quickly and do what I can there to prepare for the times to come. Like I said, I have peace. Peace in God's plan for my life. I pray that plan brings me back to you all in the times to tome with the training I need to do so. I love you all so much! I will be overjoyed to return home at Christmas. I already have so much I want to say and ask!

Love, Gabe 20150811

This is my third letter by the way :)
In case one got lost and this seems out of context...
I am basically sending you my journal!

Colorado mountains tall

18 August 2015

Colorado mountains tall
Capped in pearly snow
A gentle dry breeze through aspen trees
There I long to go
Colorado open skies
Deepest heaven blue
To see for miles and miles around
Is what I long to do
Colorado mountain home
Peaceful in the hills
Home cooked meals, that joyous feel
Each snowfall brings a thrill.
Colorado family,
Friends and freedom
Living life with jubilance
No one can defeat 'em.
Colorado mountain slopes
To hunt for deer and elk
Feet to crunch through quiet snow
Whiter than pure milk
Colorado open range
Fields of golden grain
Fading into forest hills
I long for them in pain
Colorado home
Is where I long to be.
Soon I will return to stay
My soul again be free.

To worship you, oh Lord

20 August 2015

To worship you, oh Lord
Is what I long to do
In the mighty Rocky Mountains
To give my soul to You

To sing about your greatness
Above all earthly things
To dance like none are watching
Peace and Joy to bring

You save me from depression
You make my body strong
You bring me home to
    mountains tall
You give me words of song

Your spirit sustains me
In this wretched wasteland
I will survive this test
For your love, there's no replacement

And while I'm here, oh Lord
Far from my true home
Bless my family and friends
Wherever they might roam

Give them all great peace
Give them endless joy
Be faithful even when they aren't
Your endless love employ

I pray the time is soon
That I'm returning home for good

To protect those who I love
Like You know I would

I do not long for violence
But a fighter needs a battle
And what better cause for love
For a cowboy in the saddle

My God, My King, you make me
What I am meant to be
You place in me the will to fight
To make your enemies flee

I will fight until the end to
Fulfill your each request
So take me to my mountain home
Where I can fight my best

I will go wherever
You see fit to take me
But in the end let me defend
Those I love so dearly

So still I pray and ask
That the time be soon,
In which I find my true call
Some snowy afternoon

Grant to me the strength
    and skills
To do what must be done
And when the world falls apart
Let me be the one

Who from mountain
    tops proclaims
Your joy into the world
As I crush your enemies
Flying your colors unfurled

And let my family and friends
Be with me all the way
We will rely on each other
As in your will we stay

The hero stands alone

31 August 2015

The hero stands alone
On frosted mountain top
Armed with mere sling and stone
All evil he will stop.
Hordes advance toward him
But he feels no fear.
They mean to put the sword to him
But their end is near.
On one side endless danger
The other a peaceful home.
The hero stands on the border
Eyes glint like polished chrome.
The fighting becomes thick,
The hero finds a blade.
Angelic fire flows through him
Coming to his aid.
He lifts the ancient saber
From the bloody ground,
And with a mighty labor
Makes a fierce sound.
He slaughters all his foes
Protects that peaceful place
And staggers home to recover
For his next great race.
Now some people wonder:
How did he fight on?
What drove that fierce rage?
What made him so strong?
To protect the innocent,
To return to those he loves
Is motive for his passion,
And strapping on the gloves.

But evermore he fights
With assistance from on High,
And until that help is ended
Never can he die.

Letter from Gabe's dad – August 2015

30 August 2015

Hey Gabe!

How's it going this week? I'm sorry I haven't written to you before now. I've sure been praying for you and Delta Company a lot, though. I trust you are finally getting to learn some of the things you signed up to learn. I'm also praying for your feet, hands, and anything else that may be getting exposure to adverse conditions. I have full confidence in you and in God's plan to prepare you – spirit, soul, and body – to be the best soldier and the best warrior the army has in any given situation to which your service is requested.

Thank you so much for writing the letters to us. We all take our time to read every word, and I can picture you in the context of your experiences. You really are a gifted writer. I am so proud of you, Gabe. Thank you for sharing your experiences from your heart without censoring. You are a good, Godly man. The One who called you to be a warrior in the likeness of your namesake is teaching your heart to guide your strength and training your mind to see beyond and beneath the status quo. Just like in David's day, when the enlisted men were afraid to step forward and challenge the enemy's champion (actually, I would bet they were ordered not to engage, by their superiors, because the king was afraid to engage the giant in battle), in a similar way, you are being conditioned to obey orders. Yet, because of your keen sense of justice and your strong will to protect the freedoms and liberty of the people you love, you may find yourself questioning certain things along the way.

Don't be afraid to ask the tough questions. If you or your buddies find something during your training that seems contradictory or out of place, and it's important, ask the Lord for the right words to ask the right person at the right time (in the right way). He will answer you.

You have always been a strategic thinker, and God's spirit of wisdom has been heavy on you from the time you were in your momma's belly. You have had some time to reflect on your pampered life, and I have a strong suspicion God has given you some serious downloads about who He says you are, and who He says you will be. There is a reason you chose the most difficult path. He is smiling at you right now. ☺

The poems/psalms you sent are profound! Keep cultivating the gift, and it will produce an abundance of fruit from the Spirit from which it was born. That gift was given to you by God as a protection against the cynicism and negative spirit that pervades the place where you are being trained. He gave it to David, too, and it kept the spirit of murder from tormenting Saul on more than one occasion. David, who from his current vantage point can see your present and future, is probably cheering you on every day. He experienced the same emotions you are now experiencing. Keep pressing in to the Lord; keep humbling yourself; keep esteeming others as better or more deserving than you; keep choosing the difficult thing; keep smiling, keep encouraging the weak; keep being generous and kind to those who don't deserve it; keep proving to the principalities and powers that be that you are the <u>real</u> <u>deal</u>; keep demonstrating by your conduct that men were designed by God to reflect His character as warriors who never give up or give in to the enemy; keep making your superiors look like geniuses; keep writing letters; keep drawing pictures; keep writing songs, and sing them in your mind to the Lord (or your future wife, or whomever you write them about); keep remembering you are loved deeply and many people are praying for you; keep doing your best, regardless of others' performance; keep getting 100 percent of the training, and don't let up; keep getting as much rest/sleep, food, water, and quiet time that you can.

This training is going to fly by, beginning now. Don't waste an opportunity to make real friends with good people (superiors and other trainees). As you have already begun to recognize, the guys you are going through Basic with are providing an entirely different aspect of training that you would not otherwise have received. In the same way, don't be afraid to share your heart with trustworthy people. Some of them will be strengthened by your words, and some will become lifelong friends. Be fearless in everything you do, and watch God do some amazing things through you. Yes, you will make mistakes. Don't worry about it. Shake it off. Forgive yourself. Ask forgiveness. Make things right if you can. Move on and don't let it tangle you up.

Okay, done preaching at you.

Man, I miss you! I can't wait to hear the things you will have done in the next three months as we enjoy elk steaks on the deck.

You will have stories to tell… ☺

You know, God has been really nice to us. The Facebook page for D-Company 2-19 put up about 25 photos of basic training in progress, and we got to see your shaved head in at least three of them. ☺ You look good, even though they were taken about the time you were feeling ill. It was GREAT to see you, though. (God likes me, and he knew I would praise him when I saw you in training exercises!) I sure hope you are enjoying it now. That sounds kind of odd, but you can experience some serious joy in the midst of severe circumstances. That kind of joy only comes from God; otherwise it is a form of mental illness. ;) [The text emoticons you used in your letters made me LOL. (LOL) That's funny.]

Anyway, in the current events section of this letter are the following really important items that you have missed out on because you are in Georgia, and these really important things happened in Colorado:

1. Tesa's birthday was Friday.
2. I was up all night wondering where the sun went. Then it dawned on me. ☺
3. Your mom volunteered me to be the road rep for our street. So I got to meet a lot of people up here. There are several former military guys. Good men.
4. What do you call a psychic midget who escaped from jail? See #7 below.
5. Olivia came home from CCU on Friday to do laundry and to see Valjean [Olivia's cat], but Valjean was mad at her for not writing to let him know where she went.
6. Prill had six friends over Friday night. They sang songs around the fire pit, giggled, roasted marshmallows, … you know the routine.
7. "A small medium at large"
8. I mowed the whole front and back yards (except the cattails).
9. Mom made some stinky farts.
10. Prill made some amazing cupcakes (Mom helped).

I love you, Man! Do well and finish <u>strong</u>!

Love, Dad

Thick white mane whipping

04 September 2015

Thick white mane whipping
Behind him in the wind
Streamlined, swift, smooth,
Ears to his skull pinned.
Crystal water splashing
Around his mighty limbs.
Giant hooves come crashing
The valley belongs to him.
Coat like purest snow
In the dead of winter.
Branches break before his might,
Ancient trees they splinter.
Tail like liquid pearl,
Flowing in the air,
Rippling muscles, glistening sweat,
More fierce than a bear.
His eyes are deep and black,
Piercing the soul,
Barrel chest and smoky breath;
The hills behind him roll.
The mighty stallion runs
With hooves that sound like thunder,
Returning to his herd
In the mountains, to his plunder.
Galloping in the field
Oh majestic beast
He glorifies his Maker
With his strength released.

I wish that I could tell a story about love

09 September 2015

(Gabe said he wrote this poem as a song, obviously not about him, but he hoped it would bless somebody.)

Chorus:
I wish that I could tell
A story about love
I wish that I could say
I've always had enough

But my fate is not so fine
As to have such lucky cards
So I sing this humble song
Until my life departs

When I was just a boy
My hand came to the gun
It has been my only friend
While I am on the run

When I was 17
A man I chose to kill
To avenge a puppy's life
A human's blood I spilled.

Chorus

When I was 25
I was driven from my home
Times were tough, work
    was scarce
Other countries I roamed

No matter where I went
I found a hostile fight

Men would leer and women scoff
From morning until night

When I did return
To the place of my beginning
I was spurned by all I knew
For my life of empty sinning

Chorus

When I was 34
I thought I found love
in a woman just like me
but more peaceful than a dove

One day when we were walking
A robber tracked us down
Knocked me out, took the cash
As we lay upon the ground

In the hospital I learned
My woman had been killed
So I found the robber
And his blood, too, I spilled

Chorus

I wished my life would end
There behind that garage.
My life had been so empty
A poorly made collage.

I put the pistol to my head
Tried to pull the trigger
But it would not move
As my tears grew bigger

I looked and there beside me
A man had caught my finger,
He pulled the gun out of my hand
And there a while lingered

The scars upon his hands
Across his beard and face
Could this be the man
That would end my days?

Chorus

He did not say a word
But as he stared at me
I felt the hatred wash away
I felt loved and I felt free

And then away he vanished
In a flash of brilliant white
He took away my pistol
And gave to me new sight

I wished that I could tell
A story about love
I wished that I could say
I'd always had enough

And now I finally can
Redeemed by those scarred hands
He brought me out of hell
And showed to me his plans.

I was not saved
By success or good behavior
But by the love of Jesus
He who is my Savior.

He trains my hands for battle

10 September 2015

He trains my hands for battle
He trains my mind for war
It will not be long
Before I settle a score.

There is evil in this country
That I am called to end
I cannot be stopped
The Almighty is my friend.

And evil shall be vanquished.
Wherever He sends me
I will do His will
To keep His people free.

For though I falter
Though I fall
I will remain
Through it all

To fight evil
Wherever birthed,
And to bring
The righteous mirth.

And evil shall be vanquished
Devils flee before my blade.
The Lord goes before me
And He guides my rage.

I will be vindicated
For my righteous acts

And evil shall be vanquished
When God tells me, "attack."

Through it all I stay
Humble, patient, pure
My heart will remain clean
Of this you can be sure.

And after every fight
Each loss or heavenly win
To my home I will return
Until I'm called to fight again.

I will protect that home,
And the people that are there
They help keep me strong
As in God's love we share.
And evil shall be vanquished
Try us if you dare.

Tell me, Lord of your plan for me

12 September 2015

Tell me, Lord of your plan for me
Share with me your victory
Tell me how I should proceed
Help me daily, your word to heed
Remind me of your faithfulness
And show to me your will
Help me, Lord, through trial and pain
You've given me the world to gain
Make me strong, make me bold
Make me wise before I'm old
Keep my heart safe in yours
And make me calm and still.
You've granted me your blessing
Of leadership and sight
So help me when I use it
Help me to choose right
Surround me with my people
Family, friends and more
So I can love life with them
On eagles wings we'll soar.
Give me a position
Of great authority
And guide my every move
As daily I report to thee.
Train me in your ways
Sustain me by your hand
Grant to me great courage
Let me return to my land.

With the strength of 100 men

16 September 2015

With the strength of 100 men
He got up and fought again
None could stop his rage.
A "monster" some said
This creature they dread
Cannot be locked in a cage.
Whence comes this great power
That drives him for hours
To win despite the odds?
Providence they guessed,
Yes, God did the rest
Gave him his shield and rod.
So onward he fights
To his last bit of might
To protect his mountain home
He does what is right
There in plain sight
No flaw to a fine tooth comb
The training he's had
Some hard and some sad
Has brought him to this place.
These skills he employs
To bring others joy
And he is saved from disgrace.
Now he falls to his knees
Of the Almighty he pleads
"be with the ones I love"
He surrenders his soul
Completed his role
And is given the peace of a dove.

But a choice he is given
To keep on livin'
Should he desire new fate
So he drags to his feet again
Renewed and ready to win
Because of love so great.

Give me a cut (high and tight)

27 September 2015

Give me a cut
High and tight
Shaggy on top
Short on the sides
I'm a soldier now
So hear me out
I gotta be strong
I gotta be stout
So give me a cut
A high and tight
Hurry now
I gotta go fight
I'm a soldier now
So listen well
And watch me damn
Bad men to hell.
So give me a cut
A high and tight
America rules
Her future is bright
But the barber said,
"now listen Son,
Somethin' tells me
You're on the run
I'll cut your hair
I'll make you square
But I hope that you
Will learn to care.
Go ahead
Fight your war
See what death there
Lies in store
I'll cut your hair

I'll make you square
As off into the
Dark you stare.
But tell me, Son,
What strength have you?
Is there anything you,
Alone, can do?
I'll cut your hair
I'll make you square
While I make
A subtle dare.
So the barber gave the cut
A rugged high and tight
As he quietly hoped and prayed
That this young soldier would see
    the light
He cut the hair
Made him square
The soldier silently
Began to care.
When the cut was done
The soldier asked the man,
"so what's your strength,
Where's your plan?"
The barber stopped the clippers
And responded with these words,
"as for me and mine
Our hope is in the Lord."
The soldier walked away
Puzzled and in thought
He did not yet realize
God, his heart, had caught
So give him a cut

A high and tight
Hurry up
He's gotta go fight
Yeah give him a cut
A high and tight
Teach him what is wrong
    and right
Give him that cut
That high and tight
And send him off to see the light.

Atop a giant steed

27 September 2015

Atop a giant steed
Which stamped and pawed
   the ground
The hero ready to bleed
As evil gathers 'round

A giant sword does gleam
In the hero's hands
His eyes are sharp and keen
As he makes his stand

His faithful horse now charges
Into the angry horde
The hero's righteous rage
Flows through his mighty sword

He hears the crushing impact
Of metal against bone
Back, near 20 meters
10 enemies are thrown

In pieces when they land
not as they had planned
the hero swings again
and in the stirrups stands.

The battle's going well
The hero feels a win
But then a lucky arrow
Pierces where the armor's thin.

He falls from his warhorse
Who's slaughtered shortly after

Bitter tears fill his eyes
Surrounded by evil laughter

From his knees he cries out
"Lord could this be worse?
Why must they defeat me
And even kill my horse?

You promised vindication
You said that I was chosen
Now am I to die
Alone and deeply frozen?"

And God replied that moment
A stillness filled the air
"How could you, oh little faith,
Believe that I don't care?

I have molded you and trained you
From the day that you were born
I bought your life with blood
When I wore that crown of thorns

So now could you just trust me?
Put your pride away
You have no hope without me
But with you I'll always stay."

The hero sat in awe
And replied most humbly
"My life is yours oh Lord
My faith in you will be."

Slowly he begins
To remove his armor
Wincing with each movement
In the battle clamor

He drops all his plates
His gloves and helmet too
Then he pulls the arrow
From his side where it's
    gone through

His scream of agony
Is heard in heaven and hell
The evil men close in like
Sharks when blood they smell.

But light bursts from the wound
The hero's strength returns
He lifts the giant sword
With a brilliant peace it burns.

Now he screams again
But with triumph and rejoicing
And evil flees before him
As words of praise he's voicing.

He mows through the horde
Stays his righteous course
Strengthened by the Lord
    his God,
And avenges his murdered horse.

So remember when you're strong
You can be brought low
And when you are weak
The strength of God will show.

How can the sun when it rises in the morning

28 September 2015

How can the sun when it rises in the morning
Be so cold when it shines on my soul?
How can the moon when it rises at night
Warm me much more than that first bit of light?

How does the earth spin through the days
When I am lost deep in this haze?

How can the sun when it rises in the morning
Be so cold when it shines on my soul?
How can the moon when it rises at night
Warm me much more than that first bit of light?

How does my body continue to move?
When I am trapped, what have I to lose?
Powering on through the fire and fear.
Courage and strength when you are near.

How can the moon when it rises at night
Warm me much more than that first bit of light?

How do the birds sing from the trees
When the earth is riddled with disease?
What is that strength, what is that power
That keeps them happy hour after hour?

Answer to none and sleep with the sun
Fly through the sky, get ready to run
How much more does He care for you?
With every fight He'll see you through.

The mighty knight did kneel

Early October 2015

The mighty knight did kneel
Before his lord the King
With broken sword still dripping
With dark, dark red blood
The cowboy tips his hat
To the tired rancher
Dual revolvers smoking
And boots still caked in mud
The soldier renders a salute
To his country's flag
In his heart still fighting
Through the pouring rain
The fighter raises up his hand
In lonely victory
Wheezing, coughing, choking
But triumphant all the same

The knight was given wealth
The cowboy won his bounty
The soldier got his honor
The fighter's wins are mounting

Through it all a child watched
Enamored and enthralled
He wanted to be one of them
A hero brave and tall.

He practiced from a young age
With swords, and fists and guns
He would be the greatest
Hero under the sun.

And when he was old enough
He left to join the army

Pursuing his grand destiny
He was handsome, bold
    and charming.

Will his fate turn out to be
As he had predicted?
Will he fight and win a war
Or will he be conflicted?

Would he be the best?
A hero big and strong?
Will his life be quick
Or will it go on long?

Will he get to fight
For things he thought he would?
Will he ever marry?
Will his life be good?

So many questions he has
As he misses home
As he lives in the south
And dreams of mountains to roam.

Through life he'll always learn
Each step he'll grow some more
He'll always fight to vanquish evil
To free the oppressed and protect
    the poor.

He'll do all he can
Invest in this time he borrows
He'll be a hero one day
A mighty man of sorrows.

The strength that now pours into me

06 October 2015

The strength that now pours
    into me
The fight that fills my bones
The force of will that guides
    my feet
I am surely not alone

The Lord who gives me joy
Has flooded me with power
Beware my bloody blade
If you are evil in this hour

They flee before me now
Those with twisted minds
But they will find no solitude
Their leaders are all blind

They turn now to face me
Reinforcements on the way
They think that they will take me
But God will win this day

Their bitter arrows hurt
Their sharpened spears cause pain
But their attacks will never
    break me
The Lord helps me through
    the strain.

More and more they come
My body wants to break
My sword I cannot raise
The pain I cannot take

But in that darkened day
Salvation comes my way
A legion of His angels
Through clouds dark and grey

They pick me up and set me
Upon a horse of white
Return my blade unto my hand
Its edge now gleaming bright

A voice from heaven calls
"Finish, now, your fight!
I'll not let them break you
You are a son of light."

The vision then just vanishes
I'm here on bended knee
I look up across the bodies
They form a bloody sea

For while I dreamt of angels
The Lord did guide my hand
He raised my sword when I
    could not
He helped me save the land.

They don't understand people like me

Mid-October 2015 (before family visit)

They don't understand
People like me
We'll never turn out
How they want us to be

We're strong and smart
Loyal and true
A strong sense of justice
Through and through

We run with the jocks
And think with the geeks
We play in the band
All life is our peak

We know how to fight
But we know when to run
The outdoors is our home
Where we go to have fun

I hunt, I fish
I throw bales of hay
While physics and calculus
Nourish my brain

I've driven a Toyota
I've driven trucks
I ride long boards
I know how to ruck

I can engineer solutions
To technical flaws

While I talk with the socialites
About politics and laws

So come at me now
Come test this strength
You don't know the breadth
You don't know the length

For it comes from beyond
Your realm of thought
It comes from One
Who can never be bought

He guides my steps
Trains my hands
Gives me wisdom
To understand

Lord, they don't understand
Guys like me
I'll never turn out
How they want me to be

So vindicate me
And hold my life
And teach me how to
Put an end to strife.

When the world is standing against you

Mid-October 2015 (before family visit)

When the world is standing against you
When it's trying so hard to up end you
When you need someone to defend you
Remember I will be there

When you're surrounded by the vile and mean
When your body grows tired and lean
When you need to let loose a scream
Remember I still care

When you've got no one to believe in
When the weight on your back has you heavin'
When the wrong in the world gets you steamin'
Remember I'm always aware

When the dogs attack you and bark
When your future is looking stark
When you're scared and lost in the dark
Remember what I have declared

You are strong and brave and bold
With you, I broke the mold
I've allowed you to fight through the cold
The weight, I'm helping you bear

So don't leave now or ignore me
With your chest held high stand before me
Come, from your heart now implore me
And follow me if you dare

I've chosen you to be great
But be patient, you may have to wait
Though you know I'll never be late
To my love for you, none can compare.

The days drag on

October 2015 (before family visit)

The days drag on
Or they fly
I soldier on
By and by.

It will come
To pass quite soon
Evil will flee
Women will swoon

I will be great
But not alone
Helped by Him
Who has the throne

Stooping low
To lift me up
Does not allow me
To give up

Picks me up
When I fall
Strengthens me
To stand tall

He guides me on
a righteous path
Instills in me
A holy wrath

He will bring me
To my home
Give me mountains
Again to roam

There I will
Be again
Thriving with
Family and friends

Sooner rather than later
This I pray
I will not linger
One extra day

This purgatory claims
My time for now
But to men
I will not bow

For it is God
Who sets my fate
Upon the Lord
I will wait.

There's a fiery wind comin'

19 October 2015

There's a fiery wind comin'
Burning through the plains
Crashing over the hills with
A sharp and searing pain.

There's a fiery wind comin'
Baptizing the earth in flame
Killing all the weeds
Gaining deserved fame.

There's a fiery wind comin'
To devour all the dead
Refresh this ecosystem that's
Filled with wicked dread.

Whence comes this burning breeze?
And where is it directed?
Comes from the Lord of Hosts
Toward any injustice that can be detected.

This purpose is but one
Of many that it serves
The white hot gusts of purification
To the holy, calms the nerves.

It tempers anything that
Is of metal borne
Holds me to fulfill
The oath that I have sworn.

There's a fiery wind comin'
To save me from my doom
Forges me into something great
As in my heart it blooms.

The child wore his cowboy boots

19 October 2015

The child wore his cowboy boots
Hung his cap guns on his belt,
Wore the hat of the wild west
Spoke exactly how he felt.

He grew in height an knowledge
And soon became a man
With bright and wild eyes.
Guided by God's hand,

He donned the uniform
Of sacrifice and blood
And went to fight a war
Out there in the mud.

He struggled long and hard
To become the best
With a rifle in his hand
And silver wings on his chest.

With his old cap guns
No longer he plays
Now he marches tall and proud
And wears a green beret.

When the time is right
Back from war he'll come,
He'll wash the blood off his hands,
His heart will not be numb.

And he'll change into his cowboy boots
And wear an old .357
He'll don the hat of the wild west
and ride his horse to heaven.

(Note: This poem is not about me. It is just based on my life. I intend to do a lot more during and after whatever war to which I'm called before I ride off to those pearly gates.)

Teach me what you know

20 October 2015

Teach me what you know
What you do
What you see
Teach me how to grow
How to fight
How to bleed
Teach me how to live
In the woods
In the hills
Teach me when to give
When to shoot
When to kill
Tell me why you fight
why you run
why you cry
tell me of the light
that is there
when you die
show me how to build
how to guide
how to save
show me how to fill
this purpose
and be brave
Show to me my life
What I'll do
Where I'll be
Show to me my life
Live for you
And be Free

(Note: This poem is one person talking to those he looks up to and wants to learn from with several of the stanzas being questions for God.)

Rising up above it all

24 October 2015

Rising up above it all
Like a mighty eagle
He observes the battle
    ground below
From his perch so regal.
Diving now into the fray
He draws his lightning sword
The organ player see his leap
And strikes a powerful chord
Thunder crashes a he lands
His blade now flashing bright
Evil flees before his gaze
Darkness runs in fright

The people look in hope
Will they now be saved?
Will they finally be rewarded
For everything they gave?
But then evil rallies up
Return in frightful power
Our hero is growing tired
In this fateful hour
He's doing all he can
To save the tiny town
But he takes a knife to the ribs
Now he's going down

His vision blurs
His feeling fades
He slips into a haze
His heart is hurt
His mind is made
And he begins to raise

To his feet again he crawls
When he hears a scream
Sprinting through the pain
A lustful man he reams

The girl stares in shock
At the bloody glowing sword
As he pulls it from the man
And starts against the horde
She watches every move
As he fights and falls
And always rising to his feet
He's more than given all
One man against an army
The odds were never good
But such is the risk when
you fight for love, fight for good

He was called home that day
In a final lightning bolt
Destroyed the final evil foe
And left here with a jolt
The day may come again
When a hero's once more needed
And one will come as that day
When the town pleaded
For there are still a few
Who are called to such a fate
And God will raise them up
And make them heroes great.

Oh how the hours drag on

03 November 2015

Oh how the hours drag on
While the days fly by
Born to fight, live to die
Tell me now, why do you cry?
I won't be gone too long
Crawling through the muck and mire
Fighting to make the world free
Be the soldier I was born to be
Shedding light, the darkness flees
Such is my desire
Eager now to fight and win
Push on through the pain
Hair and beard a lion's mane
I am he, Goliath's Bane
I'll rise to fight again.

What power now consumes me

08 November 2015

What power now consumes me
While I sit and wait
What might is coursing through me
As I dream of fate

This is a lull in time
Here I wash off all the grime
And prepare myself for the fame

I'm guided by His hand
Shielded by His strength
He gives me authority in the Land
Of Living days He gives me length

Whom have I to fear?
The Lord is at my side
I rise above my peers
On Eagle's wings I ride

They come at me in malice
They seek to crush my soul
But I have drunk from the Chalice
That lets me fight their pull

I am weak, but ever growing
Tired, but ever steeled
A winter crop I'm sowing
My ears are keen, my eyes are peeled

Watchful I remain
Ready to make war
Flinching not for any pain
Until I settle the score

The old man sat and pondered

09 November 2015

The old man sat and pondered
His life up to that point.
The many miles he'd put on
His tired, weary joints
He remembered growing up
In a home where he was loved
Riding shotgun with his dad
Hunting deer, shooting dove.
He remembered all his friends
From high school days long passed
All the crazy things they did
All the frights, all the laughs.
He thought back on those days
Of innocence and fun
Before his mind turned to his time
Fighting commies with a gun.
His eyes drew distant and grey
A tear slid down his face
As he remembered those who fell
Beside him every day
He slowly bowed his head
And wiped away the tear
And thought about the times
    since then
And the woman he held dear.
Forty years they lived together,
Raised a child all their own
But not too long ago the
Good Lord called her home.
The child has grown up
And moved quite far away
But keeps in touch when he can
And visits on special days.

The old man now has grandkids
With children of their own
And they too come sometimes
To his humble mountain home.
They find him there still busy
Working livestock and land.
They walk with him through
    the hills
While he holds their hands.
Some say his life is good.
He's lived it long and well,
Raised a loving family
Been through war, been
    through hell.
But while he lived in joy
He has one final wish
To find just one lost soul
And teach them how to fish.
He thinks about it all
Still sitting on his porch
As the sun sinks in the west
Casting shadows on the
    wooden floor
Just then he hears a voice
It tells him he's done good
That he has indeed taught men
    to fish
As he hoped he would.
Then he got up from his seat
And walked off toward the sun
Walked all the way to his
    final home
At peace his work now done.

Here I sit

16 November 2015

Here I sit
Waiting and bored
This extra time
I can't afford

Here I sit
Still in place
I need more drive
I need more grace.

Here I sit
Impatiently
But then a voice
Says to me

"I know my plan for you
Trust me, give it time
Strength will rise as you wait
Turn toward me your mind."

Here I sit
Tired and bored
When the music in my mind
Strikes a mighty chord

"I'll finish what I've started
You've got a while to go
From you I'll never be parted
I'll light your path, I'll help you grow."

Here I sit
Wondering why
The evil live
And righteous die

"Their numbers must be filled
The martyrs and the saints
The evil will feel my wrath
On the judgement day."

Here I sit
Deep in thought
Will my actions be remembered?
Will they be forgot?

"My hand is on your life
I'll lift you when you fall.
When you follow me
You'll rise above it all

On eagle's wings you'll fly
Above all planes you'll soar
The wicked will flee before your blade
When you trust in me, your Lord."

All my prayers answered,
All my worries gone.
He is training me for war,
Making me grow strong.

Saved from dull complacency
To live outside the lines
Called to fight, defend the weak
Hope my soul now finds.

Here I sit
Waiting on the Lord
Home behind, war before
I know what I'm fighting for.

Journal Note – November 2015

November 2015

My time in Purgatory is winding down to an end. The future is yet unclear to me, but I have a sort of peace and excitement about it. I know not how long I'll be in training or where I'll be going after, but I know that by God's grace I'll be in the right place at the right time with the right training for the mission. I will see death. I will kill. I will have to make sacrifices, and all this I will do according to God's plan for my life so that I may save many lives. I still have much to work on, but I will be ready. The Lord will complete his purpose in me.

PART 9

POETRY AND SONGS FROM AIRBORNE SCHOOL

US Army Airborne paratrooper training in Fort Benning, Georgia

November 2015 through January 2016

I sense hollow

27 November 2015

I sense hollow
I sense false
I sense a creeping darkness
My nose it does repulse

I sense sinister
I sense fake
I sense an emptiness
Makes me want to break

Away the barriers
That thousands have put up
To speak into their souls
Help them give it up

The façade they put on
To face each empty day
The mask that they all wear
To keep the ghosts away

A rage builds inside me
I want to end this game
To see people as they are
Because right now they're all
     the Same

They live their phony lives
Their achievements all for naught
They sell their souls for status
Their minds are quickly bought

They have no will or gall
They are rotting inside out
They are slaves to their own bodies
They are neither brave nor stout

They profess an outer strength
They say "now look at me"
But they fade like wilting flowers
Like smoke upon a breeze

And just now to think
To think, to know that I
Would fight so they could live
Would fight and even die

Do you know my sacrifice?
The pain that I must face?
"Support the troops" you say
While your life is a disgrace

I would give my life
To save your wretched soul
At least show me who you are
And tell me of your goals

I'm sick of all the empty
All the acting all the masks
But I can't live your life
I've got other tasks

If someday you wish
To truly understand
Go ahead and ask
I'll gladly lend a hand

Until then be gone!
All you sleeping slobs
Move aside and get behind me
While I do my job.

Follow me!

30 November 2015

Follow me! I say
As I charge into the fray
My ammo is all gone
But I've got a course to stay

I run forward without thought
Of the muzzles aimed toward me
This small American town
   will live
Will live and will live free

There is no earthly power
That can match this might
The Lord has trained my hands
To fight for love, to fight for right

The bullets whiz on by
Striking down my men
My heart is filled with sorrow
And a burning will to win

The fighting grows more thick
No chance of escape
But the foe must not advance
Here I'll stop their pillage, here
   I'll stop their rape

The power coursing through me
Is such I've never felt
As Russians crumple 'neath
   my blade
Under every blow that's dealt

I don't feel the bullets
Ripping through my chest
For the Spirit that now guides me
Does not need to rest

My friend fights on behind me
When I see a thrown grenade
I shield him with my body
While I lead this black parade

The shrapnel stings a little
But there's still work to do
Another burst of power
My heart remaining true

The world begins to glow
As light gleams from my eyes
The angels lift me up
As my body dies

A roar now fills my ears
It's coming from my mouth
Reinforcements now appear
Coming from the south

But their help is not needed
God has won this day
I give my soul into his hands
As for my home I pray

One final punch I throw
Leveling a tank

Before my heart explodes
And the Lord I thank

I collapse upon the ground
As my vision fades
I listen to the choppers
The thumping black parade

Now I float above
Looking at the scene
The earth is dark with blood
But the trees are bright and green

The morning sun is shining
Upon the battle ground
The fighting now is over
I don't hear a sound

Until I hear His voice
Filling me with joy
"You've done well, my son
Now follow me, my boy."

He leads me through the
Stars, galaxies and more
Past the empty planets
That I once wished to explore

"The time is coming soon
That we will return
You will fight beside me
There's much for you to learn.

On that glorious day
We'll make the world free
Come and draw your sword
Unleash your love and follow me!"

And follow Him I will
By His side I'll be
For I am in the Lord's
Mighty infantry.

Warrior banquet

December 2015

Come join the warrior banquet
join us in our feast
our time is done, yours to come
we toast to all our feats
Come join the fighters' party
join us while we sing
our time is done, yours to come
wear our crested ring
Come join the soldiers' celebration
join us in victory
out time is done, yours to come
wake up to the revelry
The world is facing a darkness
that you must soon fight
follow in our steps
make known our sacrifice
until you come to rest
and join us side by side
for freedom we have bled
for liberty we fought
drench the earth in red
for the legacy we wrought
Then come and rest a while
join our ready ranks
once for love you've bled
and from the cup have drank
For soon the Lord will lead us
in another noble cause
to save all of his chosen
from the devil's grimy paws

Then we will fight together
the soldiers and the saints
to make the world free
the sunrise we will paint
Come join the warrior banquet
join us in our joy
Our time is done, yours to come
we toast your courage, boy.

He surrounds me

December 2015

He surrounds me with people of virtue
He guides my voice and hands
He gives me peace and joy
He shows me favor in all lands

His face shines gladly upon me
Proud of His work I've done
He leads me in His righteous ways
He strengthens my feet to run

In all I do, to Him be the Glory
In all I say, my wisdom is His
With all my might, I praise his glory
With all my soul, he's given me this

Proclaim His goodness you saints
Take joy in His will you soldiers
Sing to the Heavens of your liberty
And the weight he lifts off your shoulders

The Lord of Hosts is my triumph
In Him my trust will stay
Praised be the God of Creation
Through gladness and pain each day

The Lord Almighty blesses me
Gives me all that I ask
So I praise his name, worship the same
And with joy carry out my task.

Through mire, swamp and grime

December 2015

> Through mire, swamp and grime
> The hero stays his course
> He fights with passion and courage
> Vanquish evil with no remorse

Lord, I need your help. Anxiety tries to take hold of me as I think about the trials to come. I long for peace and joy. For home. It's as though I know my time with them may be short. I know you will protect me and my family, that you will guide us and deliver us from tribulation, but there is dissonance in my spirit, or nervousness, or apprehension … I don't know. Please give me confidence and courage and excitement.

GOD!!! I want to feel the hero I long to be! I want to be through the grueling training and get to the grueling fight. For in training, it is hard to find a purpose for the suffering. There is no immediate threat or enemy attacking and forcing us through a gory fight. There is only the knowledge of future battle and the need to be prepared. I want to be there, at the fight, done with the nonsense, ready to carry out your wrath with joy. Help me Lord. I need motivation, conviction and drive, the kind that can only come from you. Help me God, for I can feel the next wave of contractions and birthing pains coming in my transition, and my body dreads the pain. My spirit fights for control, and my mind is torn.

Help me God, for you are my hope, my savior, my deliverer. Without you, I have nothing. Do not hide your face from me or let me face this reforging alone. Save me Lord, in my weakness, in my sorrow. Give me strength, let me feel your joy.

I love you, my God. And I thank you for your love for me. Nothing I can ever do will be worthy of your love for me. Thank you Lord for your grace. Thank you for your peace.

Where have all the men gone?

December 2015

Where have all the men gone?
The fighters and the saints
Where are all the leaders?
Why is everyone so faint?

Where have all the men gone?
The Braves who hunt and kill?
Where are all the big and strong
Who live to do God's will?

Where have all the men gone?
What happened to the tough?
Where are all the patriots
With edges grizzly and rough?

Where have all the men gone?
Have we fallen so far?
They sport skinny jeans and girlish coats
Their skin is free of scars.

Where have all the men gone?
Will they return someday?
Our way of life will soon be doomed
If we don't hit our knees and pray.

Where have all the men gone?
That ready, rugged Breed
We're here and eager to fight
When the nation admits their need.

"Where have all the men gone?"
Say the weak and broken down
"On our way," is the reply
"We're heading into town."

There's gonna be hell to pay

08 January 2016

There's gonna be hell to pay
When they go too far
When they take our rights
The warriors come out to play

There's gonna be hell to pay
When there is no justice
When freedom is dying
The warriors will have their day

There's gonna be hell to pay
When fear is too far spread
When all aspirations are dead
The warriors come out of the grey

There's gonna be hell to pay
for all of the evil and wicked
for all the injustice done
to vindicate the victims and virtuous
until the coming of the Son

There's gonna be hell to pay
When the warriors return to stay.

Names to remember:
CSM Billy Waugh

Off I go again

08 January 2016

Off I go again
To dive into the dark
By Him each step illuminated
To His call I hark

Off I go again
To leap into the fray
The Lord Almighty guide me
Through each dying day

Off I go again
To push beyond all pain
For it does not compare
To what I will gain

Off I go again
My heart is pounding hard
I trust in the Lord my God
To be my shield and guard

Guide me Oh my King
Train me in your ways
See me through the pain
Walk with me every day

Help me Oh my Lord
Down the path for which I'm called
Grant me mighty will
Grant me fearless gall

Thank you Oh my God
For your hand upon my life
As you train my hands for war
And end all of my strife.

Forgiveness I beg

10 January 2016

Forgiveness I beg
Of You oh Lord
Do not let me fall
By the edge of the sword

I fall and fall again
But you raise me up
Onward I fight
I will never give up

Forgiveness I beg
Of You oh Lord
I try and I try
To live by your word

I rise and rise again
until lambs become lions
You've given me strength
To slay the giants

That torment this earth
To free the oppressed
To defend the weak
In you my soul will rest

I have no strength
But what you give
In you oh Lord
My soul will live

Salvation I beg
Of You oh Lord
Keep me from harm
Fulfill your word

My body craves
Such evil things
Forever my soul
Of light shall sing

For though I stumble
Though I fall
I will remain
Through it all

I will live my
Life for you
To your word
I will stay true

So pick me up
When I am low
Make my spirit
White as snow

Clean my mind
Clean my soul
Make me strong
Make me whole

Remind me Lord
Of who I am
As in your will
I will stand

Thank you God
For your grace
Run with me
This final race

Forgive me Lord

January 2016

Forgive me Lord
For I have sinned
With heavy guild
My soul it rends

Please remove my iniquity
Fling it far from your eyes
Bathe me in your blood anew
Out of shame my heart cries

I want to live my life in
A righteous way
To bring Glory to your
Name every day

But I am not worthy
With this lustful, festering flesh
So please forgive me and help me fight it
In you my soul will rest

Forgive me Lord
For I have sinned
Clean me and bring me
To your Glory again.

You there get up!

January 2016

You there get up!
Pull it together man
You have to keep on fighting
It's time to make a stand
Your body your mind
It was all just a loan
So don't just lie there
Before your enemies prone

You there get up!
Get back to your feet
You have to keep on fighting
There are more still to beat.
There are people relying on you
On your will to win this fight
Your life is nothing if not for them
So give it all, unleash the light

You there get up!
The spear has missed your heart
Wrench it from your chest
And complete this bloody art

You were designed
To protect the innocent and weak
You'll not fall until they're safe
So get back up and let the bullets speak

Even if it claims your life
You know where you'll go
Another will rise to protect as you
This you surely know
So be at peace
Should the Lord call you home
But until then get up!
And sling another stone.

Rise, Rise again...

January 2016
(inspired by Ridley Scott's Robin Hood (2010) motif)

Rise and Rise again until Lambs become Lions
Get on your feet there's much left to do
Rise, Rise again until Lambs become Lions
Have strength little child, fight and be true

Rise, Rise again, your destiny is calling
Fight to the end, the world around you is falling
Rise, Rise again there's evil yet to slay
Rise, Rise again until the judgment day

Fear not all the pain and suffering you feel
Before this day ends your spirit will be steel

Rise, Rise again until Lambs become Lions
Have strength and break through, your heaven now awaits
Rise, Rise again until the world is silent
Fight to the end for it will not be late

Long, long ago a prophecy was spoken
They told of a day when chains would be broken
So Rise, Rise again and lift away the darkness
Get on your feet until the angels harken
Slay all the foes, and wicked in your path
Open up your heart, O vessel for God's wrath

Rise, Rise again until Lambs become Lions
Get on your feet, see this fight through
Rise, Rise again, don't pass away in silence
Look and you'll see there still much left to do.

Oh Lord hear my prayer

February 2016

Oh Lord hear my prayer
And come to my aid
For I am lost and wandering
My mind is bent and frayed

I am in a desert
With you my only hope
Yet I'm walking not toward water
Toward mirages my hands grope

Aware not of my thirst
My body screams in pain
But the illusions are too real
As my soul they drain

I look for satisfaction
In every empty vice
And continually crave more
And each time pay the price

Even now in writing
My mind is far adrift
There's a world out there waiting
Waiting for my head to lift

So God please pull me out
Of this sickness, sandy slime
And save me from my sins
Like You do every time

I love you Oh my Lord
And I follow where you lead
Forgive me my transgressions
Remind me of my creed.

I am a warrior

February 2016

I am a warrior
I fight to free the oppressed and enslaved
I fight to defend my home and loved ones
I fight for my brothers at my side
I fight to end tyranny and uphold justice
I am prepared for conflict, and I pursue peace
I am a guardian of justice and a defender of freedom
Evil cannot flourish under my watch for I keep
My heart pure, my mind focused, and my body strong

Compassion, mercy, and kindness are traits I hold equally
Important as ferocity, violence, and fire power
I will prevail against all enemies, foreign and domestic by
The strength of the Lord Almighty and with my weapon necessary
There is no foe too great, no battle too hard, no enemy too powerful

I am steadfast, trustworthy, and loyal
I will gladly give my life to protect the innocent and weak
Without me there would be chaos, but with me there is war
For war is my art and my calling, and should I die,
Others will rise to take up my fight

The battle is the Lord's and I fight with His guidance and
Blessing, a vessel for his wrath
I am unstoppable
I am invincible
I am eternal
I am a warrior

Cowboy in a dim-lit room

February 2016

The cowboy lounged in a dim-lit room
A layer of smoke on the air
Keen eyes scan for evildoers
from behind a cigar in a leather chair

A black bandana marks the target
Wanted for rape and slaughter
Sylvester Cain was a wicked man
Killed a farmer and his daughter

The cowboy watched his movements
They were confident and quick
The cowboy put out the cigar
On the wall of brick

Walking to the man
He readied his hand to draw
But unprepared was he
The knife he never saw

Falling to his back
The cowboy coughed up blood
Cain stepped on his right hand
With a dark boot caked in mud

With an evil sneer he said
"You thought you'd kill me?
But I'm already dead
And you're the one to bleed."

The cowboy grunted his reply
"It's not finished bastard"
And with a movement spry
Pulled his left gun faster

Cain collapsed, unmoving
A bullet 'twixt the eyes
The room completely silent
Except a baby's cry.

So bold

February 2016

So bold
in the cold
oh heart of gold
and prepare for judgment day

Grow old
as foretold
and break the mold
there are giants left to slay

Strong hold
steel that's rolled
your soul is sold
So now hit your knees and pray

Be bold
in the cold
Oh heart of gold
And then, fade into the grey

Where do you go

24 May 2016

Where do you go
At the end of the line
When death comes to all
In its due time?

How do you live
At the world's end
With nothing left to give
Filled with empty sin?

What do you do
When all is lost?
Your time is through
You can feel the frost.

The answer, friend, is simple
Call upon the Name
The Name of He who gave
    you life
He who makes the wild tame

His power is not wanting
His forgiveness ever deep
So as you die there grunting
Turn your eyes on high and seek

The troubles that once held you
Will be far beyond the sea
And the Spirit that compels you
Will drag you from the deep

O weary, bleeding soldier
Fret not upon life's end
At your call, the King of all
A heavenly host shall send

Oh weary dying warrior
Fear not the growing grey
Surrender to His loving arms
Until the judgment day

Worry not for trifles
Things you left undone
The blood you've spilled
    is acquitted
By the blood of the Son

Where do you go
At the end of the line
When death comes to all
In its due time?

You go where you deserve
Unless you call His name
He's saved sinners worse than you
He'll save you the same

So, weary, dying soldier
Don't fret upon life's end
For even in the growing grey
There is nothing He can't mend.

PART 10

JOURNAL ENTRIES FROM DEPLOYMENT

Written during deployment to Afghanistan
(various provinces and districts)

15 September 2017 through 30 April 2018

Vose Bruhs, Afghanistan, 2018
(Gabe is standing on the far right.)

Emails from September 2017

Sep 19, 2017, Gabe wrote:

Texts seem to have trouble getting out here despite the fact that I have service, so I'll try an email. I made it to the Stan, and I'll be bouncing around the country for the first few weeks here, so I won't have a solid address, but after that we should settle in to a rhythm doing what sounds like a very exciting mission. There is definitely a spiritual as well as a physical haze over this place. Smog and dust brown the air making the surrounding mountains look like jagged black walls against a putrid sky. A wind blew through today briefly lifting the smog revealing stark crevices on an intimidating mountainscape. It has a sort of desert beauty and the vertical relief is quite the relief from the flat emptiness of the true sand desert of Kuwait. I have been dreaming, but I rarely remember what I dream. I haven't yet dove deeply into biblical study as I intend to, due to the business and travel. Thank you all for praying so much. I feel peace and grace going forward. Please continue to pray, as this is the epitome of a Godless country and attacks in the spiritual will no doubt outnumber attacks in the physical. I love you guys and I'll call soon!

Love, Gabe

Sep 20, 2017, Gabe wrote:

Those are some good scriptures, thank you! Calling and texting remain sparse but thankfully the data seems to be working for email, if only intermittently. I've been told I can't say anything at all about our mission set, so I suppose I'll just give you all updates on the weather: it was sunny and dry with copious smog again today.

So far deployment feels like an extended, less obnoxious version of the June escapade. My feelings about the looming likelihood of future firefights range from ecstatic anticipation to a dull, aching apprehension. I have no doubt God's shield of protection around me and my unit will hold strong, so I shrug off the apprehension quickly when it leeches in, but it annoys me to feel it at all.

Thank you for continuing to pray! I love you guys!

Prill and Liv, I added you guys to the email so I can talk to you all at once :)

Deployment Journal 9/29/2017 - 10/8/2017

Friday, September 29, 2017 (first journal entry)

We left Alaska on the 12th so I suppose that means we have been gone for a little over two weeks. We spent a couple days total on travel along with a 3 or 4 day stay in Kuwait and 2 days at BAF [Bagram Air Field]. We arrived to camp Pamir a little over a week ago and already we are getting into a steady rhythm of activity. And by rhythm, I mean a frenzied mixture of chaos and calm spurred by last-minute security missions and monotonous tower guard shifts. However, deployment thus far isn't without a good number of perks. We are working with an ODA from 10th group special forces on a tiny camp in a tiny ANA [Afghan National Army] compound in the Kunduz river valley. So uniform standards are pretty nil. Mustaches, un-bloused boots, sweet hiking boots, combat shirts, no hats, no patches. That's not the only plus, though. The other day we went out for .50 cal crow system and mortar familiarization. I got to line up a mortar shot, set the charge, hang the shell, and fire it a few times. It was awesome. On a single charge, an 81mm mortar will hang in the air for 27 seconds to travel 500 yards reaching a peak height of almost a kilometer. The following explosion is addictive knowing you were the orchestrator of destruction behind it. We also did IVs [fluid administered intravenously] yesterday which was fun. I think I'm over any squeamishness I once had with needles. However, I'm also pissed at everyone who's ever fucked up an IV in the past. Shit was easy.

Anyway, we were supposed to go on a 6 day mission to kill bad guys on the 1st of October but it looks like that may be pushed back to later in the month. We'll only be at camp Pamir until the first part of November, but hopefully we'll have CIBs [combat infantry badges] before we leave. If not I'm sure we'll get them in Nangahar. I hear that place is real hot these days.

I dreamed about Emily the other night. I've been thinking about her a bit much perhaps. Time away from normal civilization has my imagination running wild. I only hope it doesn't affect anything negatively.

Signing out for now. More updates to come.

Sunday, October 1, 2017

We left the wire today for a longer drive than we have yet been on. I drove an MATV [Mine Resistant Ambush Protected (MRAP) vehicle] with the PL [platoon leader], the SF [special forces] Team Sgt [sergeant], and one of the EOD [explosive ordnance disposal] guys. We drove to Kunduz airport to check up on the flight line or something. It wasn't too bad overall, apart from some weirdness with the coms [communications] systems. Upon our return we spent an hour and a half going over the trucks and the coms systems to make sure everything was set for next time. Who knows how long our corrections will last considering the nature of army radios, but at least they are good to go for now. Oh, I was complimented on my driving again today. So that's cool.

In about an hour we have to get ready to go pick up 31 people from the HLZ [helicopter landing zone] on the ANA compound where our camp is. More driving. I'm sure I'll get tired of it eventually, but for now it's still new enough to be entertaining. At 2300 tonight I have a 4.5 hour tower guard shift. Gonna be a late night. Rumor is we have that 6 day mission coming up on the 8th. Also, I've heard 150 isis [Islamic state of Iraq and the Levant] clowns have moved into Kunduz. Things are shaping up for an eventful month.

I had a dream last night that I was on a bus going somewhere else in Afghanistan. We were at a stop, transferring bags, when we got shot at and found out about a bomb threat. I knew some of the semi-truck/bus drivers were part of the attack so I started looking around for my SAW [squad automatic weapon] but couldn't find it. I saw some pogs [people other than grunts] cowering next to me in the back of one of the semis we were loading and one of their long-barreled scope-less SAWs. I picking it up, racked it and sent some rounds through the window of one of the cabs belonging to the bad guys. The SAW jammed, so I racked it and shot a three round burst before it jammed again. I saw blood sprays in the cab, so I racked one more time and pumped a couple more rounds in as the SAW jammed once more. Infuriated, I threw it down and ran to where I figured my SAW would be. As I sprinted I prayed for YHVH's [English spelling of God's name in Hebrew] protection. I felt power. I saw some of the men I am here with wandering around, not yet fully aware of the situation. I didn't have time to stop. I ran until I found my SAW on the ground next to some others. Picking it up, I racked it and prepared to lay waste, then I woke up. It was a pretty cool dream.

Tuesday, October 3, 2017

So I was going to start a fast today, from everything technology except email and this journal. I forgot about that until a few minutes ago as I finished an episode of SAO [Sword Art Online]... oops. I'll start it properly tomorrow, assuming I remember to. I want to go deeper in the spirit as I have before. I want to hear from YHVH daily. I want to walk in supreme confidence and trust in His provision. I want to walk in a constant, raging inferno of spiritual strength and purity. I want to feel the invincibility that comes with being in the middle of YHVH's path for one's life. I feel all of that on some level right now, but it feels dulled, numbed. It is as if there are layers that must be ripped back in order for me to feel the spiritual wind. It is almost like listening to a soft song while wearing earplugs, or walking at night with sunglasses on. I want the blockades gone, my eyes and ears opened, and my spirit set free to roar with the fire of the saints. So for this I will pray, and starting tomorrow I will begin a fast to show my intent. I wish I could do a food fast without the problem of needing food to sustain the amount of work I have to do daily. So a tech fast (apart from email and journal) it is, along with daily Bible study. I will read as led, but I want to go over the Psalms, or maybe the gospels, or maybe the story of David again. I should, and will eventually, read more of the bible than those three favorites, but I feel like they hold lessons most relevant to my current locale and occupation. Well, to the Word. More journaling when the Counselor speaks.

Thursday, October 5, 2017

The fast is off to a rocky start. People playing videos on their phones directly in front of me, blaring music in the tent, mostly stuff out of my control, but the temptation to immerse myself in a show or other form of virtual entertainment is strong. I did have a dream last night, though. I believe it was an indicator of where I am at in the balance between my spirit and flesh. Unfortunately, the balance is near favoring the flesh. I thought about it for most of the morning and prayed a bit, asking forgiveness of my sin. I must not be like Lot's wife who longed for her life in a den of sin and so looked back upon its destruction with remorse. I must starve the flesh and feed the spirit so my true nature may grow strong, and my baser drives will lessen. I pray YHVH will strengthen my spirit and make known His glory in my life to flush out all uncleanness. I pray He will forgive the sins of my eyes and mind. I pray that He will advance His will in my life and drive out all temptations. I also pray He will soon make known to me my future wife.

> His sword shines white with fire
> His garb now dark and red
> A crown of gold where thorns once stood
> And a voice that wakes the sleeping dead
> Behold, he rides from heaven
> Black storm clouds in his wake
> Followed by legions of mighty souls
> Yet victory is His to make

Friday, October 6, 2017

I had an interesting dream last night. We were finishing some vehicle training with MATVs and RGs [mine-resistant light armored vehicle] and we all climbed into the back of one of the RGs. I was in the driver spot with a SAW that was not mine in front of me, but there were enough weapons in the vehicle that I didn't need to go grab my own. It began to rain. Pettet was driving then, and I was holding onto the back, looking over the top. We went to a muddy driving course with steep hills. Pettet took the first one too fast and then tried to brake once the front tires were already airborne. As we hit the ground on the downhill, the vehicle caught and began to flip/tumble. I let go of my place on the back, and spun to catch some rock outcroppings. My foot/let was caught in the vehicle door, and I bore the full weight of the truck to stop it from falling. It righted itself to its wheels and attempted to drive backwards up the hill. It couldn't make any progress without falling on its own, so I began to leap/climb with it hanging from my leg. I prayed to YHVH for strength and powered up the hill. For some reason, people didn't notice or seemed unsurprised that I had just pulled a multi-ton vehicle up a hill.

Today during a brief snooze, I had another dream. I was home on leave with the entire family in a minivan just like our old one. Mom was driving. For some reason, there was a giant hill in the middle of town that appeared to be steeper than 45 degrees. I guess it was a shorter rout to our destination to go over it so mom gassed it up the incline. I warned against it, but to no avail, the front wheels came off the ground and the van began to tip. It didn't roll over, but it skidded back to the bottom of the hill. I said we should go around, or she shouldn't gas it up the hill, but go up at a crawl instead to that the vehicle wouldn't flip. For some reason, my words were not heard or no one listened, or I couldn't finish, because Mom gassed it up the hill again, I leaped out of the van prepared to push if she took my advice and slowed down before it tipped back. Instead the van tipped even further and began to roll back, I stepped clear as it landed on its roof and slid to the bottom upside down amid sparks and screeching metal. Immediately I ran to the driver side to see if everyone was okay. They were fine, but mom was quite flustered. I pulled her from the car with gentle strength so that her foot didn't so much as nick the door frame. Dad and Liv were already getting out and seemed surprisingly calm considering what had happened. We all were. Although, I was annoyed that no one had listened to me, and that it was a mistake that had already been made once on that hill, and I thought it was stupid for us not to have learned from their mistake. I then went to get Prill out of the back seat. She was just fine and waiting happily for me to lift her from her upside-down seat. I knew she was doing so for fun, so I lifted her free and swung her through the air in a circle before setting her on her feet. As we discussed what to do, Daniel Raak showed up and spoke to my dad, I heard him and walked around the inverted van to greet him. I felt joy and seeing an old friend, and was excited to see the rest of the guys and have some good old times over the course of my leave. Then I was made aware that I was dreaming by shifting briefly into the half-asleep zone. Before I left completely, I saw all my closest loved ones from my past and present there in a group in front of me. I addressed them with sorrow knowing I would soon leave them to wake up in my cot. I said, nearly with tears, "I wish I didn't have to leave you all now. I wish I could stay on this leave. But I'm not actually here right now. I'm… deployed…" At this word, I woke up and set about a detail for which I had been called. There were a variety of emotions in the dream. At the start I was excited, but mildly worried. Then I was cautious, then aggravated, then briefly scared, then relieved, then joyful, and then somehow sorrowful and joyful at once. I woke up with a faint longing for home. I pray YHVH shows me the meaning of this dream and the last one. That's two dreams in row where a vehicle I was in or attached to failed its users and began to roll. In both I played a role of rescuer. In both dreams, I saw disaster before it befell. In both dreams, I knew how it could have been averted, but I was unable to change the outcome. In both dreams, the outcome was fine, people were safe, and I had joy. But I want to know the specific event or events these dreams reference. YHVH I pray to you, tell me the meaning. Give me another dream or vision. Speak to me clearly. Let your purpose be made evident and show me how to act to avert disaster if it is possible. Either way, thank you, YHVH, for your favor, your peace, your joy, and your protection of me and my loved ones.

Sunday, October 8, 2017

This morning I had a very intense dream. YHVH, give me wisdom and authority in the spirit, and protect my loved ones. YHVH give me the interpretation of this dream so I may act.

I was with Emily and a few others in a room resembling a hotel lobby or a barracks building here in Afghanistan. I was laying down and Emily was beginning to be drunk. She had a crazy look in her eyes, but I let it go longer. There was a sound of screeching or screaming that was drowning out the sounds in the rest of the room. I asked her what was wrong. She said she didn't want this, but she just needed something or someone. I told her we should talk outside. Before leaving I was looking for my shemag so I would have something in case she got cold. Once we were outside, I realized I had no shoes. I apologized and said I would be right out. She said she'd be waiting. I ran to get my shoes. I threw on my combat pants and boots without socks and ran back outside. I found Emily near some tents similar to the ones I'm staying in and apologized for being late. She said "Sorry this, sorry that – sorry, sorry, sorry" mocking me. I said "Fine I'll stop saying sorry," trying to laugh it off. She said "No! you'll apologize until I say not to." I then noticed Emily's mother and sister under a fighting position with sandbags similar to the ones here. Some conversation about a devil came up. Emily's mother said the devil was in Emily's heart. I rebuked the statement in the name of Yeshua. And spoke words of power in the spirit over Emily, redeeming her as a woman of God and rebuking the evil that had been forced upon her. As I spoke her face turned from a frowning sneer to a peaceful, innocent smile. All the while, people behind me were shouting, and I was hoping she wasn't listening to them because their words, though encouraging on the surface, were wrong and deceitful. Seeing the chaos of the people now screaming in argument, she began to step forward, but a wise old man stopped her and shook his head. A leery, thin man came up to me afterward and was staring. Emily pointed him out. He was growling and whining. In a voice low enough that the crowd could not hear, I growled back "Leave," and he walked back to his truck. The same man approached again while I spoke with Emily's father, and he placed parts of a large torn sticker in the shape of a "T" on Emily's father's forehead in "thanks" for the words of purity I had spoken. I was wary, and I did not trust the man's attempt at an innocent guise. He began to place more of the torn sticker all over the large RG that was Emily's family vehicle. At that, I rebuked any curses against Emily or her family and commanded they fall back on the attacker ten-fold and take no effect on Emily or her family. The stickers turned into long metal pipes that moved like tentacles and turned on the man who placed them, whose screams were suffocated by the curse. I awoke laying on a bed in a large room, and thought how that dream was good practice in spiritual warfare. Then on the ceiling I saw a notebook, much like one I had in basic and the same color as one I have now, clinging to the ceiling opened halfway and frozen in place, as though the page hadn't fully turned, held there by demonic force. The breath caught in my lungs. I had been staring at it but did not notice until now. I knew if I could speak YHVH's name, the demon would leave. I pointed at the notebook and then at the ground, still struggling for breath. The notebook shook, and then fell normally, at which point I awoke speaking YHVH's name in a desperate voice. I prayed as I woke up more fully, and though a little more shaken, I thought "that was some good practice in spiritual warfare."

Prior to this dream, I had a dream that I was getting ready with my family to go to an event with or for Emily. After leaving an event with my family (where my sisters and I left a couple times to play a video game), I noticed my boots were torn and frayed. I needed new ones for the event, or maybe just wanted them really badly. We went to a place where I had bought the last ones and asked for boots. All the women who worked there talked subtly about having relations with the geezer who ran the place. We walked into the basement where they said they had the boots, and we came out in the hotel lobby where the next dream began.

Email Thread October - November 2017

Oct 23, 2017, Gabe wrote:

It has been a while since I last emailed everyone, and I have a bit to say to all.

Firstly, I hope everyone is doing well – all things considered. I have utmost faith and confidence that YHVH will keep all of you safe and guide you in all things.

Mom, I have been praying that you would receive complete healing prior to surgery such that the surgery would not be necessary, and I will continue to do so. I also believe you should seek healing prayer from someone who has that as a specific gifting. However, as with all such matters, the "Your faith has healed you" clause holds true. YHVH's mind is beyond my knowing, but I know His Wisdom said that what we ask in His name will be granted and that all things, no matter the apparent origin, work together for the good of those that love Him. He will bring Glory to His name through thus. However, the timing is in His hands. For sorrow may last for a dark time, but joy returns with the light. Sorry if I'm preaching to the choir, I really do believe YHVH has it already planned and handled. So, through it all, I will pray for His grace and peace to envelop you.

Prill, I got your email about your dream and I will reply to it more later, but rest assured that such a situation is unlikely, even though a tech blackout for two – or even more weeks at a time – is possible.

Liv, there are no more donkeys because we moved to our permanent location.

Dad, Happy Birthday!! And thank you for sharing the interpretation of that dream, it made obvious sense after I read it. I had another one during the same timeframe that I will share in a separate email. It makes four dreams of great significance, and while I have pondered and asked for interpretation, I am at a loss for much of the meaning.

In other news my memoirs are off to a grand start of fourteen pages so far. By the time this is over, I should have enough for a book that will make tons of money so I can be rich and famous and buy a ranch. Although much of what I do seems mundane, I am allowed to share very little over email or phone when it comes to my job. At least that is what I have been told. But I can say that I will be switching positions from machine gunner to RTO [radio telephone operator] (does stuff for the LT and handles all the radios) in the next month or so. I'm not a fan of the change, but hopefully it will play out well, since I'll be working much more personally with my leadership. Also, the RTO is automatically the go-to guy for all manner of tasks, so it seems my well-roundedness will be put to use. Even though I was kind of used that way already....

Oh, and I have a mailing address now. No telling how long it will take to get here, and I have no idea how to send mail out, but here's what you write to make it get to me:

SPC Conde, Gabriel [address redacted]

Feel free to share it with a limited number of people. I have a finite amount of space in my bags, so don't have people send hygiene items, food, or other basics. I have access to all of those things here. I may have requests as time progresses, but for now, I really don't need anything. However, the poncho liner from Lee and Terri, you mentioned, will be a welcome addition to my gear in the near future as the weather grows more brisk.

Oh, please do not post that address anywhere online and do not let the people you send it to share it any further. Thanks!

I think often of home, and I pray for you all daily. It has been a rollercoaster in both realms here, and to be honest, I'm very much enjoying it. I will try to call soon. Trying to arrange a free hour or so at a time when you all will be available is proving a challenge. Fret not though, I shall make it happen by next weekend, if at all possible. I love and miss you guys a ton!

Your son, brother, hero, slayer of beasts, grand adventurer, the fleet-footed, yet steadfast, utterly fascinating machine gunner, inherited RTO, winner of stuff, champion of things, ever gallant, strikingly handsome, the noble and utterly modest,

Gabe

PS. Prill, if you need to terrify a scrawny turd who's never seen a barbell, I can now bench 285 pounds, deadlift 435, and squat somewhere near 380. It's not much compared to some freaks of nature, but those numbers are steadily moving upward, and I have 7+ months with nothing better to do over here than plot the demise of some sniveling twerp.

You know, just in case :)

Nov 17, 2017, Gabe wrote:

Hello mi familia!

I apologize for procrastinating so much on this email. Nothing very eventful has happened since I called last, and now I hardly have time to write about the blandness of the past couple weeks because I am about to travel elsewhere for a few days. Hopefully, it results in some excitement or good fun. However, a number of days spent in boredom or doing monotonous tasks is equally likely, if not more.

Apart from this upcoming escapade, I've done nothing but sleep, eat, work out, and participate in silly training put together by my leadership. I've done a little writing and reading here and there, but not much worth mentioning. I hope life has been treating you all wonderfully and YHVH is pouring out His blessings on you. I have been praying for you all, especially for Mom's recovery.

I gotta get going, so unfortunately, I'll have to cut this email a bit short. I will write more later! Oh, and Prill, I will reply to your email properly when I get back from this outing.

I love you guys and miss you a ton!!

Love, the paragon of all things masculine and peak of human evolution,

Gabe

P.S. I would really like a bar or two of Duke Cannon soap. It's literally called Big Ass Brick of Soap. Duke Cannon is the brand, but it is sold by Duluth Trading. Also I have been hankering a Rocky Patel Vintage 1990 cigar or two. I can't think of anything else I need at the moment. If either proves too difficult to obtain, no worries, I'll be fine either way. Well, I'm gonna be without my phone for a while, so I won't get your replies until later. I'll talk to you shortly after that, hopefully! Love you guys!

Nov 18, 2017, Gabe's dad responded:

Hey Gabe!

It is great to hear from you! Thanks for the update on your boring life. I have a feeling that you have a feeling that something is about to change where that boredom is concerned. Nonetheless, I hope the few days does not turn in to a few months. Considering the scenery is about to change for you, I know how to pray for you and the others going on vacation from boredom. Try to stay away from the ag industry while you seek ways to mollify the mundane.

I am just sitting in front of a peaceful, mesmerizing fire in the wood stove downstairs. I woke up to stoke the fire, and I saw you had emailed. I had been dreaming about your mom right before I woke up. I don't remember the details, but I remember thinking how beautiful she looked. She had been doing something active, and she was very happy and full of life.

Prill talked to a boy on the phone and then washed the dog last night before she went to bed. The critter had been sprayed by a skunk (the dog, not the boy). Even in all the boredom, just remember that at least you are not sitting next to a dog that was sprayed by a skunk.

Olivia went to lunch with me yesterday. She seems to be doing very well. She starts a new job the Monday after Thanksgiving. We are going to miss you over the holidays. By the way, she published a new album a couple of days ago. It is on the interweb. She can send you a link.

Your mom is definitely healing up, but she seems to have difficulty staying inactive so she can heal faster.

If you ever have a chance to do research on the inter webs, take a look at the relationship between Ai and blockchain. Being a math genius, you might find it fascinating. Perhaps YHVH will give you some insight regarding the acceleration of certain things the next couple of years (think exponential advancement of specific tech).

Well sir, we will be praying for you the whole time you are on vacation, and we hope you will communicate as soon as you can. Watch for YHVH to demonstrate his power and authority in unique ways. Your times are in his hands, and your life is hidden in his son. Please keep writing down the dreams he gives you. You are surrounded by his favor like a force field. Literally, the safety of those around you depends on his favor. May he bless you and keep you. May he cause his face to shine upon you and be gracious to you. May he turn his face toward you and give you peace.

We love you and miss you so much, Gabe. I'm praying you will do your job better than anybody else could do in whatever situation you find yourself. I continue to pray for your wife, too. She probably longs to see you as much as you want to see her. Stay the course. She is worth the wait.

I love you, man!

Dad

By inference, the father of the paragon of all things masculine and peak of human evolution

A dragon's curse on ancient gold

09 October 2017

A dragon's curse on ancient gold
Took one lone man hold
He wielded the power of a king
But unto greed his soul was sold

Years rolled by, on and on
Near all who knew him were dead and gone
Loneliness was his company
And silence, the throne he sat upon

The days grew dim
His figure slimmed
His beard grew long
Was never trimmed

He lost all care
For fresher air
In his hall
In his lair

Until one fateful day
A young lad did pass his way
To explore the crumbling castle
And find a place, the night to stay

Giant doors creaked slowly apart
To reveal muted gold and dusty art
And midst the mounds of treasure high
A wretched form gave the boy a start

The king looked up, under crystal crown
And saw the boy now searching around
In his heart, a feeling grew
That seemed to cut the darkness through

But the dragon's curse still held sway
And smothered the king's feelings true

He rose from throne with reptilian growl
And let loose an inhuman howl
"Begone you pest, you thief, you scum!"
The cursed king screamed with a scowl

The boy set down the delicate chain of silver old
Which till then in his hand did hold
And turned to face the wretched king
For a peasant boy, he was far too bold

"Oh king," he said, with a shaking voice
"How dare you, in this treasure, rejoice
This chain was my mother's before the dragon's rule
So I leave you with a fatal choice.

Pay the price of her fiery death
End your reign and cease your breath
Or grant me just this single chain
That with my mother, it may rest."

The dragon's rage burned in the king
Upon standing up, the halls did ring
With golden chimes upon the stone
But the king didn't hear a single thing

The dragon's mind was strong and vile
The king's mind by gold beguiled
Given wholly to unholy drives
The dragon's breath seeped from an evil smile

The boy did not step back
He braced for the dragon's fiery attack
Stoic and calm, unswayed by greed
In clueless courage, he had no lack

But behold! Strategy was foreign not
To the peasant boy whom hardship begot
He dashed 'cross the room with agile speed
As from the king's mouth, dragon fire shot

Diving, he slid behind a pile, though short
Made of countless coins, the silver and golden sort
For he knew the dragon dare not harm the treasure
And correct he proved, as the burning breath stopped short

Why this particular stack
Of shallow coins and money sacks?
There were others that were bigger
More suited for stopping the dragon's attack.

Because upon his arrival, the boy did see
A dull and rusted mystery
And the boy in wit and haste did figure
An object of great importance, it to be.

For in a castle that glimmered and shone
With the cold light of metal and stone
A tarnished blade was out of place
Even so far from the dragon's throne.

The boy's hunch was proven true
Whence comes this mighty, fearless youth?
He hoists a blade of nigh five feet with a single hand's embrace
And a righteous flame in his own heart did brew.

The king ceased movement down the hall
For by not his nor the dragon's fault
He had forgotten that ancient blade
But its visage now caused his breath to halt

The youth, prepared, took up the lull in fight
And leapt over the treasure with shocking height

Never was his movement delayed
And from the sword flashed a brilliant light

The king screamed in agony, his eyes accustomed to the dark
The boy's aim was deadly true, and the blade struck its mark
It cleaved the ground before the king, its edge finer than a hair
The boy then spoke and commanded the evil king to hark

"There was a time you could have been
A great leader of valiant men
But you fell prey to the dragon's greed
Which took your noble soul to rend.

This, your sword, was cast from you
Its deadliness the dragon knew
So it was buried and rusted 'neath golden beads
Lest you see the burning light of truth.

Know I have no love for you, though you are my father
For you let me go quite long ago for the glitter of another
You sold your soul to greed and malice
You let the dragon kill your wife, my mother.

So now know this, you foulest of beasts
If I can't free you I can kill you at least
So drink you now, from my wrathful chalice
Oh dragon king, this man release!"

With that he drew the mighty sword now shining pure and white
Spun around toward the dragon and swung with all his might
The edge of gleaming steel cut through the lizard's armor
Cutting through both bone and flesh, the dragon the boy did smite.

A hush fell over the room
As the light from the blade lifted the gloom
The now feeble king began to stammer
Like a dead man raised from a darkened tomb

Once more the youth drove the blade into the floor
Its hilt gleamed like ruby sand on a sunlit shore
Its blade seemed to sing and spark like the hammer
Which smote the blade of white fire fresh from the angels' forge

The boy turned and walked away swiftly, but paused ere the door
He reached and lifted the hair-like silver chain
from the coins midst the floor
Its single bright blue gem was etched with an ancient name
A name that meant courage, and all the weight which that word bore.

The same name was burned now into his hand
From when with the sword he took his stand
The hilt etched with the word of courageous flame
Had left its mark like a cattle brand

So the boy whose name meant brave
Walked away from that treasure filled grave
Left the king to regather his mind
Without so much as a word or so much as a wave

In doing so he fulfilled the prophesy once spoken:
"When king by dragon's greed is broken
When eyes by gold are blind
Youth with sword of light awoken
The dragon's bones will grind
No treasure taken but just one token
For heart of courage, bravery kind
Free the king, no word spoken
And leave his home, his fate to find."

Deployment Journal 10/10/2017 - 10/22/2017

Tuesday, October10, 2017

I had another interesting dream last night.

I was here on camp Pamir doing army things, or going through some tests while pulling security or guard (basic dream versions of army stuff). At some point there was a water slide, cleaning stuff off a toilet, and some other oddness before the real dream began.

We were driving out to go on an adventure. Instead of with the army, my family was behind me in a different vehicle. I started out in a truck, but it turned into my Corolla. I was far ahead of them and didn't know where they were. I was in Colorado, but taking a route unfamiliar to me, when all of the sudden traffic stopped and people started scattering or pulling U-turns or driving off the highway. I slowed to a stop and looked ahead to see what looked like a mushroom cloud. Thinking it was just an odd cloud formation, I prepared to weave between vehicles, but then I looked behind me and saw a true mushroom cloud above where northwestern Longmont would be. I looked back at the first and could see it was real as well, and located over Loveland. Then looking behind once more, I saw a full nuclear explosion where southern Longmont would be and then another bigger one where Denver was. Shocked into near disbelief, I got out of my Corolla and began assessing what to do. I knew the radiation would be the biggest killer in the area where I was, so I found a reflective blanket in the back seat that I turned into a jacket. When I put it on, the burning sensation on my skin ceased, but I knew I would need more permanent shelter. I didn't try to call my family, keeping faith in YHVH that they were safe. All the same, I made sure I had my phone, and then found my knife and wallet in the back seat and put them in my pocket. I realized anything else I could bring would be useless, so I set off across the highway toward the east to seek out a safe route back to my family. On the way, I came across what appeared to be a military camp. I did not mention that I was in the army, since I noticed the camp to be off in some way. The leader of the camp asked me questions which I answered with intentional ignorance of rank and feigned civilian politeness. He assumed me to be just a normal young man wandering around clueless. He said he would help on my quest, but I didn't believe him. On the way through the camp, I found two people of like mind to myself who became my helpers on my mission to find my family, gear, and important information and clues. As we were being shown around by the camp leader, we noticed a man who was former or current US military who did not answer any questions the leader had asked and had been tortured for it. At this point, we knew we must escape, which we did by leaping down from a guard tower when no one was around. As we progressed, I realized I needed a new jacket, since mine was now soaked in radiation. I managed to find some ponchos or tarps tied together with zip ties, so I ripped one free and threw it over my shoulders. This happened on the way back from trying to find answers about what had happened. There were three parts of a key that we needed to accomplish our goal. One was a small journal, another was a map, and the last was a key or computer code of some sort. We had memorized the first two somehow. When the journal and map fell into enemy hands as our unwitting villain caught up to us, I hid the last small leather case holding the final key, knowing we no longer needed the other portions. (We were at a sort of animal shelter or orphanage where I, or another member of the group, had friends that helped us find the last key. The residents were intelligent ape children. One of them had been taken by the invading force to serve in their military, but escaped to return; only now it looked more human and with blonde hair and clean teeth, though still with apelike posture and excessive body hair. The man who was my helper had come from this orphanage and spent long enough in the military force to become fully human.) The leader of the camp who had caught up to us searched frantically for it, and we allowed him to take the first two parts of the key but feigned ignorance as to what they actually were. We managed to escape without him discovering we had the final part.

After I had found the poncho, and we continued on our journey, the dream tapered to an end. Someone similar to a soldier I work alongside began to speak about the explosions and radiation. They said I did not need any more protection from it since it would dissipate quickly. There would be no severe fallout. This was not a nuclear apocalypse, despite what it would appear. YHVH created this land, and who are humans to think they have the power to destroy it with their paltry bombs? I was encouraged by his report and pressed forward without fear of radiation or sickness, confident I would find my family and achieve my goal.

I will be praying that YHVH shows me the meaning of this dream.

Wednesday, October 11, 2017

We have a mission coming up tomorrow night that will last 48 hours. High chances of a CIB [combat infantry badge]. I'm so stoked!!! I will create a comprehensive journal entry documenting the mission upon return.

Sunday, October 15, 2017

It was... uneventful.

Monday, October 16, 2017

I had some more dreams last night of which I can't really remember the details. I have had many dreams about women lately. I want to believe I have met my future wife in some of them. Whoever she is, I miss her.

Speaking of girls, Kiah finally replied to my email. She seems to be doing ok, but struggling with some stuff like sickness and stress. I will pray for her and send encouraging words in my next email.

We are leaving camp Pamir soon. Sometime within the next few days. Hopefully we see some good fighting at our next location.

Sunday, October 22, 2017

We have been at Camp Vose for about three days. Very little has changed day to day, except for the fact that we are now inside BAF. No me gusta. If we step foot outside our gate, and we don't step foot back onto camp Vance across the street, we have to go full potato, meaning full retard, meaning full army gayness. On the bright side, the gym here is level, clean, and with decent weights and machines. Much lift. Such swol. Wow.

I slipped the past couple days. I allowed myself too close to the precipice and if not for YHVH's grace, I would have tumbled. I do not believe a fast to be necessary. I simply need to let my yes be yes, and my no be no. I have sworn an oath and I will uphold it.

In other news, I am going to be RTO. F—K.

My God, My Salvation, My Lord

22 October 2017

My God, My Salvation, My Lord
Before you I kneel with
    broken sword
The music of my soul strikes a
    dissonant chord

And my spirit is grievously torn
Splotches of blackness rend
    my form
Deep in my mind clouds brood
    for a storm
YHVH my God, this can't be
    the norm
Steeped in filth and heaped
    with scorn

The putrid slime drips from
    my head
Corrosive and burning, my soul
    it shreds
It won't cease its attack until my
    body is bled

YHVH! My God! Save my
    wretched soul!
My lungs draw air in
    painful breaths
My mind is dull and stinks of death
The smell pervades my flesh and
    seeps out on my breath
The stench I cannot stand
    so I kneel before you less
    than whole.

YHVH! My God! Save my
    wretched soul!
The shame on my head is like
    burning coals
My spirit, neglected, is
    shivering cold
My body is covered with sores
    and mold
YHVH I can't afford the price of
    the toll
I've sinned.
Creator, my Father, I've sinned.
Accepted the filth of a
    regretful decision
Shunned and forgotten my
    heart's circumcision
Lost sight of the pure and the
    right, of my calling, my
    future, my mission
Between You and I, I caused
    this fission
I failed to acknowledge, I failed to
    listen, failed to use the vision
    You've given me
So now I acknowledge, I lay bare
    my shame,
I have transgressed Your Will. I
    have dishonored your name.

And I beg, YHVH, for your
    mercy and grace.
I beg You, YHVH, do not hide
    your face

I beg You, YHVH, I won't move
from this place
I beg you, YHVH, forgive
my disgrace.
I renounce my sin of lust, of
adultery, of pride
Of blindness, of deafness, of
anger, of snide
Of harshness, of lying, of
dishonest words
Of dullness and complacency, of
my eyes that burn and my
tongue that curse
Forgive my transgressions,
YHVH, Creator
And clean this miserable frame.

Behold, explodes now from
the Throne
A burst of brilliant light
Thunder claps, and
lightning strikes
A fearful, dreadful, beautiful sight

Clouds of fire form over my head
And pour out a rain of blood
It cuts to the bone, burns with fury
And washes away the mud

It rebukes the shame
Casts out the grime
It sings a great Name
And it cleans to the time

It pierces my soul and lays bare
my spirit

It fills the holes where infection
once gripped
It envelops me, cleans me, wraps
me in light
And leaves me, just me, fresh and
clean, new and stripped

YHVH places a garment of grey
across my shoulders
It shines like silver in His glory
"Humility, righteousness,
resolute strength
For your cleanness, for My Glory.
You are forgiven, your sin is
no more
You are free, and wild, my blood
has made you pure
Feel the fire of my Spirit
inside you
Go in peace, and sin no more."

His words are simple, and they
burn my heart
His mark is on my spirit, to His
call I hark
I break down there, and weep
Out of love, relief, and thanks
YHVH saved me from
the darkness
And raised me up before I sank

His goodness is immeasurable
His Wisdom always endures
His faithfulness is astounding
And of this you can be sure:

YHVH, Creator, Lord of Hosts
    has granted me forgiveness
I was fallen, filthy, and putrid, but
    in His blood, He bathed me
And He will do the same, for
    any who call His name, and
    approach His holy throne
Behold He loves, He purifies, He
    forgives, and by His blood, I
    am set free.

Deployment Journal 10/23/2017

Monday, October 23, 2017

Today Rogers and I studied radios with the 18E. He's a pretty decent guy and seems eager to teach us everything we can possibly absorb. Personally, I intend to learn all I possibly can from him, despite what feels to be an unnaturally slow start. Now, in my normal tone a slow start would mean that the rate of learning is lacking in satisfying my brain's capacity, and comprehension of thus is somewhat of a bore. However, in the current context a slow start refers to my own ineptitude in satisfactorily comprehending the nature of the devices with which we were working. In short, I was challenged, and it thrilled me. My brain was forced to work, to surge in processing and computing large amounts of both input and output. Rogers, having prior experience with radios over 7 months of learning them the hard way, found the tasks to be much easier than I, and so finished them much more quickly and with better information retention. For him, the class today was a bit of refresher course. Despite my best efforts to keep up with him on the second round of programming the radios we were given, I found myself meagerly finishing preset station six while he had already finished the tenth and moved on to filling COMSEC [communication security]. Far from discouraged by this, I am finding motivation and encouragement in the competition and comradery. These masterfully intriguing devices which can communicate across the room or across the world have earned a bit of realism in my eyes today. The methods behind their security and functions are have been made slightly more clear. I would fain learn more and quickly as the days progress. No happier, am I, at the prospect of becoming the RTO of 2nd PLT [platoon] Able Company; however, knowing the trade of the position prior to entrance is a welcome idea.

If the astute reader has noticed a sudden change in structure and diction of this most recent entry, a far cry from the unorganized notes and unfinished thoughts of some prior, fret not for the sanity of I, the writer. For this morn, nigh the breaking of the fast, I found myself enveloped in the sparkling commentary and poetic prose of one J.R.R. Tolkien and his collection of lost tales. At thus, I was reminded of the wonder that filled the world in my youth, and yearned for such fascination once more. Writing in such a way as to reflect the poesy which flooded my imagination in those days is but a vain attempt to revive the spirit of a more innocent, more wonderful time. However, neither vain nor imaginative is the secondary reason for my new chosen voice of pen and key: that I may reactivate and tune some deep crevices of my brain long unused, but aching for complexity and beauty once more. Better refined and elaborative entries will not appear in these memoirs with complete consistency, as a tired mind finds it easier to jot ideas in duller color, but when energy and time permits, expect to be regaled by vivid descriptions and deeply thoughtful digressions as I weave the story of my adventures across the globe and save them for future reflection.

Behold yonder mountain peaks

Thursday, October 26, 2017

Behold yonder mountain peaks
Their countless jagged crags
Which weave a wreath of
    ominous height
Round the dusted desert lands

No drop of rain will fall for long
No cloud will blot the sky
The desert barren, without song
Save the lonesome grey dove's cry

Behold the shadows, deep
    and black
Midst the towering, rugged walls
If of good vision, your eyes
    have lack
Hearken to my words, enthralled

For midst the canyons, dark
    and long
Lurks a lowly form of life
They plot in secret profane acts
They sharpen each their
    twisted knifes

See now how they laugh,
At a lamb caught twixt
    the brambles
At the shepherd boy
    now struggling
On his feet, not even sandals

They move in for the kill
The lamb they'll carve and
    then devour
And if not stopped they'll harm
    more still
They'll filthy the boy that has
    no power.

But behold once more and see
The justice of the hills
For a lion leaps first, upon
    the sheep
Which it swiftly kills

Now it turns, glares at the men
Who approach behind the boy
No normal lion is this beast
And weapons to him are toys

A man of meager strength
Shoulder's rifle now to fire
But the lion's gaze is steady
And filled with bloody ire

Fear strikes the hearts of the
    wicked men
And flee they back to shadowed cave
The lion stares now at the boy
Whose body shakes in fear
    and wonder, grips his
    shepherd's stave

But the innocence of youth
Grants a certain witless
    courage then
One that conquers
    primordial fears
And turns boys into men

Behold the boy, he raises voice
And speaks unto the lion, he
"Sir you've killed my lamb
Which was neither marked
    nor flawed
And you've cast away my enemies
As with the eyes of a god

But sir you were mistaken
And my anger flares at thee
I'd rather you have taken mine
Than the life of the lamb so
    precious to me."

And lo! The lion now replies
For no normal beast is he
"Come to me my child
There is something you must see."

The shepherd boy, the brave naïve
Approaches now the lion's feet
And there from 'neath his shadow
Comes a sweet and milky bleat

The lamb unharmed, springs to
    the boy
Over a pool of scarlet red
And its wool seemed a brighter white
Which shone near like a crown
    about its head

Hush now, and listen,
For the lion speaks again:
"A man without flaw was sacrificed
And His blood leaves not a stain.

As your lamb has done today
So did He in the ancient times
Bled that others may be saved
Yet some failed to see the signs.

Behold, my child, your lamb
    now lives
And so does He who has
    saved mankind
For he conquered sin and death
    that day
That they who seek may know
    His mind.

Little one, it is not without cause I
    tell this tale
For greater salvation than
    you've seen
Today will be granted if you
    follow me
To where the water is wide and the
    grass is green.

For lo! As you love your
    flawless lamb
Greater love have I for you
My sacrifice for you was made
Come and see, my words are true."

At this it dawns upon the boy
The fatefulness of his
    encounter, divine

Without needing explanation
He leaps and darts after the Lion's
    unearthly shine

The boy and his whole herd
After the Lion did follow
And arrived at paradise
Where no heart was left
    with hollow.

The mountains stand on, ever tall
A wreath of jagged earth
They ever watch the deeds of men
From their death, back to
    their birth

Their crowns of snow near catch
    the stars
As summer day to winter night
Falls the sway of all creation
At the fading of the light

But the little shepherd boy
No longer do the great hills see
For gone is he
To a land more free.

Other mountains there do rise
And touch the Heights of Glory
And their wreath of
    wondrous majesty
Mark the ending of this story.

Deployment Journal 10/27/2017 – 11/12/2017

Friday, October 27, 2017

This eve ere the middle watch of the night, our party shall embark upon a quest to a nearby camp. Our method of travel to be grand metal beasts of the air. Russian in origin and convoluted in design, the mammoth rotary winged sky transports are heady, but perform at a level which satisfactorily suits our needs. If the night proceeds as expected, it will be one of vague and stifled blood lust waning into sleepy dullness nigh the break of dawn. Should there be time allotted for the closing of eyes and the resting of mind, the winks will be a precious few. I have grown to expect such monotony from ventures into "combat" zones. The first mission to such a locale in which I was privileged to participate resulted in two drearily boring days. Even as enemy gunfire occasionally crackled from a few hundred meters afield, and as the stray enemy mortar splashed dirt against our forward wall twice or more, naught was I permitted to do in relation to my duties or my desires. I felt no true presence of danger, nor did I flinch at the idea of such. For when steeped in blandness of view and experience to such an extent as we, one craves the possibility, even the likelihood of a proper attack in which the skills of the soldier become truly necessary. I would fain tonight be full of glorious battle and grand deeds of valor, but alas, the probability of fate allowing the savagery and violence I crave is slim, even in the scope of the several months which remain to me in this mountainous desert. Should excitement erupt from the sullen plain of readiness, certainly I will share tale of the events to follow in glittering detail. Though be aware, dear reader, that an occurrence of any magnitude is unlikely, and it seems that Providence sees fit to belay the christening of my blade until a more ideal time.

Monday, October 30, 2017

So…, that happened. I'm too tired for poetic words and ornately contrived musings so I'm just going to share the events in my regular voice with limited embellishment. Just after midnight on the 28th we flew to camp

Dalkhe to be QRF [quick reaction force] for a mission that some of our guys were a part of. Upon arrival we were told that there was a fallen angel (SOF personnel KIA). Apparently, a Chinook crashed in the middle of Taliban territory and the pilot was 160th SOAR [Special Operations Aviation Regiment]. As such, three ODAs and their uplift (us) were sent to secure the area, retrieve survivors, and destroy the wreckage. There was some oddness with the flights to the LZ [landing zone] and some Haji pilots did us dirty by flying us around then dropping us back off at Dalkhe. We finally arrived on location at 3:00 or 4:00 AM. Then, moving into the village where the wreckage was, the show really began. We worked our way to a defensible compound atop a large hill overlooking a wide, ridge-cut valley to the north and east. We stayed at this location until late last night with the exception that six of us uplift were sent to a house 70 meters north for the first night to maintain security for ODA 0215 who didn't have many of their own uplift (we are attached to 0214). The first day was uneventful, with the occasional bomb strike and distant sound of gunfire as the ANA worked through the surrounding area. The night was cold, dull, and sleepless until early morning. The following day was much the same except for a few pop shots taken at our compound. The assholes fled before we could PID [positively identify] their location to return fire. Sneaky jerks. I hope we get another opportunity to see those human scum put in the ground. I still need to fire my SAW in combat before I become RTO. Definitely got a CIB now, though still not under the circumstances I was hoping for. At least I was able to experience rounds cracking overhead. It was definitely a bit of a rush; one that I will not be telling my family about until my return. (Future Gabe: That was a lie.) Hopefully there are many like it to follow which result in the slaying of the enemy by my hand and by YHVH's guidance. Anyway, late last night we moved back to the crash location, cleared a few compounds on the route to the new HLZ, and were sand blasted thoroughly by the chinooks that picked us up a bit after midnight. We flew back to Dalkhe where we waited for a short while before boarding a C130 to return to BAF. Due to some stupidity of which I never discovered the cause, we waited at a single location crammed into this plane for over an hour waiting for the ANA dudes with us to unload. Once they finally did, it was a four minute flight to BAF and then a thirty minute crazefest of trying to find our way back to VOSE by walking. We finally stepped back into our own rooms at about 0430 or 0500 in the morning. Hell of a time.

Tuesday, October 31, 2017

Happy All Hallows Eve.

I am not one for celebration or festivities on behalf of evil spirits and legends of putrid origin. I dislike its popularity amongst otherwise upstanding individuals. Glorifying death, demons, and the dark, grizzly ideas of twisted minds is an activity that ought to be reserved for such persons as hold those things in high regard, and not for those of us who value life, honor goodness, and love the light and its Creator. However, this is a meaningless gripe. No amount of want or opinion will change the status quo. Frankly, it is only faintly that I feel the convictions aforementioned. There is little reason to truly care.

My mind is dulled today. I feel weak, pathetic, emotional. I have caved to temptation and the guilt weighs upon me even after knowing YHVH's forgiveness. My flesh is a ravenous dog on a chain, refusing to be tamed, spilling its own blood as it strains for things it is not meant to have. In the name of Yeshua, the Son of YHVH, my God and my Lord, I repent of the wickedness of my flesh and the uncleanness of my body and mind. I renounce my sins of lust, polluting of the heart, and voluntary uncleanness. I rebuke these sins in Yeshua's name. BE GONE FROM ME. Forgive me, YHVH, and make me clean before your eyes once more.

It is more difficult than I want it to be, this pursuit of spiritual cleanness. It is a lament I have written of before. Never did I think myself one to be swayed or shaken by the ways of the world. I pray YHVH returns me to a place of spiritual strength so that I never will be swayed or shaken again.

Wednesday, November 1, 2017

Drama rears its ugly head.

Beyers is a decent leader and I have learned a lot from him both good and bad as with all leaders I have ever had. On the negative side, he takes things too seriously and personally, being quite taken in by doctrine and regular army standards of appearance that hold no dominion over fighting prowess. More positively, his view of "it's easier to just play the game" is understandable, and he is reasonable about his corrections and requests of us from what I have seen. In addition, he is proficient at his job and a good managerial type, making sure tasks are understood and his guys are squared away. However, reasons aside, he is often stressed and really does take things quite seriously, which has a negative impact on morale and people's view of him. I don't particularly like that aspect of his leadership, but I've learned to deal with it and get along with him quite well. (future Gabe says: How politically correct of you past Gabe ....)

Roybal is Beyers' counterbalance on a spectrum of army leadership. They are very much equals and opposites, but far from yin and yang or a zen middle road of balance, they are oil and water, fire and ice, clashing wind currents that under prime conditions cause a tornado. Roybal doesn't care about appearance or regulation until he gets called out on it, at which point he will fix himself, but not without a copious amount of complaining .... He is adamant and argumentative when he has an idea that he believes to be correct. I have learned much from Roybal as well though, and he is one of the best team leaders I have had. He is extremely tactically proficient, has a hardballer common sense approach to things, and is unafraid to make his voice heard and his opinion known no matter the consequences.

So both my leaders have good and bad sides; they do things I will imitate later in my career, and things I will avoid. However, as truly common ground, they both lack the ability to communicate well. They're good enough at expressing ideas or giving directives ..., but when it comes to empathizing or reading the implied versus the spoken, or reading body language and atmosphere, they both are not up to par in my experience. As a result, their conflicting personalities, which should cause honing and balance, cause strife. I find it a little sad since if they worked well together they would accomplish amazing things. Beyers is just too traditional ..., and Roybal is too headstrong. If instead they would blend their better parts, with Beyers being steady and predictable and Roybal being assertive and quick thinking, I don't think a better squad/team leader duo could exist (future Gabe: lies).

From my first day at Able company, 2nd squad, my squad, has always been the best squad of the best platoon of the best company of the best battalion of the best brigade of 25th ID [infantry division]. I do not shy away from saying we, as a squad, are at the top. I have no doubt that this prestige is in no small part due to the favor of Providence. I believe it will continue to stay as such no matter the leadership or manning so long as the spirit remains. This spirit of aggressive performance, savage desire for glory, and reveling in exceeding all standards set by others will remain. All else is irrelevant in the eyes of the army, in the eyes of war, and in the eyes of the world. Aside from the spirit of 2nd squad, the only thing relevant about us in God's eyes is our faith. If I may in boldness profess: as long as one or more member of this 2nd squad retains a deep, pure faith in the Living God, His favor will remain, and our legacy prevail. I hope and pray that Beyers and Roybal settle, and harmonize in their jobs. However, I know that no matter the outcome, the squad will remain unchanged in a fundamental sense.

And that's what I have to say about that.

Oh, and tomorrow is my birthday. Yay me.

Dang, this is the 24th page of these journals. I'll have enough for a proper book by the time I'm done here.

Monday, November 6, 2017

I don't know why it's been so long since I last wrote. I suppose the rhythms of life caught me up in their sway. Not much news apart from the usual day to day nonsense. Waiting on a cool mission.

I did have a couple interesting dreams recently. In one, some guys I know from various places (including the army) were trying to figure out the meaning of a dream from a written journal, a drawing, and a map. The only thing I clearly remember (other than some vague conversation in which another person called us dumb, and we decided [unrelated] that the drawing was an unnecessary piece) is that I saw the map change before my eyes until it was all depicting a charred, barren, desolated wasteland on a stretch of land similar to the front range of Colorado (mountains on the west). However, in the middle of the map jutting out from the side of the mountains was a ridge with a circular valley at the tip surrounded by thin, towering mountains that acted as a wall. There was an opening like a doorway facing the plains. My first and only repeated thought was: It's a safe haven from the destruction.

Well, hopefully something noteworthy happens soon that will make a good, entertaining entry. True actions are always more captivating than thoughts or even dreams.

Thursday, November 9, 2017

Still nothing of note to really write about. Just a bizarre dream.

Apart from the bizarre dream, the only news is that the ODA we are with left today for a QRF mission without us. They will be gone for a couple weeks. Our leadership here has found it pleasing to schedule daily training while they are gone – most of which will be focused on topics of which I already have a firm grasp. Boring. Life is growing boring. Nothing exciting to write about. Nothing exciting to do. I could talk about how my shoulder and knee are healing nicely, but since I never mentioned the injuries in the first place, bringing it up now is a waste of time. My spiritual journey feels plateaued in a state of stumbling forward in pursuit of cleanliness and righteousness. I am not in a bad place by any means, but I want to move further onward and upward; to dive deeper in my relationship with YHVH and feel the surge of His presence and power constantly. I will pursue Him to this end. No matter the stagnation or the bore of regular life, no matter the spiritual stumbling blocks, I will pursue Him.

Sunday, November 12, 2017

Supposedly some new guys were supposed to leave Alaska on their way here today. I've heard some bad rumors as to their demeanors, but it could just be SFC Herron's ever famous exaggeration and judgmental bias against anything that doesn't fit his paradigm of what the army should be. However, if it's true they have irksome personalities, and haven't adapted to their new occupations, they will be in for a sore surprise upon arriving to Camp Vose. Able is known for not going easy on people we deem unworthy of our ranks – 2nd platoon even more so. If these new guys have bad attitudes and haughty countenances, rest assured it will be fixed, or they will be gone. There is still a week and a half left before the ODA returns from their QRF mission, which means a week and half more dumb training and boredom. As a result, these new guys' arrival is the most exciting thing happening for a month probably, assuming they will indeed leave today and arrive within the month. I wish another mission come down and result in beautiful chaos and close combat. However, I suppose I must fight and win another battle before such an adventure may occur.

I want to create something. I want to forge metal, carve wood, bend elements to my will to create something beautiful and powerful. I want to do something. I want to push my body to its limits, drive onward for a noble cause, succeed in shaping an event that will have echoes across the globe for eternity. I want to make something. I want to leave behind a story, a life, a legacy so bold and wonderful that all who follow after me are in awe of the story and the miracles of YHVH therein. I can't do all, or any of this right now. However, as the start of a blade is with fire and ore, so the start of my story, the start of my doings, my creations, my legacy, is within the forge of YHVH's temperance and spirit. I'm afraid I have proven a tiresome metal to work, but nonetheless, I am willing and seeking the time at which I will be refined, sharpened, and put to use.

My shoulder has been re-aggravated by my own actions. Those reading take note of what may be viewed as sense common even to a fool, yet had escaped me, or rather been ignored in my desire to regain what ground I have lost. Do not, if at all avoidable, perform the same action which has caused an injury under any sort of major duress or strain lest the injury worsen. This morn, the joint between the acromion of the scapula and the clavicle seemed excessively sore. Such a soreness is preferable to a sharp or pinching pain as there had been some days ago, yet it is an inconvenience to know that the joint is not healed enough for heavy load. As I have never injured a ligament or tendon before, much less one in my arm or shoulder, I am unsure how to remedy it with exercise. I am certain that there are movements that may be performed in order to speed the healing process with a strengthening or a stretching of the surrounding tissues. Not knowing what these movements are, and thus having to ad lib my own based on an educated guess as to what may be helpful, has been a rather tiresome bother. I will pray YHVH heals my shoulder soundly before its full strength is necessitated by circumstance. In the meantime, I will continue with my improvised treatments in hopes of some success.

Hopefully some adventure arises before I become too bored. All the reading, watching of shows, and writing cannot replace doing what I have been trained for in a real-life setting where actions truly matter. However, I should really pursue deeper study of what non-fictional books I have brought in an attempt to gain deeper spiritual, strategic, and medical insight. So I suppose I shall do some of that now.

Deployment Journal 11/13/2017 – Short Story

Monday, November 13, 2017

Short story ideas: post apocalypse sword fights, presumed death and a journey home, dual world existence, new addition to the Creature's story, wilderness survival, fantasy/sci-fi war, drama and political intrigue but all the main characters get assassinated before they can do anything, war but just the boring parts, multiple points of view surrounding one event (such as a chaotic occurrence in the streets of some downtown city during an enlightened medieval age)

Start of a story: (added details over the course of several weeks)

The man stood well near seven feet tall. A loose fitting black coat that hung from his slumped, yet broad shoulders only added to his intimidating visage. The hood drooped low over his brow, just short of covering two piercingly green eyes that darted to and fro with an uncommon alertness. His hulking frame drew stares as he sat alone at a table toward the back of the barroom. He wore twin .454 Casull revolvers, their dark gleaming eight-inch barrels just visible at the edges of the unbuttoned coat. The only other weapon the man carried rested on the table in front of him. It was a sword. A mammoth blade nearly unwieldable to a normal man seemed to flicker with the red glow of its ancient temper in the lamplight. Most men of the era carried both a gun and a blade for the purpose of self-defense. Few, however, used them as often as the giant at the rear table. He was an assassin. His unnatural size kept most people from picking a fight, but his agility and reflexes were on par with a wild cat. He could choose whether to eliminate a target with finesse, or to barrel through their defenses leaving a river of blood in his wake. Never had he failed to bring down his quarry.

The batwing doors creaked with the chime of a bell signaling the entrance of a new customer. The bar was already filled with the steady din of voices and song, with the night reaching its peak of activity. The assassin's eyes instantly assessed the newcomer, and he drew a breath of fear. To the untrained, or inexperienced rather, the man who had just entered appeared utterly normal. He wore plain jeans and boots, a waist length brown leather jacket with no notable features, and an old-fashioned baseball cap probably made in the '20s. His face was relaxed, calm, with a vacant gaze. He was a fairly average height, maybe six feet give or take an inch, without a noticeably girthy build despite quite obviously powerful legs that yielded a swift and sure step. These observations were normal enough, and could have been made by a novice. However, it was not these that caused the giant to gasp quietly. He had noticed one thing amiss: the man carried no weapon. For a man to walk around unarmed in the 2080s was practically suicide. No law reached the countryside, and the cities were amuck with up and coming mobsters intent on taking advantage of the post-war chaos. Muggings and murders were so normal that families would have eight or more children in hopes that one would survive to the age of 20. Yet here was a young man who seemed unscarred, and worse, unafraid of the world around him despite his lack of weaponry. This small detail terrified the hulking assassin because the ordinary, apparently defenseless man happened to be the next on a list of targets. The assassin had never met a man who could survive in this world without weapons. Even children who neglected to carry a pistol or knife died quickly. The strongest brawlers could not rely on muscle to stop a bullet. Death was a fact of this life and here was a lone man defying it. Defying the very law of nature. So the large assassin gasped silently in fear before quickly redirecting his thoughts to the mission, his gazed fixed on the unarmed man.

The stranger walked confidently through the batwing doors of the bar and scanned the room in one sweeping glance. Nothing of great importance or potential danger stood out to him save one shadowy character near the back of the room. Rather, it was not the shadowy character that stood out as a potential threat, but the great red sword that sat across the table before him. The man did not think much more of it; however; it had been a long time since a sword had been capable of harming him. Truth be told, he was a little sad that adrenaline seemed such a rare hormone in his blood these days. As he walked to the bar, his hand subtly brushed his left jean pocket out of habit. The small billfold was still in place. He carried no other possessions. Upon reaching the counter, he ordered a beer, paid on the spot and sipped thoughtfully as he surveyed the room in the shelf mirror. Out of the corner of his right eye he could just barely see the large shadowy figure with the red sword. The stranger didn't focus long on the assassin, but noticed easily enough that the heavy man's bright green eyes were locked on him. The man smiled to himself behind his raised mug, thinking about the scenarios that may play out in the next few minutes. His daydreaming was cut short when the fifth scenario played out almost perfectly.

Once again the batwing doors chimed a new entrance. A woman, scantily clad in a form fitting, red silk dress, braless, with the form of a goddess, and the grace of a swan, waltzed brazenly into the male-filled room. She, an assassin by training but a con artist by trade, immediately noticed two things amiss with the barroom scene. One: a rather simple looking, unarmed man was not staring at her. Two: a shadowy figure with a mammoth sword wasn't either. Every other eye in the bar molested her very visage as she glided to the counter. A breeze from the closing doors caused her nipples to stiffen; the men began to drool. She sat next to the unarmed stranger and ordered a scotch. She threw a sultry glance with her shining blue eyes, trimmed by long eyelashes and a gently curved smile, at the normal looking man. In the same glance, she noticed a few more details about the shadowy figure in the corner. It seemed he was here on a hit, and from the direction of his gaze, she was certain that the target was the man next to her. This was an unfortunate development since she was here for the same man, but to drug him and turn him in to her employer alive. She brushed the stranger's leg with her own as she shifted on the stool.

The stranger knew one of two things would happen at that point. Either she would use the contact as a segue to conversation and then kidnapping, or she would attempt to kill him right there without anyone noticing. She chose the former. He humored her for a while, even looking into her eyes and staring for a while at her shapely bosom. She leaned against him, pressing her boobs against his arm with a flirtatious laugh, after her second scotch. He neglectfully turned his attention from the entire room to the woman next to him. No matter how much he froze his heart to the world, some instincts never change. Hurriedly correcting his mistake, he turned his face toward the shadowy figure in the corner to check on him. The shadowy figure had moved. Impossible. In a mere split second he had lost sight of the only person in this bar that posed a potential threat. A normal fellow would have felt his heart sink and begin to race, but the stranger just shrugged and went back to his beer. He easily tasted the tranquilizer that the woman had slipped into his drink. It ruined the flavor, but he was determined to play along for just a few moments more. It had been a long time since any drug affected him. It was likely that none could.

The assassin swung the great sword downward as forcefully as he could. The ensuing mayhem of blood, gore, and screams would provide ample opportunity for escape. The stranger's back was turned to the hooded giant and his head was drooped over his beer. The brawny assassin stood over four feet away, with the blade tip nearly touching the ceiling. The woman seemed not to notice, or care, that a 5 foot long blade was about to split her target in half. What a waste, the assassin thought, that the woman's arm and part of her leg would be caught in the blow. She was an alluring sight, but not worth the bounty on the stranger she clung to. The blade began its downward path, gleaming red in the lamplight. Less than 20 thousandths of a second later, it smote an empty stool.

The stranger was somewhat disappointed that the blade had not dealt with the annoying broad. He never knew how he managed to move so quickly, or how he knew about attacks from blind spots, but he didn't really care. What concerned him was that the woman seemed to have similarly quick reflexes. Perhaps she was even faster than the stranger, since before he could reassess where the assassin was, she was already sinking a thin blade into the giant's chest.

The assassin, impressing both the woman and the unarmed man, caught her hand before the blade had gone a full inch, and broke it in his grasp. The woman screamed in pain and anger and drew a derringer with her other hand. The assassin was not quite quick enough to dodge a bullet. To his luck, the first shattered against the large sword, and the second merely lodged in his enormous shoulder. It hurt, but it could wait. With a hand quicker than a rattlesnake, he loosed a shot from one of the behemoth revolvers that rode at his hips. As if mirroring the woman's aim, his shot landed at her shoulder. However, just as lion dwarfs a housecat, so the massive ball of lead from the giant's gun did far more damage to the lady's small frame than the quaint .30 caliber derringer did to his shoulder. She fell backwards onto the table behind her unconscious and bleeding, one full breast visible where the dress had fallen after being torn at the strap by the bullet.

The stranger watched the split second exchange of gunfire with a detached interest. Though, a pang of pity did dance fleetingly across his heart when he saw the woman's blood-sullied body sprawled across the table. He didn't have time to contemplate the emotion since the assassin's second sword swing was already slicing the air toward the stranger's side. The unarmed man figured he would let it hit him this time. He was bored and hoped that, by some happenstance of fortune, this big man might prove entertaining. Less than two seconds after the first blow had cleaved the empty bar counter and stool, the second connected cleanly with the stranger's upper arm and began to burrow toward his ribs. The stranger sighed when the shattered blade tip lodged itself in the wall behind him and the room fell silent. The unarmed man looked quietly at the giant who was staring at the broken red sword. The stranger looked down at his own arm. No cut, no bruise. It was as if the blade never touched him. He walked up to the assassin, weaving easily between the barrage of bullets, and struck the giant with a mighty uppercut to the diaphragm. His fist broke flesh, shattered bone, and shot out the big man's back. The shockwave from the speed of his movement prevented any blood from staying on his hand or clothes. The large assassin fell forward, dead before he hit the ground. The stranger looked at his watch. The entire ordeal had only lasted 6 seconds.

The woman awoke some time later to one man groping her breast while holding a cloth on her wound, and another pushing her legs apart while toying with her thong. Both men dropped dead with slit throats. She winced as she sat up, her left arm dangling uselessly at her side. Perhaps she should not have killed the groper, it seemed he had been holding pressure on her wound and now, with an open hole on each side of her shoulder, the blood flowed freely. She felt as though she might lose consciousness once again. Suddenly, a shooting pain shocked her mind back to alertness. She attacked mindlessly, and her knife was easily wrenched from her hand by the unarmed stranger. He was stuffing a cloth into her wound on each side. He then wrapped the shoulder with a long strip from another cloth and cinched it tight over the packed wounds. She looked at him in confusion. He should be unconscious at least from the drug, she thought, or dead from that big man- her thoughts stopped short as she saw the giant assassin laying on the ground in front of her with a hole the size of a bowling ball in the center of his chest. She looked in shock at the man bandaging her. He didn't seem to notice.

The stranger knew he should probably leave town. If the dull populace of this rotten city began to spread rumors about the incident at the bar, it could result in disaster for his future. Once the smart men, the malevolent men who pulled the puppet strings, caught wind of these rumors, the stranger's identity would be known. There were not many men in the world with abilities like his, and even fewer that openly used them. The stranger was not one of those reclusive fiends, seeking only to justify their own sense of self-righteousness by claiming their shut-in behavior was for the safety of others. Neither was he one of those openly self-righteous monologists who dreamed only of attention while lamenting the burden of their powers. The stranger was simply himself. He walked where he wanted, did what he felt like, and never sought out trouble. Yet trouble is what always seemed to find him. Case in point, the woman before him now had a look in her eye that he had seen many times before, and it was trouble. She looked shocked, as was expected, but there was a glint of awe in her eyes. Awe always turned to worship, which depending on the person might turn into a twisted form of love. This twisted form of love was the trouble the stranger hated most. It caused pain. Fights, assassination attempts, starvation, being kicked to the curb for differences too great for the mindless sheep of the world to reconcile with their own lowly ideas of rationality. Even death itself was not painful for the stranger. Twisted forms of love, though, hurt how he imagined the woman to hurt now from that bullet wound. It occurred to the stranger that he had locked eyes with the woman for some time now, so he turned away without a word and drew a glass of water from the bar and drank it. The woman seemed put off by the blatantly un-gentlemanlike behavior, meaning his goal was accomplished. He drew her a glass and brought it over.

The woman drank slowly, once again reeling from the pain in her shoulder. She and the unarmed man conversed with short sentences. Smalltalk. She revealed too much about herself, perhaps, but despite the fact she had attempted to drug him, the man seemed to her quite trustworthy. She noticed the pain in her shoulder fading, and for a moment the world seemed a perfect place. She imagined the stranger smiling warmly at her and holding her with a gentle embrace. She felt warm, safe, as if it were the perfect time and place for a long, long nap.

The stranger knew when he had dressed the wound that the woman was doomed to die. The nearest hospital was an hour trip at shortest whether by hovercar, train, or land car. The amount of blood on the table and floor around it, and the size of the hole through her, made clear the end from the beginning. In fact, he had unwittingly presumed her dead before she leaped off the table, slashing the throats of the men that were poking around her body. It was then he decided to ease her passing in what way he could. So he packed the wound, brought her water, and avoided appearing a hero. The last part was selfish, though. He didn't want her to hold him in awe, or love him for saving her, because that would have caused him pain. The pain of watching someone die who trusted you.

Most of the bar had emptied at the start of the shooting; most of what remained fled when they saw the stranger's fist explode from the giant assassin's spine. The two men the woman had killed were a drunk who had woken up because of the ruckus, and the bar tender who had cautiously poked his head out when all was quiet only to see the bare breast of a potential corpse just inviting a quick feel. The stranger was glad they were both dead. Fewer men to tell the tale of what they saw. He left the woman laid across a pool table with a regular table cloth draped over her face and body.

Walking into the street, the stranger noticed three things. First, and most obviously, he was surrounded by police. Second, and most importantly, a woman who looked exactly like the dead one inside was staring at him from beside a cop car. Third, and probably most interestingly, none of them were pointing guns at him. They were just waiting. The stranger had no desire to play along with any more annoyances on the part of those who sought his life, so he walked down the street toward where the gathering of policemen was the thinnest. They shouted, screamed through megaphone static, and flashed holograms in different languages, all in an attempt to make the stranger stand still. He refused. A policeman drew a firearm and combat knife and advanced toward the unarmed man. The rookie cop was told to stand down repeatedly, but the adrenaline of fight was already thick in his veins. The stranger sighed. In a flash, the pistol and knife were no longer in the young cop's hands, but in the stranger's. He fired once, killing the young man who had attacked him.

The rest of the police force drew weapons and opened fire at the stranger, who had already dropped the weapons he had taken from the rookie policeman. A gale of explosions echoed through the empty street like thunder in the mountains. No one heard the woman's cries to cease over the din of gunfire.

The woman had awoken in the car on the way to the bar, her last memory being of the stranger who had bandaged her. It was a toilsome thing, being a downloadable soul. She had died in copies of her own body so many times that she began to think that true death might come as a relief, when such a time came as the higher ups saw fit to let her die. This bleak outlook was what gave her cool composure, and the ability to do anything to anyone without true feeling or emotion. So why, then, was she screaming for the sake of a man who she—well, her previous copy—had just met. More worrisome, why was she rushing toward him when her own employer had changed tunes and now wanted him dead? Why would she waste another copy of herself on this seemingly plain man? Why did she want so badly for him to survive? And... where was he?

The view of the city from the sky at night was a beautiful thing if one did not consider the evil that dwelt there. This contrast is what the stranger's thoughts lingered on as he fell toward the earth from the peak of a jump that had launched him a bit higher than expected. On his current trajectory, he would land a few blocks down from where the police were firing at an empty bar front. His landing left a rather large crater in the ground and the handful of onlookers that witnessed it hadn't time to overreact before the stranger was gone, sprinting down the road. The gusts of wind caused by the air displaced by his movement were strong enough to shatter glass in a few storefronts. He felt a twinge of guilt, knowing that he could not stop and repay the owners for the damage. Time was of the essence and the stranger's plan did not include parley with strangers over broken windows. He grinned in thought as he ran. Things could progress in one of seven ways from this point forward, and all of them resulted in an enjoyable clash of force. His plan was simply to force the decisive battle upon those who attacked him so that he could enjoy a peaceful dinner (it was early morning and the stranger had no plans to eat lunch). The company that sought his capture or demise was likely to have equipment on hand capable of pursuing and possibly even subduing the stranger. The man laughed. No, the men pursuing him could not subdue him no matter the equipment. However, if he wished to pursue his current plan, he would need them to think it possible. So he changed course and attacked the confused cluster of cops from the rear. A few well-placed punches resulted in two demolished cop cars. A light tap on the chest of one of the braver policemen ensured he would not have the use of his left lung ever again. The stranger paused. These men were fodder compared to the foes he was used to. He should not use his full strength, lest he murder an innocent. A bullet seemed to slow as it advanced toward him, he dodged it by a fraction of an inch, but feigned being struck in the shoulder. He grasped the intended place of impact with his left hand and ran away, slow enough to be seen and followed.

A few minutes later the stranger encountered a road block on the highway leading out of town. He repeated the scene at the bar front, this time faking an injury to his leg. He continued on his way, even slower, until he reached an area far enough from the city for a proper fight. The fields were beautiful in the current midmorning light. Full of tall wheat and corn, near shimmering in the sun of an early summer day. The stranger was sorry for the destruction that would soon overtake such a pure plot of land.

The woman rode in the back of an up-armored ground car. The auto-drive kept them in perfect synchronization and spacing with the other vehicles in the convoy. A few cars ahead of her, a large cargo truck hauled the organization's secret weapon for use against the unarmed man. It was a particle destabilizer. Well, that was the fancy term for it. More specifically, the weapon was a relatively small laser mounted on an auto turret that could track a railgun bolt with ease. The laser itself was powered by four enormous fusion generators (hence the cargo truck) that supplied an obscene number of gigawatts. Put that kind of power behind the laser's ultra-high frequency (in other words, a midrange gamma wavelength) and 18 inch beam diameter and most things were incinerated within seconds; shattered nuclear bonds in non-radioactive elements produced more of a fizzle than a bang upon breaking into their respective byproducts. The danger was in accidentally pointing the weapon at large quantities of heavy metals or at anything remotely radioactive to start with. If such a mistake was made, the resultant radioactive shine or, even worse, atomic explosion would kill anyone within a certain radius. The woman was sure that the weapon would not miss, and the sureness caused her heart to sink as though struck with fear. She was far from understanding the feelings she harbored to this stranger who had shown one of her bodies kindness. Having been put through programming after programming, she wasn't even sure if the feelings were her own. She had never had proper emotions before, save the rage or lust she used when luring or eliminating targets. Such was the fate of downloadable souls; they were emotionless, robotic, and lethally efficient. This preconditioning considered, what could be causing the faults that now appeared in the flat plane of her feelings? Her conclusion terrified her more than the weapon that was now aimed at the unarmed man. Love. Not romantic love, not infatuation, not even brotherly love or broad human love; rather the love that one feels for a person who has shown them kindness. The simple, appreciative happiness directed at another in return for an unwarranted good deed. She had never felt it before, yet it was nostalgic. Despite being carved down, honed, trained, indoctrinated, and programmed beyond any hope of humanity, her original human soul now cracked its cage just enough to allow a glimmer of that feeling that is native to all mankind. The particle destabilizer fired with a roar like thunder as the capacitor discharge ionized the air around the weapon. She looked frantically to the window to see the stranger's figure vanish in the beam. Human tears rolled down the cheeks of her cloned body. The manager that sat next to her typed a few words into a com-pad, signaling the end of their experiments with both the weapon and the woman.

The stranger strolled casually behind the weapon as it disintegrated nearly half of a 10 acre corn field. He did not know how it was he avoided calamity, how his body could move quicker than physics should allow, or even how he would remain cancer free despite the radiation burn from where the beam had nicked his arm. He did know, however, that the woman who died in the bar was now bawling her eyes out in the car behind the weapon, and he wanted to know why. There was no real sympathy or even concern in his vague curiosity, simply a desire to see what miracle could have resulted in 1) the woman being alive, and 2) an assassin crying over the death of a target. His first question was answered quite quickly as he strolled past the second trailer behind the weapon. The open side of a container revealed frozen, sleeping, perfect copies of the woman who sat in the car behind. A few men were tending to them, or… the stranger's breath caught briefly before he resumed his detached observation; the men were not tending to the clones, they were disconnecting them. The stranger knew he should not get involved any further than needed, but the fleeting sadness he felt at the destruction of such beauty, even if only copies, compelled him to act. The men were paralyzed and unconscious a few seconds later. The stranger observed the clones more closely as the particle destabilizer whined low and hissed, signaling the full drainage of its power sources. Encased in cryogenic gel behind bulletproof glass, the statuesque bodies of the woman he had treated at the bar revealed a troubling truth. The woman was a downloadable soul. A human taken from birth and trained ruthlessly to the point of machine-like perfection in their occupation and then taken from their body and implanted time after time in clones until their employer no longer had use for them. The original body would then be killed, eliminating the soul, and allowing the clone bodies to be disposed of without much effort. At this moment of realization, the stranger felt a very strong surge of sorrow and rage due to the injustice of such a slavery. He had seen slavery, in its raw form before it was abolished, and then again in a more modern from as it evolved underground, and even again when it was reinstituted as a legal practice, but this form sickened him more than any other from the past three centuries. He resolved then to do something he considered properly crazy. He would retake up the torch he carried in decades passed, and fight for freedom. From the depths of his chest there brewed a strong sensation, one he had not felt in nearly fifty years. His platonic, disinterested eyes flickered with the flame of passion. The emotions which he had long shut in the darkest corners of his soul now surged to the surface. Justice dealt for the sake of justice had dulled his mind, living for a thrilling fight had left him empty and bored, but now a cause was placed before him that shattered the veil. The stranger made sure the clones were safe and walked back to the weapon as crews were prepping to leave. They barely uttered the first sound of alarm when the stranger bellowed with a voice like a lion's the battle cry of his younger days, and with a single strike, demolished the entirety of the weapon that had been made to kill him. Dashing to the vehicle in which the woman rode, he tore the door from the hinges, paused, and held out a gentle hand. With a grin on his face as wide as a child's on Christmas, and with the inferno of righteousness in his eyes, the stranger said, "Come with me."

The woman was too stunned to answer at first, but her cloned body reacted in a way which only a true human should be able to. Reaching up, she took the stranger's extended hand and stepped out of the car with a tearful smile.

The following pursuit and climactic battle was one that rivalled any of which the woman had historical knowledge. It seemed that one moment the organization had cornered them, and the next moment the stranger was having them dance to his own battle rhythm. These fabled gods, men of renown, superheroes, the woman had never witnessed one in the flesh, much less seen their tremendous capacity for violence. It stunned her, scared her. However, she realized — after a few shots in her direction mysteriously never struck anywhere near her, and after each underling of the organization was left ambulatory with a mere broken arm or leg — that the stranger which fought before her was indeed one of noble character. She had seen that, she recalled, the first time they met. He had seemed impervious to the tactic of seduction that had infallibly lured every other target to their demise. In addition, he had bandaged her dying copy and provided her comfort, even peace, in a process that had only ever yielded pain. She found yet another nostalgic emotion crack through the shell of programming from the depths of her soul: joy. It was a grateful, inspired, heartfelt joy at the prospect of being saved by a true hero.

It was in no such heroic lens that the stranger viewed himself, however. He felt duty-bound and humbly grateful to embark on such a mission as human freedom once again. With his goal in clear focus, and time sensitive at that, the stranger made short time of mopping up the pawns and moving in to attack the heart of the organization. In truth, calling it an organization was a bit of a stretch. It was closer to a loose, failing conglomerate of three small tech companies who happened to have a couple of geniuses on board. The chief stockholder decided that a man with "abilities" would make a good addition to the research subjects, and boost stock prices as a plus. The stranger was lightly amused by how vastly they had underestimated his "abilities." Perhaps one day he would give himself up for study under a more ethical team of scientists so that he may have a chance at understanding his own body for the first time in his nearly thousand-year life.

Upon reaching the main headquarters of the organization, the stranger noticed the woman wince in pain and place a hand over an eye. The proprietors of the establishment must have begun to remove the downloadable soul's original body from life support. Wasting no time with the small fries, the stranger asked the location of the body from the front counter. The secretary gave it out quite readily while staring wide eyed at the path of destruction behind the unarmed man before her. Once more, the stranger wasted no time, skipped both the stairs and the elevator, and simply jumped through the floors with an amount of power that conveniently landed him directly on the level where the woman's body was kept. It seemed that the owners had gotten a clue as to their own incompetence, and abandoned their efforts to clean up and discard of sensitive information and dirty little secrets. He walked across the nearly empty lab as the last of the research team were fleeing. The woman's body floated serenely in a tank of life support fluid. Electrodes with wires extending dotted her skin. Electrical stimulation pulses and renewable tissue implants kept the body in good health in case clones were eliminated faster than they could be produced. The stranger flipped on the few switches that had been flipped off on one of the control panels, and the grimace of pain on the woman's face and that of her original body disappeared. The woman now stood behind him, having taken the elevator. The stranger realized he must have been staring for a long time. He turned quickly away and nearly blushed, nearly. He commented to the woman that she looked quite peaceful, and beautiful.

She looked at her original body, and then at the one she wore. The clone body she had grown all too comfortable with now made clear its faults. She could not feel the air around her as keenly as she wished. She could not touch her own skin without cringing slightly. Even looking through the perfectly copied eyes, she felt as though a thick pane of glass lay between her and anything she saw. She looked at the stranger. He was the only person who had ever stood out clearly to her and even now he seemed to fade…

The stranger caught the woman gently as she collapsed. He lay the clone body carefully on one of the medical beds nearby and walked to the glass tank. The woman blinked slowly, and then met his gaze through the amber fluid. Gesturing to the control panel, the woman began to pull the wires, attachments, and tubes from her body. The tank shook and gurgled as the fluid was drained. She stumbled slightly when her bare feet touched the ground, caught herself, and pushed open the unsealed door. The stranger stood with a hand outstretched and she took it. It seemed as if all the programming, all the indoctrination, all the layers of firewalls built into her soul by training and killing melted away. The very real touch of the stranger's hand and the very real look of compassion in his eyes overwhelmed her in a way unimaginable to one who has spent their whole life experiencing such real interaction. She shivered with the cold of the air on her skin, still dripping with life support fluid. The stranger immediately, almost with an embarrassed look, wrapped a large towel around her and handed her a folded blanket before leaving to find clothes for her.

Around the same time, as the entire adventure of the stranger and the woman had only taken a mere day and a half, a giant of a man drew a sharp breath from the floor of an abandoned bar. The hulking assassin sat up and stared blankly at the nearly closed hole in his chest. He rose to his feet, wincing slightly, but had regained a kingly demeanor and powerful stance by the time he had walked the few feet to where his broken sword lay. He picked up the hilt end, and pulled the tip end from the wall. Laying them both upon the bar top, he mumbled some quiet words and extended his hand over the blade. "The life of me for the life of you, till the day you run me through, bonded ever our spirits be, never dying, never free," the giant boomed. The red steel began to glow and spark as though fresh from the forge. In a blinding flash the two pieces were rejoined and the crack vanished. It was a strange thing, the magic of downloadable souls. Most people used them as slaves, as weapons and tools. However there were some who became such an existence voluntarily, and some who were capable of bonding the souls to objects that would survive it even should the host body die. As a result, the objects obtained a sort of immortality that passed to those who owned it, but only if the wielder gave his own soul to the bond, in a way that made their life forces, their spirits forever bound by fate. The big assassin whispered to the blade, speaking gently to the soul which it held. It was a fierce one, beautiful and terrible to behold, it was the soul of the giant's best friend who had grown up with him, and become an assassin with him, and died a violent death on a mission, but not before speaking those secret words that tore his very essence from his own body and embedded it in his friend's blade.

He walked out of the bar and squinted at the midday sun. Over twenty four hours it had taken him to heal. He was impressed with the unarmed stranger. Never before had the giant met one of those legends, those superhuman fighters of old. It was an experience he would not soon forget. Abandoning his contract and his target, the assassin set out westward for the hills. It was time for a period of reflection and training. The stranger may be one of the fabled superheroes that once conquered the world, but the giant would not be so easily trampled over again. There was strength, and untapped power in his blood, and in the binding of two spirits. Blade and flesh, downloaded soul and conscious mind, became one in the big man and his sword. A challenger had arisen that finally called for his greatest effort. The giant had no desire to kill him anymore, or even to harm him. He solely wished to meet him in glorious single combat, and be seen as equal.

The wilderness of 2085 North America was a contradictory thing. Holographic displays danced through the national parks and along hiking trails, the ghosts of plants and animals long extinct from human negligence. There were speakers that poured out woodland sounds and occasionally a narration of the region's history. The large man thought it was sad that the enslavement of the land and the overuse of technology therein was what people now called nature. Thankfully there were spaces left. Spaces yet untouched by the oozing, outward spread of civilization from its hubs. There were places on the globe, even here in North America, that no human, grown up and grown soft with all modern comforts, dared go. The giant man had never had the comfort of technology or civilization. His size and demeanor set him apart from a young age, and his family were what was left of a dying breed of farmer. He worked the land, using his hands instead of automated planters and reapers. When he reached the middle of his teen years, he killed a fellow classmate in just three strikes. It was quite accidental, the big adolescent hadn't known his own strength. Despite the ruling that it was self-defense, the assassin was shunned from his town and his home, and taken in by an unlikely group which taught him all that he now knew. It was back to this group that the giant now traveled, ready to see old friends, train with old masters, and tell them of his adventures and his triumphs. So he walked onward for days, leaving behind the urban sprawl and commercialized parks, and entering the utter quiet and dark of the true wilderness.

After a week of wearisome trudging, the supplies in his pack long expended, the big assassin arrived at the looming gates of his old guild. They opened without a sound, though made of thick oak and steel, due to enormous greased ball hinges. Most of the assassins that lived and trained here were large folk. Burly men with hulking frames and women resembling Nordic goddesses were the norm, but even among these hearty people, the giant of a man stood tall and intimidating. As he walked through the open gates, the guards rushed to greet him. These were friends from the old days, fellow trainees, and teammates on missions, all of whom were glad to see their brother in arms return safely. One of them asked where his partner was. When the giant had struck out to make a name for himself, his best friend had followed and they had become famous for their effectiveness as mercenaries. The giant man only looked to the ground in silence and then placing a hand on the hilt, stared long at the deep red of the blade which he carried. A look of understanding, sorrow, grief, and acceptance came over the faces of the old friends that saw his subtle motions. Pushing the matter aside, they welcomed him into the large cedar hall at the center of camp. A large fire roared at each end of the building, and a banquette table, ever set with the fruits of the land, lay spread for a feast in the middle. A return of a comrade after time abroad was always cause for celebration among this unique group of killers for hire. They held to the old style of martial virtues, accepting all useful strategies from deception to brute force, but not denying the necessity of emoting as the basis of human nature. They were a group of men and women that time had forgotten, and who themselves had chosen to forget the sickening materialism of the world in which they lived in favor of a strenuous existence that toughened the body and tempered the soul.

Deployment Journal 11/16/2017 – 11/30/2017

Thursday, November 16, 2017

I had a dream last night about a few things. There was a battle royale between a number of ultra-powerful individuals that all had very powerful followers/fighters. The clash took place on and around camp Vose. I was one of the fighters, but was on par with the superior beings. I don't remember many details.

Another dream was based off the anime series called Fate. I remember explaining the Grail war and servants to my dad or someone else. There was a nefarious plot among one or two of the servants and *mages*. I could sense a demonic presence for much of the time. I used the name of Jesus to cast it away. There was still something wrong after the most potent one was gone, though. The whole dream felt off in some way. Even the fun parts like chariot races and dramatic intrigue were blurred by a film of dissonance.

Overall, I am unsure what to think of these dreams. I pray YHVH tells me what they mean and gives me wisdom on how to act.

I received word yesterday that there is a mission coming up on Dec 3 that could yield multiple kills. I am excited, but cautious. The mission is to last 20 days total, until Dec 23. Nearly three weeks away from "home base" will no doubt feel like much longer. However, if even a few of those days are filled with glorious battle, YHVH's protective hand and Spirit of Power, and the destruction of the enemy, I will be quite happy. I am excited to learn what true battle, true warfare looks like. I am excited to do my job, my true job. I hope that I will be able to deal a lethal blow to the enemy force. I wish to singlehandedly bring down enough wicked men to cripple their force. I realize there will be others with me that have similar desires, and I hope we all get to see those desires come to fruition. However, to obtain perfect victory we must be clean. I, at the very least, and preferably all those of faith, must be spiritually and ceremonially clean at the start of the mission so that YHVH's favor may provide a forcefield to cover us all as we advance against the foe. As David told the priests at Nob when they asked of the men's condition before giving over the consecrated bread and great sword of Goliath, "The men's things are holy even on missions that are unholy."

Friday, November 24, 2017

Brace for idiocy:

We were supposed to be at Gibson for four days. Two for travel, two for shooting. We ended up staying for a week since our leadership doesn't listen to us or care what we think. While there, tensions rose, as I knew they would, and Roybal got himself in a little heat with the honchos. Usually this wouldn't be a problem. His reputation speaks for itself, and a confrontational personality comes along naturally with his aggressiveness and intensity in work. Unfortunately, he and the higher leadership lack sturdy communication skills. Hence the heat. Turns out they were completely sick of his attitude/personality/sense-making, so they decided to ship him off to a completely different base where his skills as a leader and an infantryman will be wasted. As a result, we of second squad will be losing our primary nonsense deflector, advocate, and go-to man. Roybal did well embodying the spirit of second squad, leaving yet another reason he should not go. Our leadership, in their great and infinite wisdom (sarcasm), decided to move him in just three days, right before a huge mission. So we will be in a bad mood, and have a non-combat-tested team leader going into the longest mission of this deployment and to the most dangerous area thus far. Brilliant. In addition, no one was consulted. The one joe that was asked wasn't even on Roybal's team. I thought the PL was a level-headed guy, but it appears he has thin skin just like every other army leader above E-5, and so he decided that he didn't want Roybal picking on him anymore. Of course Beyers rolled over and accepted it, despite knowing that we will be losing our platoon's (most likely the company's) best team leader. Sissies. Weak, thin skinned, sad excuse for infantry leaders, Sissies. I understand that they don't like Roybal's attitude, and how he does what he wants and fights back on things that sound dumb or pointless. I understand that they don't like how he can be obstinate, argumentative, and insubordinate. However, they need to get over themselves, because he was the best they have access to, and they just threw him away.... Oh, and now a new training calendar is coming out .... No doubt it will be full of useless training and wastes of time with no one to shove reason into the equation. Our team-level leadership will consist of a laid-back Pembrook, a quiet Canfield, and a new-to-the-squad, (potentially yes-man) Minton. (Nothing against him. He's a decent guy, but I've never seen or had him as a leader, and I don't see him being very assertive with those higher than him.)

In all of this, I was never asked, never consulted, never given the courtesy of knowing what was happening with my team leader until it was done. Oh, I'll be fine. It doesn't matter where I go or who is there. I'll just do what I do, but they can kiss my trust in them goodbye. They can kiss the morale of second squad goodbye for a long, long time.

I will cool down from this eventually, but for now the burns are fresh. I intend to do my job better than anyone else, as always. I intend to perform at the peak and keep second squad on top, as always. However, I will not do it for my leadership.... I will not laugh at their jokes, join in their conversations, or listen to their rambling anymore. I will … maintain a peaceable existence ….

In other news, … well there really is no other news. Just the stupidity. Utter stupidity.

Saturday, November 25, 2017

I had a dream last night about a girl who was similar to Sarah. We were sitting close and talking and she said something along the lines of "I know you haven't heard it yet," or "I thought I wouldn't have to say it out loud," or "I figured you would have already acted but…," then she said, "I trust you" as she looked deep into my eyes. I stumbled over my words a bit as I smiled and leaned in. I assume that the woman in my dream represents my future wife. I don't know why she was given the image of Sarah in the dream. Perhaps because Sarah is a fun, sweet gal that I know from my past, but I am not very close with her. Perhaps this represents the current conditions between my future wife and I. Perhaps she has known for some time that she "trusts" me. Maybe we have been walking the same road without knowing it and it simply must be revealed to me. Maybe we are friends or acquaintances who are already close in spirit without fully knowing it. So many possibilities. So few answers. I pray YHVH makes clear the meaning so that I may act if need be. In the meantime, I'll savor the feeling of that dream.

The attitude of the squad is as predicted. Miserable. No morale. No jokes. No laughter. Gayness returning from upper leadership. No stupidness deflectors. Yes-men team leaders. Roybal is already checked out and ready to leave. Feelings of abandonment and distrust. Overall dissatisfaction with leadership and negativity of mood. Not a good state to be in as we head into our next mission.... Totally oblivious to what is right. Totally oblivious to the condition of their dudes. Totally oblivious to the annoyances they are pushing downstream. And here I'm stuck acting happy and playing pretend to keep peaceable relations and avoid excess nonsense. Forget this.

YHVH in the name of Yeshua I ask this: that you salvage second platoon. That you impress upon our leaders a feeling of guilt due to their actions and that they would see the correct path to take. In the name of Yeshua, help me keep the guys safe despite the negativity that now brews. In the name of Yeshua I ask you, for my sake and for the sake of my squad, allow Rogers to stay on here at Vose as team leader. Please have Minton be sent to Gibson with first squad. Please, YHVH, do this to salvage what is left of my morale in this squad. To salvage the one constant I have left in the physical. Rogers is my friend, but I would gladly work for him, and I have faith in his leadership ability. YHVH I do not think that my trust in him is unfounded, so please in the name of Yeshua, keep him here as the next team leader, send Minton to Gibson, and chastise our upper leadership for their lack of wisdom. Please give me Wisdom, YHVH. Please tell me and show me when and how to act to prevent the downstream flow of idiocy, and to protect the guys with me, and to salvage the parts of this squad that I still appreciate. YHVH, as I have done before, so I do now, and place this series of events, this situation, in your hands. YHVH, you are the orchestrator of my fate and my destiny, and all things work together for the good of those who love you. I love you YHVH, and if I have found favor in your eyes, please honor my request. I will do what I can in the physical when the opportunity is given. So please give the opportunity, YHVH, and give me wisdom to speak, and cause those words to be heeded by my leadership. I pray all this in the name of your Son, Yeshua. Amen.

Sunday, November 26, 2017

Church was alright. The pastor says the right stuff, has the right passion, has the right knowledge, but he seems… discouraged perhaps? Maybe just tired? I couldn't tell for sure, but it seemed forced, as if he wanted to feel the joy and the power in the words he said, but they just echoed hollow in his own ears. As for me, I did learn a few interesting tidbits that I wasn't aware of before. So it was not a loss, and I intend to go again.

More gayness is flowing downstream from leadership again today. More CLS classes. Tomorrow is some silly physical assessment. Not a fan. Not interested.

I can't stand it. I am sick of acting the obedient little SAW gunner Conde. I'm sick of pretending I don't mind hanging out with my leaders. I'm honestly shocked that my opinion of them could change so quickly but that's what happens when their actions are equivalent to a betrayal of my trust in their leadership. My mind is horrendously stressed in managing the façade which I hate and the hate which I hide. I am so utterly incensed with the turn this platoon has taken …. I am livid that they would eject to the wayside our best team leader due to their petty personal quarrels. This anger has no outlet except this journal and working out. However, now they wish to take the latter from me as well, by forcing me to participate in a group workout, a PT event, a "friendly competition" in which I want no part. The event is pointless, agonizingly boring, and painfully long. It may sound like I'm complaining. Maybe I am. With good reason though. I want nothing to do with them, and now they are making me spend time with them. They are naively assuming that we are all just happy and everything is hunky-dory because they don't actually care what we think. Not that it matters. I don't care what they think. The difference is that their indifference directly affects the lives of those they command. They are obligated in the spirit of good leadership to seek our favor and respect. They should, in effort to maintain morale and encourage our obedience, portray qualities which we look up to and revere. Instead they are consumed with pathetic, paltry, petty, insignificant emotions of the thin skinned, and are blinded to the condition of the troops which they lead. They do not have our respect. They do not have our admiration or adoration. They do not have our support or our approval. They are toxic, and they are making us sick. If I didn't wish to stay in second squad of second platoon, if I didn't wish to remain relatively unbothered and drama free, I would shed this mask and reveal my true face. It would crush their hearts and anger them to no end, so I refrain from doing so. I don't need that kind of drama on top of the mood I'm already in.

I'm not sure what to do. Should I suffer through it or act in some way? Should I plod along like a pathetic cog in the machine with my head down, or should I rise up with the voice of the people? If I were too blind to see the end from the beginning certainly I would do the latter. However, consequences are real, and decisions must be made on the balance of pros and cons. As of now, with what limited foresight I have, the cons outweigh the pros of speaking out against these leaders. However, should their actions ever endanger the lives of the men I serve with (obviously unrelated to the natural dangers of battle, rather in relation to their ability to lead calmly under stress and make sound decisions), I will unleash my fury and relieve them of command for such a time as is proper.

Monday, November 27, 2017

YHVH has seen fit to answer my prayers! Rogers is now my team leader. Fuss is under Canfield, but I'm sure he is happy with that compared to the alternative of Minton. I am still peeved that the PL and Beyers threw out Roybal, but I am relieved that the patchwork I requested from YHVH has been done.

I am better with the acting now, and it is easier knowing my petition was found worthy in YHVH's eyes. I still do not approve of the LT and Beyers and what they are doing with this squad, but it is becoming easier to speak to them. I suppose I recover quickly, although I still do not trust them. They prove hard to hate, unfortunately, as they both appear as children in my eyes. Timid, naïve, soft, somewhat gentle, caring about the way people see them, and thirsty to control whatever they can. Not great qualities in leaders, but qualities common in common folk. I hope and pray these traits do not endanger us on missions.

Still have nonsense going down though. I did the silly PT [physical training] event this morning and the rest of it is tomorrow morning. I conveniently, or inconveniently, annoyingly, yet with impeccable timing, ironically, shockingly, pulled or strained a back muscle doing dead lifts yesterday. I'm not a fan of the pain, but it made my low scores on the PT event much more real and believable. I will probably have to sit tomorrow out except for maybe the run so I do not further the injury. The PL gave me a ball to roll out with (hard to hate the guy even though he's a temperamental weakling half the time) which seems to have helped loosen it up a touch. However, one good act doesn't stop the pointless MARCH classes or the other nonsensical time wasters. We'll see how things go this week. Really not looking forward to the possibility of entering a mission worn out because of our leadership's delusional ideas of preparation.

I've decided to do a four-day food fast. YHVH help me.

Tuesday, November 28, 2017

Fast is going well so far. Hunger pangs haven't hit as hard as I expected, but my stomach feels very empty. I have had at least two interesting dreams of which I cannot remember anything. Hopefully future dreams will stick in my mind long enough to write them here.

Start new story:

Aramathandor, known as Aram, or Randor by his friends and family if he had any, was slight of build for one of the sons of the Nephilim. His human mother had fled her hometown and given birth to him in the wild. She died of blood loss. By some chance of fate or of luck of his breed, the young giant survived. No mortal being knows what befell the newborn, or how he managed to survive, much less grow strong in the untamed wilds of the land now called Pangea. Perhaps the earth was gentler then, before the flood. Perhaps Providence found it pleasing to spare the young one's life, that his story may unfold as testament to the glory of the Creator. Indeed, none on earth knew of his existence until he had grown into a harsh brute of a man, or giant, rather. Being five generations separated from the great titans who shook the earth with their hundred meter tall frames, Aram was lowly among giants. Even as an adult among his own generation, his near eight-foot build was dwarfed by the ten and twelve-foot monsters that came to be known as great conquerors and heroes of old. He would one day challenge such beasts in combat and prevail by virtue of his hidden past, and perhaps a small amount of the favor of the Creator due to his mother's goodness of heart.

It was a crisp morning in the deciduous woods wherein dwelt the young Aram. His wolf-skin clothes hung loose about his gaunt young body. By human standards, he was maybe seven years old and already tainted by blood and death. His eyes were that of an animal, his instincts likewise, and no language was uttered from his lips. Displaying the incredible durability of his race, the child-giant had scars from wounds that would have killed a normal boy. He was on his way to drink from the lake which lay in the valley to his north. On the way he intended to kill breakfast, with his bare hands if need be. The pain in his stomach signaled that death was mere days away if he did not eat soon. However, within moments that pain was forgotten, and his adrenaline surged as he saw a great ball of fire fall from the sky and strike the earth less than a mile away. He braced for the impact of the explosion that he knew to follow such phenomena, and was startled when he felt none. His instincts screamed fear, but his human curiosity chose a sad time to overtake his animalistic side. Approaching the location of the mysterious object, he witnessed giants roaming to and fro in the woods around a shining metal vessel. They were dressed in perplexing clothes that seemed half armor, half skin. Their bodies were strong, and build for a planet with much higher gravity. As such they leapt nearly as high as the great oaks in which they were beginning to camp. The young Aram stared in awe, with no knowledge or understanding of what he saw. Then the world went black.

A lieutenant of the space crew that had stepped away to relieve himself had seen young Aram watching his men. He had done research on the people of this planet, and knew that if such a young one was living in the wild alone, he must be descended from the famous fallen angels who had strewn their seed among the daughters of men. A specimen like this would not be missed by any family, and would prove excellent for study and experimentation with the purpose of unravelling the mystery of the Watchers and the Nephilim. Not that such things mattered to the lieutenant; the scientists could have their fun, but the soldier's main purpose in abducting the lad was to put him to work. Slaves were status in their culture. The more varied and unique the slaves they took from other planets, the more honor was given their position in society. He dragged the limp body by a skinny arm back to the ship and threw him into a force-field cage along with a few other odds and ends from previous planets on this patrol.

Aram awoke with a start and a snarl, as a female of a red furred humanoid race poked his side. All in the cage cowered to the corner in fear. Most were female, some young males, and one or two self-reproducing tentacled beings that seemed oblivious…or asleep. Aram immediately killed one of the sleeping animals and ate voraciously. A few of the other prisoners vomited at the horrific scene, and one cried out in a piercing alien dialect. Aram put her to sleep with a swift kick. After eating his fill he stood to leave, only to be shocked unconscious by the electrified force field. The rest of his time aboard the craft was a blur, as any time he awoke, someone or something put him right back to sleep. He dreamed nightmares and lived them as well. Demons of the earth gnawed on his mind as they traveled with him through deep space in slumber. Yet so little was his knowledge of what the future held, that no tear touched his cheek as he looked into the blackness through a port window between beatings and sleep. There was much sleep during the month aboard the alien vessel. Dark and terrible sleep.

When he finally awoke to full awareness, the boy-giant was at a loss for even his usual grunts. The alien city that sprawled before him as his cage was loaded onto a cargo ship was beyond anything he had ever dreamed or imagined. In that moment, some deep hidden emotion welled in the child's heart, and he knew that he must conquer that place and burn it to the ground. His thoughts did not dwell long on such plots, however, because shortly the cargo ship came to a halt and his cage was dropped from the bottom, directly in front of a brilliant green mansion. He was hauled inside and the forcefield was deactivated. Gruff hands of giant aliens dragged him to a courtyard where youths of many races fought and trained. A human might see it as a sort of spartan or gladiatorial arena, but to the young Aram, it was hell. Three earth years went by as he trained and fought, killed and bled, and grew mighty. The lieutenant had begun to train him in hundreds of skills and trades and nearly as many languages. He learned fluently the alien language of the planet where he dwelt as well as the language that was spoken on earth. He learned science, mathematics, special reasoning, history, strategy, navigation, astronomy, astrology, diplomacy, magic, and many other disciplines. The lieutenant found the young giant to be quite adept at nearly anything he tried, but he excelled at anything related to warfare. Such qualified conquerors were most of the sons of the Nephilim. By the time the lad was eleven years old he was the most famous slave in his alien city. Crowds came to watch him fight and kill members of races from across the galaxy. Few could match his speed with a sword or his skill with a gun. Fewer still could hold their own in a weaponless brawl. The advanced society which donated life after life to this cruel game of slave battle had lost much of what made it strong to begin with, a fire which still burned brightly in Aram. Even the races which they plundered on other worlds held no match for the young giant's ferocity. It would be a long, long time before any could best the hero in proper close combat. And when that time came, it would be the most unlikely of the races to succeed. A human. However, that is a different story.

Wednesday, November 29, 2017

Surely the words of YHVH are more filling than choice bread, whole vegetables, or grilled meat. Surely His teachings are better sustenance than food prepared by men. His lessons, His laws are living bread and water and sweeter to the stomach and mind than the best port wine. I pray YHVH gives me grace to continue this fast until Thursday night. It will only be 72 hours, but I pray He honors it. I have chosen to break it on Thursday night so that I will be able to ease back into a normal amount of food at meals before we leave on mission. It will give me time to replenish the glycogen in my muscles and store extra calories aside for the next time I am to go without food. During this fast, I pray that YHVH gives me strength, courage, and invincibility in battle. I pray He protects me and my men. I pray that He blesses and shows favor to my family and those friends which I consider to be family. I pray for Mom, Dad, Olivia, Priscilla, David King, Heath, Luke, Kiah, and my grandparents and other extended family and friends that YHVH would bless them, touch their hearts, fill them with His Spirit, and wraps them in His wings. YHVH you are God. You are my Lord and Master, my Savior and my best friend. You are my Counselor and my Protector, my shield and my high place.

Honor this fast unto you YHVH and give me grace to continue until Thursday evening. I love you YHVH.

I had dreams that I vaguely remember last night. One was just odd. There was an antagonistic guy who seemed to be stealing or taking advantage of someone who was considered a leech by his own family. I, or he, or someone knew it was wrong and tried to advocate, but his own father did not raise his head to help, and rather took the child under his arm as they suffered to be buried in popcorn (I believe symbolic of the worlds gluttony and excess). I fought the man who was causing the injustice. He seemed tough and there was little I could do on my own. I realized I was not striking properly, so I changed my style and injured his neck. He reacted with anger and pinned me down, trying to get into a position to strike back. Either I blocked his blow or he hesitated, unable to attack me or unwilling. His demeanor was that of an insufferable, impatient big brother trying to teach his younger how to brawl and be tough. I realized I could not hate him.

Later, the dream changed. I went and returned from leave after deployment, and yet mid-deployment. I smoked my pipe as others smoked cigars.

In another vague asleep/awake dream I saw or imagined old west gunfighting of incredible speed. Then I looked and saw terrain or land like Colorado, but the hills were scarred as though a chunk had been removed. People ran down a dirt road beside powerlines toward the scarred foothill. I was going to join them but decided against it and turned back to the small fire I had, and prepared to leave. I was dressed like a cowboy, with a horse, a six-gun, and my duster and hat. I decided to head northwest over the closest foothill through the woods to hunt for food. I may have simply imagined those things vividly while half asleep, but I like to think that my future holds some excitement and peacefulness such as that.

Balaam did right in the eyes of YHVH. He was not an Hebrew, nor did he have the Law that was given to them by YHVH. However, he knew YHVH, worshiped Him as King of all, and the Almighty God. He obeyed when YHVH commanded him, and lived his life with brutal honesty and fearlessness. I must conclude that YHVH honored him due to the condition of his heart toward his Creator. In the one instance where his heart was wrong, an angel of YHVH was prepared to slay him, even as he travelled where YHVH had instructed. It was YHVH's mercy, in allowing Balaam's donkey to speak, that saved his life. This slight course adjustment of the soul caused the Israelites to be blessed in the land of the Midianites. Balaam was the one who YHVH spoke through when he said those famous words "May those who bless you be blessed, and those who curse you be cursed." This prophesy holds true even today for the Children of YHVH. So why do people teach Balaam's story as one of warning against cruelty? Why do they condemn him for his use of "sorcery" in speaking with YHVH? Those who teach his story this way are ignorant. They do not understand that YHVH had not given Balaam any laws, or forbade him from such practices. He would appear Himself or send an angel when Balaam needed to be corrected, and always Balaam responded with obedience, humility, and reverence. Indeed before ever a Christian walked the earth, Balaam was an example to us. He obeyed YHVH, fearlessly rebuked the Midianite king, blessed God's people, and even prophesied the coming of David. He lived honestly, took no bribes, and knew the truth: that YHVH was the one true God and salvation came by His will alone. I have no doubt that Balaam was imparted righteousness for the purity of his heart toward YHVH. I have no doubt that, while the Israelites had the Law and were saved by God countless times, one would have been hard pressed to find a soul as obedient and pure hearted before YHVH as Balaam was. He even knew and honored YHVH's holy number each time he built alters. He played along with the foolishness of the Midianite king so that he would have more opportunities to bless the people he saw filling the valley before him. Balaam's story needs to stop being taught as a simplistic "don't beat your animals" or "God can use anyone" story. Instead it should be taught the way it is: the story of a fearless and honest man who sought the heart of YHVH in all matters, worshiped and revered Him, and obeyed His commands; and a man by whose mouth, God blessed His chosen people, and as a result was blessed. ***Edit on Jan 15 after conversation with Dad: For that particular instance only. Following his blessing of the Hebrews, Balaam did evil by advising their enemies on how to lead them astray. His heart was turned by money. It really was more of a "God can use anyone" story.

Jesus said do not judge lest you be judged, and in the same measure you condemn another person so condemnation will be measured to you.

However, after this, He has a caveat. The parable of the brothers, one with a speck and one with a log in their respective eyes, sheds light on what Jesus meant by "do not judge." Essentially He says to fix yourself first, then fix others. First ensure that you are clean, pure in YHVH's eyes, then go about leading others to such righteousness. Do not condemn someone for their sin when you yourself are swallowed by it. A modern example would be a pastor who watches porn, and then calls out men for adulterous tendencies. That pastor would be wrong to do so; however, he would be justified if first he kicked his porn habit, repented to YHVH and his wife, and removed the source of his temptation. Thereby, he would have the experience and authority necessary to back his commands and reprimands. He would be able to call men out from their lives of sin, judging their actions as wrong, and helping the men swallowed by them, without bringing judgement on his own head. This is what I believe Yeshua meant by that verse.

I'm so hungry! Even water tastes good, and music is like food to my mind. Must press on. Must be strong. Tomorrow night when I break my fast it will be wonderful indeed, but I will remain in control of how much of what I eat, so as to avoid sickness and remain a state of Spiritual openness to YVHV for at least one more night. YHVH help me and give me Grace to last until then.

Thursday, November 30, 2017

I decided to break my fast this morning with breakfast. My entire body was in pain when I woke up and the dreams I had were... unsettling.

I went to a restaurant with an older man reminiscent of Doc Holiday—but it was actually Nolan from BHS marching band my freshman year of high school—and a pretty blonde girl who Nolan said he loved. The restaurant was a horror one, like a real life horror game where you could get injured or even die and still be alive for the next round or if you left. I survived longer than most, killing the people around me by reflecting a blue laser off a silver plate so it wouldn't hit me. The laser was coming from one of the waiter's eyes. It was as if the waiters and waitresses were superpowered zombies who we had to kill. For some reason, the people around me were rooting for my demise, so I killed many of them with the reflected laser. I had gotten the plate from the waiter attacking me when he threw it to me before he attacked, out of some code of chivalry I suppose. I tried turning the laser on him, but he stopped firing when I did and resumed when I moved the plate. One of the ladies who was a guest had a whip like a razor. She attacked me with it and it lacerated my left leg from the quad to my foot. It felt very real, and I was not fond of the game, but the adrenaline rush was incredible. The waiter fired again, and I deflected most of the beam, though it grazed my body somewhere causing a deep burning cut. The place felt malicious and evil, and I knew I had to leave now that it was round 3 or 4, and I could see that death was a very real possibility. As we prepared to leave, all the waiters and waitresses acted friendly and polite while the other guests were still undergoing the event. I walked back inside to grab something I'd forgotten and was struck on the left shin by a spiked club wielded by a paramilitary/militia weirdo who wore a foreign camo uniform with made up patches for his little club. I chewed him out for hitting me since I was no longer a part of it. When he talked back, I took his club and bashed both his legs and one of his knees. My own leg hurt, but I took it surprisingly well. I was furious and ready to leave. Once we finally left at night in Nolan's car, I was much relieved. That's all I remember. The whole dream had a spirit of death and injury over it, the kind that is malicious, but more annoying than anything else. It was fairly sickening to be surrounded by it for so long.

YHVH please tell me the meaning of these dreams, and in the name of Yeshua, protect me and my loved ones from the forces that would attack us or see us harmed. Surround us and fill us with your power and Spirit, YHVH. May curses and attacks laid against us be nullified, and instead rebound on our enemies tenfold. YHVH, please keep my body healthy, strong, and uninjured. Make me a stench in the nostrils of the enemy, and a fearless warrior in the physical and the spiritual. Allow me to deal a lethal blow to the forces of evil, physically and spiritually, without so much as a scratch.

Idea pitched: airsoft guns for all of us in the ark (our tent with a building inside it) for "training purposes"

Outcome: TBD (no opposition from folks here, but the LT wants higher-up permission...silly LT)

Edited Outcome: it was a no.

In ancient days when giants played

Friday, December 1, 2017

In ancient days
When giants played
And drank the blood of men
A man quite brave
With oaken stave
Sought to be their end

The giants nigh
Ten stories high
Their bravest fighters sent
Yet by and by
Each fighter died
Their bodies torn and rent

Still the rest did feast
On man and bird and beast
Until the earth cried under
    the strain
The bloodshed did not cease
The Creator was not pleased
Order was given to end the pain

A plague 'twas said
That killed them dead
Under a setting sun
And naught was bled
On human head
The work, perfectly done

But truth is more pronounced
And no one may denounce
That one man had a role
A man quite brave

With oaken stave
Into giants' lair he stole

Their walls of stone
And human bone
Were rubble by the end
This man alone
Limped away with a groan
His stave with a crack and bend

He knelt right there
And gasped for air
Titans' sons gathered 'round
They screamed and stared
Pulled out their hair
The man made not a sound

These beastly folk
Their teeth they broke
In gnashing at the sky
The man awoke
His fire there stoked
And loosed a furious cry

"GO HOME" he said
"Sons of these dead
And leave their bodies be
Were doomed to die
By God on high
That mankind may be free

He spared you lot
Why, I know not

So get thee gone in peace
Lest wrath be spurned
And anger burn
Make thy flesh food for beasts."

Silenced, they looked
In fear, they shook
At a terrible sight
The man was robed
In glory which strobed
A blinding, burning light

Beloved of
One up above
Took up the oak'n stave
Staircase appeared
From across the lightyears
The man went on his way

His duty done
New journey begun
He walked toward light of day
Stairs one by one
Strode toward the Son
No falter no delay

Giants' sons dispersed
Roamed o'er the earth
Their stories told today
But all have forgotten
The brave man begotten
For the titans he did slay

Deployment Journal 12/02/2017

Saturday, December 2, 2017

We should be leaving for Paktika this evening or during the dark hours of tomorrow morning. I have been informed that our primary sub-mission as a squad will be tower guard. I am not keen on spending three weeks sitting in a tower staring at nothing, so hopefully something fun happens. They will have a gym and a chow hall at least, so conditions won't be terrible. I pray YHVH turns it into a brilliant adventure, full of daring and glorious fights, joyful victories and experiences of goodness, and of course good food and warm showers. Although the latter can be limited or somewhat postponed in lieu of the others. I pray YHVH provides intrigue, mystery, opportunities for individuals, including myself, to shine and excel at our jobs and other more unique skills. I pray that each challenge is a joy to undertake, and each new turn a thrilling development. I will go prepared for boredom and/or brutality, but my prayer, if YHVH will hear it, is for what I have mentioned.

I have been thinking a lot about going on leave when we are done here. I am excited. The plans and adventures and quests that I intend to complete during those three weeks of freedom will be wonderfully refreshing, invigorating, and exhausting. I can't wait.

I will be switching from this journal to a physical one for the duration of my time in Paktika. The missing segments will be added to this collection at a later time.

Correction, I will switch after the following account:

This afternoon I had three dreams.

> In the first dream, I was with Mom and Prill, and they both were going about doing ordinary tasks in a way that didn't make sense or made them more difficult. I had to sternly correct them a couple times, but when we dropped Prill off at home, I gave her a big hug to show her I wasn't mad. Then I talked with Mom about it and explained why

I had acted sternly. She said I had incredible patience and kept very calm considering the circumstance.

In the second dream, there was a bad guy who had done something evil, and a clue was given to his whereabouts. It was said he was hiding on an island between two other islands whose names I don't remember off the coast of the mainland. Shore, Beyers, the SF 18F, and I went to investigate the island that wasn't supposed to exist. We ran through enemy territory on the mainland and took a float plane to the island. I do not remember what happened, but remember we collected recon and came back, checking some of our luggage. A civilian contractor handled moving it from on the plane to under it, as we walked the rest of the way.

In the third dream, Pembrook and I were on computers in Paktika like it was a totally normal MWR [morale welfare recreation], except we both had incredibly long wavy hair.

Email Thread December 2017

Dec 11, 2017, Gabe wrote:

Not much news from trashganistan as far as job-related excitement goes as of right now. A lot of tower guard. Living in a small room with 4 other guys. Haven't showered in over a week. Haven't changed my shirt in an equal length of time. Good times.

It's been a bit of a mess here as far as morale goes. People (including myself) are taking their turns going through the dumps of situational loathing. Short tempers are common, leadership bounces between tolerable and painfully annoying, and motivation is horribly low. I had a couple days of some oppressive anger. I shook it off with YHVH's help. Although, if credit were given where due, I can't take much of any. Certainly some level of self-awareness, introspection, and logical processing assisted; but the burst of light through the clouds of unwarranted and self-righteous wrath came in the form of a fragile bundle of adorable innocence named Bonnie. (Pictures attached)

Bonnie has shown massive improvement in just two days, evolving from a skittish, malnourished pup into quite a spunky fluff ball. We have been keeping her in a guard tower so she stays warm and out of harm's way while a military working dog is on camp. Her diet has been mostly beef jerky, but we got her some good lamb meat and fat tonight. We estimate her to be somewhere between two and three months, most likely on the younger side, seeing as she seems to still be teething a bit. There has been much discussion as to her heritage. She is quite obviously a mutt, but her coloration, bone structure and depth of voice is somewhat indicative of a large shepherd breed native to Afghanistan. I think she may have some collie in her as well. Once we fatten her up, she's sure to grow into a burly one.

The current plan is to bring her back to Vose with us and have her as the squad dog. Shore means to organize a way to bring her back to the states after deployment. She seems quite healthy for a stray. No fleas, no worms, and a lush and healthy coat of fur. She loves everyone in our squad she's met so far. Most likely we are the only humans to have shown her care. She's already quite attached, as are we.

That is the extent of excitement here, and a good morale boost for us all. I would be unsurprised if she found her way here by the guidance of YHVH for the sole purpose of steadying our temperaments and bringing the light of innocence and joy to our days. My suspicion is given credence in that she arrived in nearly perfect timing as an answer to a prayer of mine. Although the form of this answer was certainly not what I had expected, and gladly so.

Well, there's a lot of words for a singular event midst days of blandness. I thought you all would be entertained by it though.

I love you all and miss you a ton! Oh and Mom I got your text the other day, thank you for praying!

Love, the recently soft of heart due to a surprise guest, recently recovered from staring into a cesspool of darkness, and freshly rebounded to a level of situational resilience proper of a vastly superior human, Gabe

Dec 14, 2017, Gabe wrote:

Possibly gonna be doing some fun stuff tomorrow (tonight for y'all). Please pray! I shall tell vague stories and give subtle hints as to the nature of my adventure upon my return!

Dec 16, 2017, Gabe wrote:

Written word is insufficient to describe the wild events of the past couple days. Nay, even with gesture and inflexion of the voice, the picture may be too dull, or else too vibrant to match reality. There was violence, blood (at a distance), fierce exchange of fire, a potentially disastrous circumstance, sprinting, explosions, fire, and the most fun I think I have ever had in a single day. There were no casualties, no bullet of the enemy struck it's mark; RPGs [rocket-propelled grenades] flew harmlessly (if close) overhead, mortars struck too far away to injure, and fear was struck into the enemy. Many surrendered of their own free will. It was a happening that I will remember for all time, and cherish as a memory of YHVH's protection, provision, and action on our behalf.

My actions are humble in my own eyes. I feel as though I did no more than necessary, that I succeeded in performing my job satisfactorily at best. Yet a feeling of pride, not arrogance or haughtiness, but a pride in the men I fought with and myself, for the success we were granted, wells within me. The elation of victory still runs thick in our veins, and the stories grow. I have been exalted before my peers and earned the respect of men I revere. And all the while YHVH's favor is with me and evident.

It is said that after David slew goliath, women sang of how he had slain tens of thousands compared to Saul's thousands. In such a way my legend has grown to where I am credited with double what I felt to have accomplished. Certainly not due to my words, rather those of others have taken my actions to wild proportions. I have told my piece to those I work with, with no extravagance or downplaying; I told what happened as I saw it happen. I must strive to remain humble now. It was YHVH that won the day and raised me up. In kind, I must acknowledge my own shortcomings and effort to resolve them for the sake of the men who will depend on me. I intend to credit YHVH entirely should more flattery or questions arise. I do not wish for extravagant inflammation of my actions; as aforementioned I told the events with plainness. I am forever grateful for YHVH's faithfulness. Even prayers written in anger and selfishness He has acknowledged and seen fit to honor. I am not worthy of such favor, but I revel in it and am filled with joy nonetheless.

It is humbling in itself to have been given the opportunity to do what I did with men I admire. As the revelry dwindles to a hum and the congratulations finish, I am left wondering what more bizarre and beautiful adventures may yet happen upon me during this deployment. I am excited. I am content. I am ready for more.

Thank you, my family, for the constant prayers and intercession on my behalf. Thank you for the constant support and encouragement. And thank you for the fearlessness and confidence which you have taught me. But most of all I thank YHVH for all that and more. It was by his hand that victory was shaped.

I love you guys and I can't wait to call again! Until then:

Your battle hardened, spirit softened, humbled and exalted, masterful SAW gunner, mighty soldier, and favored by YHVH,

Gabe

Somewhere in Afghanistan, 2018

Deployment Journal 12/24/2017 – 12/27/2017

Sunday, December 24, 2017 (Christmas Eve)

So… Paktika. That was a hell of a time.

I may or may not insert the handwritten journals of my time there. Some may be omitted permanently in favor of a summarized entry. I experienced much in my time there and a few mere paragraphs will do little to convey the depth of emotion and heights of jubilation which I found myself at over the course of the past twenty days. For now, I will say this: I have experienced true combat. I have killed a man. I have been inches from injury or death. I have seen victory and defeat. I have known both fearlessness and fear. I have emerged from the tests a different man, yet the same in all the right ways.

Battle story one:

We infilled at about 4:00 AM and moved to a compound which the PSU [Provincial Special Unit] cleared. It was in the low ground and had no vantage point toward the bazaar we were to clear in the following daylight. So we moved to another which was filled with rubble, and finally another in which Trevor and I posted on the roof to observe the bazaar and pull security. As the morning progressed we consolidated with the other half of our group at the next compound over. Richard already had a confirmed kill from about 50 meters outside that compound. I saw the body from a distance lying in a pool of blood, fallen in a pose impossible for a living being to emulate. We moved from the compound at about 9AM and advanced toward the bazaar. We made it through three compounds/houses/shops before the shooting started. PKM [Soviet machine gun] fire danced overhead, and snaps of near misses filled the air. From my position I could do nothing. Derek, Chad, Mark, and I made a mad dash about 75 meters down the road as our sister element laid down cover fire. We arrived at a sort of strip mall which friendlies already occupied. At this point, we chose to downgrade as the sun was growing warm, and the chill of night had turned into profuse sweat over the past sprint. After hashing out a plan, we moved from the strip mall up a small hill and behind another line of shops. Our team cleared a house and a bakery atop a small hill. Suddenly, a black streak with a white tale hissed overhead. A second later a deafening boom echoed through the valley. Snaps of close enemy fire echoed off the walls, and puffs of dust appeared on wall tops and in the street. There were one or two more RPGs that flew overhead and exploded to our rear. After moving out of the bakery, I attempted to lay down some cover fire over the bazaar, aiming haphazardly at rooftops and windows. I shot at a black figure that dived behind some rocks to the right of a building about 400 meters away. We moved back a bit behind the wall of the bakery, and I took up a position where I could see the building. Derek told me there was a man to the left of it that was hostile and to shoot him if I saw him. Seconds later a black-clothed head appeared where Derek had pointed. My sights were lined up perfectly, my body was tight, my mind was clear, and I pulled the trigger. A cloud of dust kicked up by my rounds obscured my view, and when it cleared, I did not see the head, though I thought perhaps there was a red stain on the corner of the wall where it had been. I found out later that I had killed that man. It was good to have the closure. I felt it was an accomplishment. Reflecting now, I knew right away that I had hit him. Time slowed briefly, my sights had not moved, and YHVH certainly answered my prayer for true aim before I had prayed it. Following that, we moved to a garage which was a rather large storeroom for huge bags of peanuts. At this location we got into about a 10 minute fire fight with an enemy mortar team and sniper. I do not know if we killed them, but we certainly scared them off. The rest of the day was spent without much action, plenty of snaps and pops overhead or down the street, but the sources could not be found, and no friendly forces were so much as grazed. Bombs from air support had killed an injured a good many more than the ones Richard and I had merc'd. As a result, no doubt due to the favor of YHVH, more than 30 military-aged males surrendered to us of their own free will. The PSU commander indoctrinated them and made them raise an Afghan flag above the bazaar. The village elders were grateful for our defeating the Taliban in the area without civilian casualties. We took some more machine gun and ineffective sniper fire while at the square at the end of the bazaar, but not much could be done. In the end, the enemy ran. As we moved to EXFIL [exfiltration] that night and waited in a small, sawdust filled carpenter shop, I felt a surge of pride in the men I was with and myself for the victory we were granted. It was thrilling, elating, addicting.

Tuesday, December 26, 2017

Battle story two:

We infilled at night as usual and stumbled through dry rice patties and over terraces upward and northward through the valley approaching the village from the south. We skirted to the west to gain what high ground we could after passing through the "honeycomb" part of the village. ICOMS [radio] chatter indicated our presence was known. We set up shop in an empty compound filled with building materials and a huge dirt mound atop, which I set up a security position with my SAW and the aid of two GBs [green berets]. We sat on that hill behind piled logs until sunrise. We left to push toward our objective and found out quickly the disadvantage that would follow us for the entire day. The enemy was invisible. Hidden deep behind windows and like shadows in the street, no muzzle flash revealed their location, and the echoes of their gunfire made it seem as though the mountains themselves were against us. We took fire as we ran across an open field. We took fire again after clearing a couple compounds on a hill in the middle of the valley and began moving southeast. A 18D from another team and I ran a hundred meters back to our previous location to see if we could spot the shooter. I stayed crouched behind a log and a rock, head up and scanning, but saw nothing. The GB stood and openly invited enemy fire, mocking the shooter's aim with fearless abandon. A bullet snapped in a wisp of dust off a rock in front of me instead.

We continued to move from compound to compound, ever wary of enemy fire, ever trying to see where our ghostlike attackers struck from, and to no avail. Bullets snapped overhead, off the dirt to our side, front, and rear, although it was not so dramatic as I know you will imagine. The pace of combat in real life is quite variable, and often slow. Machine gun fire is intermittent and in small bursts. Not the constant "spray and pray" of the movies. The enemy doesn't open fire with a line of troops with common aim and goal, they move between buildings and take sparse shots when they can from rooftops and windows, always trying to avoid detection, and often succeeding. So under regular and close enemy fire, we moved to our final compound after chasing mere phantoms of enemy fire, and our only return fire being for suppression or the warning of civilians.

Once set up in our individual compounds, medevac birds came for two people from another team (ODA [redacted], ours being ODA [redacted]), but the two were Afghan partner force, not American. The birds took fire, we tried to suppress, we took fire. After they left and a couple aimless airstrikes had been pursued, we began to take effective sniper fire at both compounds.

An Afghan policeman five feet from me was shot in the shoulder. I ducked down as the 18D next to me began to give the man aid. For a moment, a minute, maybe two or three, I was given pause. I was not startled or scarred by what had happened, nor was I afraid, or perhaps some fear reared an ugly head to be quickly suppressed by thoughts of anger. I was aggravated that I could not see the source of the gunfire. That I could not do anything to help the wounded man. That I could not slay our attacker with my own hands as his phantom bullets seemed to materialize halfway along their flight, leaving no sign of their origin. And yes, there was a twinge, a touch, a prick of fear that I shoved away. A quickly dying thought of mortality, hopelessness, and a supreme desire for nightfall, when the world in darkness was our domain. Even thoughts and prayers for the enemy to be consumed by fire, struck dead by a lightning bolt from heaven danced through my head, but to no healthy end, for I was, by these things, distracted from my purpose. I went "full potato."

But as quickly as the shadow arrived, it passed and I found my service to be needed, having been yelled at for a reply, in transferring information for the 18D while his headset was off. Once more my mind was clear and instinct took over in a familiar and comfortable way. I relayed what information I could when asked, fired at the hillside where the sniper fire was said to have originated, and stayed low, stayed alive.

As the wounded man was lowered to ground level, I was called across the compound to the side closer to the hill. Bullets whipped off the top of the wall above my head as I knelt among the GBs and Afghans gathered in the small space. I fired more at the hill, suppressing, aiming at likely sniper hollows, praying that I could kill the man who attacked us, and praying that he suffered. I believe it was an airstrike that finally brought down our foe, or perhaps he fled after finding out we had bombed eleven of his wicked brethren to their gory deaths.

The air fell quiet and we medevacked two more Afghans: the one shot in the shoulder and another from the compound below us who was shot in the head. His helmet saved his life, but not without letting the bullet leave a gaping, skull deep wound in his scalp. The rest of the evening was quiet. I stood freezing on the rooftop, staring into the dark, hoping to see a native man with a gun even as the light faded, and I knew the Taliban went home to their beds. We exfilled at 2150. We had spent 8 hours under regular enemy fire. One of which was spent being pinned down by a sniper. I left with the joy of having survived and fought once more, but also with the evil taste of having been denied the opportunity to slay the enemy properly, to riddle their bodies with lead, and see them fall, never again to hurt or harm. May YHVH bless our next mission, and allow us to see justice done upon the wicked men who oppress the weak, and oppose the patriots who we support. I am ready for more. I crave it.

Still December 26

Christmas was alright I suppose. I stayed in my room much of the day, relaxed, watched Lord of the Rings. It was good. It is nice to have rest and comfort.

Last night I had a demonic visitation. What appeared to be a part ninja, part clown, part repairman ran with bowlegs up to a doorway, and blocking it with his frame, stared at me with a malicious grin. The breath caught in my lungs, and I knew I must say YHVH's name, but air would not pass my lips. I awoke as I finally pressed the sound of His name from my throat and began to pray and rebuke the evil presence.

In another dream, I was in jazz band again with Canfield, Shore, and someone else our age. Farus [Gabe's high school band instructor] said that Shore (and me if I chose it) had the potential to be the greatest trumpet players if we put our talent to use and worked even a little for it. Then he talked about school schedules and things we had to arrange with other classes for daytime performances. I pointed out that Shore, Canfield, and I weren't in high school, having graduated years ago, and we all laughed. Farus chuckled and said it didn't apply to us then, and that even as we were much older than the others, we were welcome in the band.

My sleep last night was fitful, and I felt exhausted and tired even as I slept.

Wednesday, December 27, 2017

I struggle once more against a sin of the flesh. Against temptation and falling I scramble along a slippery rock face. YHVH my God forgive my wickedness and my dishonor. Forgive my vile acts and hold them not against me. Forgive me and wash me, make me clean and worthy of your presence once more. Help me YHVH and give me strength.

Deployment Journal 01/01/2018 – 01/10/2018

Monday, January 1, 2018

A new year has begun but to me it is just another day. We are going on a five day mission tomorrow morning. YHVH forgive my sins and my uncleanness and do not remove your presence from me. Forgive me, cleanse me, place in me a new heart and a pure spirit. Fill me with your spirit and wrap me in your wings. Protect us as we go out, no matter our task or goal, go before us and prepare the way. Protect those with me as you have protected me. Thank you, YHVH for your favor and faithfulness. Please give me wisdom, understanding, and an iron will to follow your path for my life. Thank you for watching over those I love and keeping them safe in your care. Thank you for being you. I love you YHVH.

Thursday, January 4, 2018

Nothing much is going on. I ended up not going on the boring mission due to the truck I was in breaking down and needing to return to BAF. The guys who went left yesterday and returned today. I've been told they just pulled security on a mountain.

I do not enjoy the act of killing. Such is the white lie I've told myself and others to keep at bay the voracious hunger in my soul. In a pedestrian sense, the statement holds true, but there are conditions under which a certain amount of elation results from the taking of human life. Perhaps it is not the taking of the life directly that causes this uplifting sensation, rather the conditions and the change therein surrounding the event may be what create the sense of ecstasy, that supreme, satisfying confidence.

I would feel the pain, the horrendous evil guilt and morose blackening of the soul that would accompany an innocent death at my hands, a death unjustified by heaven or nature. I would take no thrill from it, and it would haunt me all my days.

However, when the enemy of the weak and the enemy of YHVH stand in my scope, and lead from my gun strikes them down, there is joy. A brief slowing of time followed by a subtle question flitting through the back of the mind like a wisp of smoke, followed by a surge of joy. Not the kind of childish elation that makes one shout or dance, but a sudden sureness of self, of Providence, and of the reliability and favor that lies therewith. All emotion drains from the mind, life is laid bare and its fragility made clear, yet no fear grips the soul or slows the hand. All that stands now is the Purpose, the Goal. A half thought prayer to YHVH of Hosts in this state of giving all for the defense of life and the pursuit of evil men, is worth ten, twenty, a hundred times one said in the safety of a four-walled chapel where no challenger arises to test the courage or the will. And YHVH, not being bound by time as are we, may answer these prayers before they are muttered in a half whisper, and bring to fruition their causes before they are even thought.

It is in this state of nothing, this state of the entirety of body, mind, and spirit being focused on a common purpose with righteousness and defense of innocence, the foundation, that a man is free. It is only in this state, however, that such heroic acts or fearlessness as told in legends or in battlefield stories is possible. It is a state of action, of doing. A lack of self, and a fullness of drive.

When selfish thoughts or the desires of the flesh re-enter the mind, the invincibility is lost. Fear is allowed to creep back in. Stagnation of movement and feelings of anger, of frustration arise. Action slows and ceases. A lack of self is necessary for killing the wicked. An emptiness of the soul is necessary for heroic acts, for without this vacancy YHVH cannot fill us with His power as He or we might wish. Yeshua told his disciples to deny themselves in more than one way and on more than one occasion. Righteous emptiness and resolute and continuous action arise from, and are necessary for, vanquishing evil. And such a feeling, such purity and invincibility, and indifferent, yet righteous, fury is addicting.

So, I do not enjoy the act of killing, and yet I do. So deeply and voraciously do I crave the feeling of crushing evil and defeating that which oppresses and seeks to harm, so violently do I crave that chaotic calm of combat. It is this hunger which I must deny and suppress in the civilized world. Even here on BAF, in the country of our country's longest war, my desire must smolder in the depths of my soul, lest the flame of its full potency betray me. Perhaps I should not, though. Perhaps I should embrace the feeling that so many people call bloodlust. It may be that such an emptiness of self is exactly what I need in order to stay clean and pure midst the temptations of the modern world. I only hope that my future wife will see through, understand, and appreciate the stoicism and distance of gaze that comes with such a focus. Or maybe human emotions and intensity of personality will be amplified by the condition when the focus is not on killing. Maybe that denial of self is applicable to all situations and violently amplifies the traits needed for them. Yes, I believe that is the case. I believe being filled with YHVH's Wisdom yields such rawness of nature and purity of drive no matter the circumstance. So I will strive for thus, for emptiness to be filled by YHVH. I will remember the feeling of taking that life and relive it, again and again, always humble and thankful, always sure, always in action. For it was that vacancy filled by YHVH that brought me to a new level spiritually, and I think I finally understand why.

On a different note, I have told my family of the stressors that combat places on the physical body; however, I have not recorded my observations here. I will do so now:

First, and probably most obvious, the legs (to include hips and feet) take a hell of a beating: walking, climbing, sprinting (so much sprinting), kneeling, all up and down hills, on adverse terrain, with about 100+ pounds of equipment. (And for me and other machine gunners, some or all of the ammo on an ammo belt around our waist, restricting movement of the hips and requiring immense strength and stamina from the hip flexors, abductors, and other supportive muscles of the waist) After my first mission, which was by far physically easier than the second, I was exhausted and my legs ravaged and sore. There is need for all encompassing fitness of the lower body and core, with power being the main priority as it takes much power to move speedily under load. Secondary, but still vital, aspects are strength, endurance, agility, and balance. A myriad of workouts or a few basic ones can prepare one for such strains. One should not neglect running, nor lifting, nor any other potentially useful exercise. One must simply tailor it with power as a goal whether or not the workout is aerobic or anaerobic. In short, do everything your legs can handle and then some, because you'll have to when the bullets are flying.

Second, and fairly obvious as well, is the strain placed on the neck and shoulders. I sling my SAW around my neck for mobility, ease of use, and freedom of movement for quick reaction and weapon deployment. As a result, I spend about 16 hours per mission wearing a 20 pound necklace. In addition to this, there is a 30 pound armor vest with all its pouches and attachments, and usually a 35, 40+ pound ruck hanging off those same shoulders. Combine that with maneuvering and operating the weapon (moving, raising, lowering the shoulders), and moving under the load all day long, and obviously the shoulders will be tired. However, it is a pain that can be adjusted to, and while strength and meatiness of the neck and shoulders certainly helps, it is really more of a suck-it-up-and-be-tough sort of strain. Although working out the upper back and delts is still necessary (due to how often they are used in activities other than load bearing during the day), firing the weapon is almost always from standing or kneeling (which requires sturdy shoulders when the gun is heavy), and there is much lifting, of bags, weapons, and other gear that requires a strong back. Once again, no exercise should be spurned when addressing this stressor. Power is once again paramount, but endurance, strength, and flexibility are no less necessary.

Finally, and most interesting from my perspective, was the hands. The sheer quantity of use that your hands undergo during a daylong mission is shocking. I assumed, ignorantly, that at most you'll just be toting around a weapon and the most use your hands will see is during its deployment. However, there is carrying, lifting, climbing, holding, and a constant grip of iron around the weapon you hold. Your hand keeps you from falling off a rickety ladder under full combat load while the other grips the same machine gun it has been carrying all day and holds it in a safe direction while you climb. You lift and lower gear and equipment to and from rooftops. And you work, just work. Having a strong, reliable, enduring grip is vital for combat. As such, I have begun to train my forearms, hands, and fingers much more than before. There is no miracle cure for this strain either, but this time power is less necessary than an iron, enduring strength of grip. Rock climbing, finger/forearm curls, fingertip pushups, farmer carries, punching bag work (for the wrists), etc., are all useful means to that end. I finally understand why David said of YHVH "You train my hands for war and my fingers for battle."

Saturday, January 6, 2018

Such a wretched sinner am I. Time and time again I transgress what I know to be right, I choose evil, I am swayed by my flesh and I cave, I shun the screaming of my spirit and ignore its agony, I fall short of what is expected of me because of who and what I am. YHVH I am so sorry. My words mean nothing. They are the words of a shameful mind. So hear the cry of my spirit YHVH and forgive me. Do not hold these wicked things against me. Test me once more. Make the voice of my spirit and Yours within me scream louder than those of the temptations. I will not ramble on. I will show my resolve with Action.

Sunday, January 7, 2018

Gotta do stupid driver training today even though I already have over 24 hours driving between the MATV and the RG33. All of us have driven within the past week without incident. Most of us drove at Pamir and have driven on adverse terrain without problems. I have operated all manner of vehicles since I started driving at 12. Still Behler and Beyers don't trust us. They … roll over and submit to anything their higher-ups say no matter how worthless it is or how much time it will waste. They could use their positions to mitigate the stupidity, tell the truth, and say we have already done the driver training they require, and let it be at that. Instead, they choose to waste our day on things that won't actually help us when the roads get narrow and rough. We are going to waste fuel the night before a GAF QRF, risk messing up the weapon and coms systems, and overall waste time and resources that could have been far-better spent. In addition, they have put out no information about the mission on the 9th. I heard it through rumor and then got pseudo details when I asked Pembrook, but no information was properly put out…. I have said my piece (if not all of it). Rogers has made his position clear. No one actually wants to do this training, and we all have enough drive time even within the past week to call it completed. Literally, I did the same exact drive last week that we are going to do today. Yet still [they] turn their bellies to higher and gnash at us with their blunted teeth. "I know it sucks but we gotta do it man." No we don't. "I know it's annoying but it's battalion mandated." So tell them we already completed it, because we have. "That's enough, no more out of you, we are going to do it, and that is final." ... If only I could say what I think without risking over two years of my future. An event like this isn't worth that kind of time. I just wish they would take a hint.

If the astute reader has noticed the occasional flare of venomous, seething anger, be not alarmed. I'm used to it. And I spend a good amount of time fighting to control it or ignore it, but sometimes it simply must vent to prevent a potential explosion or outburst that would be much regretted on the future side of it.

Wednesday, January 10, 2018

So I started playing Skyrim after Pembrook downloaded it on the PS4. Now I really want it for my computer because I'm kind of addicted.

We have a short mission tonight: a POD (period of darkness). Hopefully something pops off and I can finally make a proper stack.

Not much else going on, except the continuing and increasing stupidity resulting from leaders who have nothing better to do than make their guys miserable by garrisonizing deployment. A few of them ... got banned from Vance for being gay and trying to bring regular army silliness onto a SF camp. LOLOLOLOLOL. I hate those three, so that news made me very happy. I hope they feel terrible and depressed and never try anything that idiotic again.

I am craving a mission where I can kill the bad guys again. I heard about one that the guys at Gibson had that I wish I could have been on. Apparently [three soldiers] got at least 6 confirmed (Future Gabe: that was a lie; stories get exaggerated really easily) between the three of them and one killed the driver of a vehicle and blew it up with a Gustave. (Also a lie/exaggeration). SOOOOOOO JEALOUS. I can't wait to do that kind of stuff again. I miss it so much.

That's about all the news I have.

Deployment Journal 01/15/2018 – 01/30/2018

Monday, January 15, 2018

They are taking Canfield from us. Beuron has officially angered me more than the guy that I killed. He is once again over stepping his bounds and has whined his way into getting Canfield sent elsewhere while being replaced by Minton. All this because he fell out of a movement during a night op when he was hopelessly ill. Meanwhile at full health, Minton has been known to fail runs. It's horribly stupid. I don't want Canfield to go, though he is supposed to leave tomorrow. YHVH please in the name of Yeshua, don't let Canfield leave Vose. Strike the hearts and change the minds of those that are orchestrating this utterly erroneous plan. Let Canfield stay with us so Minton does not need to come here, and so there is no further damage to the kinship and dynamic of 2nd squad.

Wednesday, January 17, 2018

Gayness has reached a point far beyond that of garrison. To the point that we are going to do stix lanes with sim rounds for training. Usually that would be fun, but I guarantee … it will turn stupid. Beyers will be all conventional, and Shore, Pembrook, and I will just stand there like "Wtf are you doing?" I will use my experience from actual combat during this training, and I guarantee that our dynamic leadership duo will hate it and think I'm not taking it seriously. Of course I won't be taking it seriously, because I can't take playtime seriously after having rounds snap off a wall a foot from my face, after watching a dude five feet from me get shot by a sniper, after having seen real combat and done the work related to it, and after having taken the life of one of the enemy. Playing army and going through the doctrinal motions are things I will never be able to take seriously again.

Monday, January 22, 2018

Still nothing neat going on. Went on a mission last night that amounted in a couple captures, but no action. The SOC, abbreviation for special operations commandos I believe, seem like decent Afghans who actually care about doing their job and bringing down the Taliban. Yet we are still pulling a roaming guard on them as a precaution since we are on a large, secure base, and higher ups are terrified of green-on-blue attacks.

Minton has arrived in place of Canfield who was sent to Mez. Luckily Minton is still the same old guy and is adapting well. I think he's having a bit of trouble fitting in, but he and I get along fine. Once he's used to the laid back rhythm here, I think he'll be a fine addition. (Future Gabe: incorrect.) I'm still sad that Canfield had to leave, though. One would think that leadership would try to avoid mix-ups in the middle of a deployment, but Beuron has to stick his nose everywhere it doesn't belong, and it almost got us separated from our SF team. He's officially angered me far more than the fighter I killed ever did. Hell, I suppose a lot of people have. Such is life. I hope he gets fired and forced out of the military somehow. He's a prime example of toxic and ineffective leadership. I honestly wouldn't even be mad if he got hit by a stray mortar. I can't wait to do the brigade command climate survey. I'm dropping names and bringing up all the stuff that's been irking me lately. It'll be a good place to vent anonymously and with potential usefulness.

Wednesday, January 24, 2018

I watched Fury today, the second time I've seen the movie, and it resonated with me. Not all of it was perfect, it was a pessimistic view of war, but much of it was true to life I believe. It was dark, brooding, shedding red and glaring light on the dark places of the human psyche in battle. Yet it was uplifting, encouraging in a way, in how it told a tale of resilience, courage, overcoming the weakness of the self, choosing the right path when it means certain death, and never yielding in faith or determination. Toward the end, when they are in a lull in the tank, Bible brings up a Bible verse in which YHVH asks whom he shall send, and the writer replied "Here am I, YHVH, send me." Tonight, before watching this scene, I uttered near the same words while on a guard shift. This simple quote said under the circumstances concurrent with its presence in the movie laid a heavy weight on the worlds I had sung. I feel now the burden which those words carry, and yet the freedom they bring. I feel the price that those words cost, yet the power which they give. It is both sorrow and joy. It is both pain and victory. Whether or not these words are said in a time of war, the weight and power of them is the same. All followers of Christ and those faithful to YHVH should have these words always on their lips, a constant promise, a constant service. They capture an important portion of the spirit of what it means to be a disciple of Christ.

Friday, January 26, 2018

I overheard a brief portion of a conversation between Beyers and Pembrook. Beyers sounded scared to go on a mission that would be more difficult or dangerous than the ones at Paktika. It sounds like he wants to keep us from going. I think that's stupid, so hopefully he doesn't get his way. However, this entire scenario could be utterly false considering how little I heard of the conversation. Either way, I hope some cool missions come up and that I am once again immersed in glorious battle for the glory of YHVH, that I may see His hand on my life in that wonderfully tangible way, and that I may see His favor and His protection evident in the physical once again as He gives us victory. I pray, YHVH, that you go out before us, weaken the enemy, and let us destroy them completely and without exception. Give us good partner force men to work with who are patriots and steadfast in their desire to bring peace to their country. Let the battles be thrilling, and once again let me deal a lethal blow to the enemy in the physical, and help me to do the same in the spiritual.

I had some dissonance in my mind or spirit this evening, and I do not know the source of it. I prayed and read the Bible, and it seems to have subsided, but there remains a trace. Some inkling of a missed puzzle piece, a forgotten item, an unfinished task still hums in the depths of my soul and in the dark recesses of my mind. I wish I knew the cause, or if the cause is one of the few possibilities I have in mind, I wish I knew how to go about resolving it. Actually, I know how to resolve it either way. I will pray, I will act. By YHVH's grace, I will be successful.

Monday, January 29, 2018

I saw on what bits of Facebook would load on my phone today that something apparently happened to [a friend of Gabe's from high school]. It would seem that she died recently, though I do not know any of the details. Another Berthoud child fallen prey to the spirit of death over that place. It is sickening. It preys upon the weak, the broken. YVHV in the name of Yeshua I rebuke that evil spirit. Send legions of angels to battle it and drive it out, to bring peace to that town and its people. Please in the name of Yeshua protect the other young people in that town and around it. In the name of Yeshua protect my family and friends. Do not let that wicked presence claim any more lives.

Tuesday, January 30, 2018

[A classmate of Gabe's from high school] died in a helicopter crash in Washington state. "A thousand may fall at your side, ten thousand at your right hand, but it will not come near you ... If you make the Most High your dwelling, even YHVH who is my refuge, then no harm will befall you, no disaster will come near your tent." YHVH I pray this verse from Psalm 91 over my family and my friends right now. The evil powers of this world have begun to increase the pace of their wicked plots. In the name of Yeshua, protect my home and all who live there. Protect my tent, YHVH. With legions of angels and the fire of your very Presence and Spirit, protect that which I love in this earth. I love you YHVH and thank you.

Deployment Journal 02/01/2018 – 02/10/2018

Thursday, February 1, 2018

Some annoying stuff is going down tomorrow. … Just gotta get it over with. Then missions coming up in March. I can't wait. I neeeeeed to go out and get in a proper fight again. I crave battle. I am sick of the utterly wasteful boredom that higher ups like to fill downtime with.

I had a dream today about a town filled with just women and children who managed to defeat a main bad guy who was trying to take their town, but a new attacker was coming that only a young boy knew of. It was the man and gang who had killed his mother and father in front of him. His father, with his dying breath, gave a .45 lever gun to his son for protection. The boy, now perched atop a hill near his ruined house and lay down cover fire to keep the bad guys at bay. He adjusted his sights so he would be ready to snipe them when they crested the ridge ahead. A mysterious figure offered him advice and aid. The man said that he raised bears, and that two or three could handle the gang of men easily. They were trained to love American soldiers and civilians, and trained to despise and attack those who had a green canteen thrown at them or carried on their person. One of the bad guys managed to climb into an RG that was parked there, and began to turn on the crow. The mysterious man began dismantling it so that it would not fire, and I scrambled into the vehicle to kill the bad guy. But my pistol jammed, I lost the magazine under a seat when I was clearing the jam, and my eyes would not focus, and my hands were weak. It was horrible. I woke up.

Saturday, February 3, 2018

After spending the entire afternoon and the better part of the evening sitting in a truck watching the Charlie company goofs bumble their way through the stix lane twice, I got a proper dinner. So I suppose I'll be lenient in punishing them for their idiocy later. I am honestly revolted by the fact that we had to do something like this in Afghanistan anyway. It was utterly ridiculous, completely unrealistic, and an imprudent waste of time. Real combat is nothing like that. I stand by my claim that if we went into combat as a unit, we would get crushed.

Things I have learned that the big army has not:

Don't maneuver across even slightly open ground. If trees, boulders, and buildings are readily available, then it could work in theory, but even then it is unwise due to the high likelihood of traps and ambush. The enemy likes to bait.

Don't maneuver on foot when trucks are available.

NEVER EVER BOUND UNLESS THERE IS ACTUAL COVER. SPEED IS SECURITY.

Don't be a sissy. When it comes to the Taliban, they can't hit much anyway, so there's no point freaking out. This is on leaders somewhat, but boils down to the overall attitude of the group.

Stay acting. Know your place and know your job. If you are at a loss, ask someone if they need help. Do not become sedentary in combat. It means a collapse of morale and effectiveness at its most mild, and a loss of life at its more severe end.

Don't clear every building. Most of the people you'll run into are just ordinary citizens trying to lead ordinary lives.

Use human shields. If you capture someone, have them walk in front of you and through doors before you. If you have to carry heavy evidence off the objective, make the captor carry it in a sealed or locked bag. You should remain mobile and agile to be most effective, but the prisoner can suffer under load.

Running distance doesn't help when you are carrying 100 pounds of gear at a sprint up a hill under enemy fire. It just doesn't.

Don't get out of an armored truck to wait out in the open. It is plain dumb. The big armored trucks we have (RGs, MATVs, MaxxPros) can withstand .50cal, RPGs, and IEDs. Leaving that safety to wait under less safety is retarded. There will be a moment's pause or so once exited and before moving to organize, but you should stage ready to file off the vehicles and into the fight. Don't stage on the ground outside.

If you can see them, they can see you. If you can't see them, they can still see you. If by some chance you can't see them AND they can't see you, they still know where you are and will shoot in your general direction.

The "mad minute" is not a real thing.

Single file is the way to go in a mine ridden area.

Don't ask for permission to shoot, you can justify it later.

Shooting prone is rare. Very rare. "Barrier" (wall or lip of roof) shooting is the most common. Ironically the only kill I have so far was taken in the prone, but who knows, maybe some stray rounds of mine knocked down one of those mortar guys or dude on the roof that engaged us in the peanut garage.

Leading to the next one: Perfect shots are rare. Suppressive fire is much more common.

If a bullet hits the car, they'll stop faster than if you just hit the ground in front of the car.

Grenades are mostly for fun. (320s included)

Yelling accomplishes nothing if you do it all the time. Speak with a cool, relaxed voice, altering the level of urgency for the situation. Do not yell until you need immediate results or need to snap someone out of a trance.

Mention anything suspicious you see and communicate clearly, but do not make conversation unless the situation warrants. It's distracting.

Avoid reacting with surprise to enemy fire. Instead react with immediate return fire, no matter whether you can see them or not (if dismounted, and in a slightly open area). The first couple times a bullet hits a rock right in front of you or snaps of the wall next to you, it will be involuntary to utter an expletive and maybe flinch, but eventually you need to know that if you see it or hear it, it didn't hit you and it's nothing to lose your cool over.

Be confident, not cocky. Feel invincible, but avoid acting like it.

Memorizing stats doesn't help you shoot.

Battle drills are useless and should not exist.

Listen to the real leaders, and men with experience in the art of battle and killing. Ignore the posers and those lacking experience, no matter the rank.

These things I have learned may not apply to all situations or wars, but they work for this place, and I would venture to guess most others as well.

I had a dream today that I was driving my truck in Alaska, but I realized that I never went to get my truck from storage when I tried reflecting on the adventure of my return. As a result I realized I was in a dream. I woke up from that into another dream where I told someone of that dream and how amusing, yet sad it was. I ended up waking from a different dream of some great significance that I could not remember, so I prayed YHVH would tell me the revelations I had forgotten. It turns out this was still a dream, and I remember words along these lines as my feet went from glued to the bed by a malicious force, to free: "We must fight the enemy on his ground, in the realm of choices."

Wednesday, February 7, 2018

I had a couple interesting dreams recently. One is written in my phone, and the other I can't seem to remember, but I know it had some significance. I wonder if YHVH is calling me to fight human trafficking. I wonder if, should I choose to do so, legality and politics will impede justice. I wonder if I would be able to change that by going in with open eyes and YHVH's wisdom. I wonder if my nose will ever heal properly inside so that I stop picking off the scab assuming it's a stubborn booger causing blood flow. I have a lot of questions. I always do. I pray YHVH answers the important ones at the right time, and more so that I will be tuned to hear the answer.

Thursday, February 8, 2018

I had a dream about Sonya today. I haven't spoken to her since Christmastime of 2016. In my dream she had darker hair than in reality, almost fully brown. She was beautiful, quiet, confident, and refreshing to see. I was in the process of giving her a tour of our living area at Vose (but a maze-like, ruinous dream version). Then I was distracted by something or someone, and Richard came up and asked about Sonya as did a couple others. A friend and I explained that I was looking to have a relationship with her. They were all happy for me. Richard commented on how beautiful she was. In that time, she had finished exploring the area, and she made toward the gate in a graceful run, smiling as she passed me. I asked if she was leaving already to which she turned around and smiled as she said "Bye." I ran toward the gate to see her off, but the dream changed. Aunt Diane was outside with David, and Daniel, and Destiny joined them.

They were driving off BAF to travel across Afghanistan, and I went with them to see them to the outer gate. I gave them directions which they followed, but then David said he knew where he should go based on maps, so I emphasized to follow those over my directions since I only knew the location of a couple exits, and they may not be the correct ones for their purpose. But David seemed calm and treated it as an opportunity to learn and see more, trusting my guidance, but aware he could turn around if need be.

I do not know what this dream means. I wonder if Sonya represents my future wife. I wonder what role this SF team has yet to play in my life since this is the second dream I have had based on Vose with members of the team there. (The other was earlier today and was about picking up brass, but not because we didn't shoot. I had to explain to some first platooners that Kevin was joking about it. The first platooners and Beyers and some others were wearing the old dumb UCP [uniform camouflage pattern] ACUs while Pembrook, Rogers, me, and the team were wearing the OCP [operational camouflage pattern] FRACUS of deployment.) As usual I wonder some good many things. I pray YHVH reveals the answers before long.

Saturday, February 10, 2018

Had a dream last night in which Dad and I were hunters or lions, and caught a large prey which we hauled off to a location that it wouldn't be found where we could subsist off it for some time. Another dream where there was some discussion and dissonance and some dark looks at the past, I was worried about which knife to carry and was concerned I had lost one. We all wondered where Olivia was (she was supposed to be with her friends but we hadn't seen her in some time). There was a drawn picture of her sticking out of a door that portrayed her laying on the ground with part of her skull missing, from a vehicle crashing into her. I was shocked once I realized what the picture was and immediately began to pray for her safety in the dream and again when I woke up.

YHVH I beg you to show me the meaning of the dreams which you have been giving me and tell me how to act.

Songs of heroes long forgotten

12 February 2018

Songs of heroes long forgotten
Weave a somber tale
By blood and pain and
    strife begotten
By broken sword and torn sail

What's more they leave out parts
That dry and dull the ears
Without thrill or merry spark
Which sometimes last for years

They do not tell of the
    lowly times
Or highlight bland tradition
They have no space for the
    daily grind
Which causes the heroes'
    high attrition

For what good would the tale be
If monotony was all it told
Save a moment or two of fire
    and glory
Which are now those legends old

It would make the audience aware
Of a truth so dull and glum
A truth so many cannot bear
And so turn to herb and rum

The truth is this, simple and raw
Without ornamental illustration

That adventures are the needle in
    the straw
And their memories, a
    grand inflation

The rest is work and
    wearisome toil
Which few ever come to savor
But satisfaction should be found,
    says the teacher
In food and drink and labor.

Meaningless though it may be
And tiring all the same
It is the lot of a man that's free
To labor on in vain.

For he takes no product with him
And hears no remembrance song
As the numbers who sing it
    grow slim
A fleeting moment of glory is all
    that sticks for long

Yet all of this is good,
It is a rightful path to follow
For without daily work and drink
    and food
Life would be sorrowfully hollow

The monotony is fine
Because it does not last forever

So keep its peace in mind
And embrace it if you are clever

For life is made of this
The boring daily grind
And spurning it is unwise
For in work there's joy to find

No, they won't sing songs
About your daily job
Their memory won't be strong
Of that time your car was robbed

They probably will forget
How neat your tie was tied
And they probably won't give
    a darn
About all the foods you tried

They won't care about
    your money
They'll forget about your clothes
Perhaps you were quite funny
But they'll soon forget your jokes

All they will remember
All they'll care to tell
Is the time you saved a life
Or the time you walked
    through hell

They'll remember one or two
Heroic deeds of yours
And all else that you
    lived through
Is so much dust on the floor

But all of this is good
So labor on in vain
But stow away no physical riches
Or try and buy memory's refrain

Instead enjoy your peace
And in heaven store your wealth
For when your breath has ceased
And death comes with
    sudden stealth

No memory will save you
No song will free your soul
The blood and pain and strife
You'll love as with the whole

The monotony and quiet
Of the long days of your life
Will be what taught you patience
And gave you rest from strife

And all will be before you
As one existence song
And by its tune you will
    be judged
And a slow melody is strong

That said don't be idle
Act, and do and chase
All things that are righteous
Live with fervor, run your race

Simply do not spurn
The times that are not wild
Enjoy that peaceful quiet
And love that beauty mild

For songs of heroes long forgotten
Weave a somber tail
Of blood and pain and
　　strife begotten
Of broken sword and torn sail

But the parts that they leave out
The happy days between
Are what gave them strength
　　to shout
And battle to be free

To carry on through tragedy
To rise back to their feet
To chase the goal of victory
After each defeat

To give and live their all
For their family, home, and God
Those boring times, the
　　daily grind
Is what made them so strong.

Deployment Journal 02/12/2018 – 02/27/2018

Monday, February 12, 2018

Finished the above poem today. Following my own advice is not often an easy task unfortunately. Lol.

Wednesday, February 14, 2018

Saint Valentine's Day

I had a dream that is written in my phone. It seems significant. Also, I am reminded of how lonely I have become.

> Party/night get together. Went to a bar or a place for takeout food. Rogers, Shore, me and some others like Siji and Michael from college. When we left, things got rowdy. It was just me and Shore off to one side. Michael was being annoying hitting people with a stick. Siji or someone else was holding a girl who was cold. I was wearing less than most others there and was not cold. A bit of a tussle started but I could tell it was in good fun. A couple of guys there I didn't know did not know it was and went to get guns. They shot at the group. One guy shot his friend in the shoulder or back and a bullet hit Siji on or near the junk. I shouted for them to stop and put the guns down. So did Shore. They obeyed and as I walked toward the location, one of the guys took his gun back to his truck. When the cops showed up I called him out as the main aggressor who actually shot people which he was. He was nonchalant. I told him he needed to tell his friend goodbye since people don't live though taking a 44mag to the ribcage. My voice was not as forceful or as loud as it should have been, but people still heard and obeyed. Shore and I neutralized the situation to keep others from getting hurt without having guns ourselves.

Sunday, February 18, 2018

FUUUUUUUUUUCK... Last night was the most miserable, useless mission I have ever been on. We came up empty handed. There were no fights. My bag broke, along with an MK 48 drum, leaving me looking like a bag of smashed ass bumbling around in the dark. We walked through freezing streams, climbed God knows how many terraces, fell off of a nearly equal number of ledges, terraces, and berms, stepped ankle deep in feces and mud more than should have been possible, climbed up the side of a mountain for giggles just to climb back down again, and so on, and so on, and so on. All with a heavy machine gun, and 800 rounds of 7.62 dangling from my shoulders and neck (80+ pounds with just the gun and ammo). The straps on my bag broke, so I carabinered it to my plate carrier, but 60 or 70 pounds of ammo doesn't play nice, so it pulled the whole plate carrier back to a point that it choked me out every time I walked more than about ten steps without readjusting and pulling it forward. NEVER EVER MAKING THAT MISTAKE AGAIN. I hope I never have to go on such a painfully aggravating mission again. If there had just been a little five-minute firefight where I got to drop a dude or two, it would have been worth it. But instead we came up dry. The intel was wrong, or everyone had already cleared out when we got there. Sissies.

Monday, February 19, 2018

I both hate this place and I love it. I experience agony for it. I suffer for it. Yet so little have I accomplished to aid in its forward progress. Indeed my actions are so feeble compared to the breadth of this conflict in both time and space that they can hardly be said to have accomplished anything at all. I have formed friendships and bonds with locals that may be long forgotten in a year. In the same manner, they will work with more Americans, get to know them, and forget me and my companions. Still, however, I value them. I have grown to detest the manner in which America is handling the remnants of this war. We shy away from rebuilding infrastructure, from making forceful moves against governmental corruption, from pushing the Afghans toward self-sustainment.

For peace in this country to begin in a true sense and end the turmoil of the past 30 years, Afghanistan needs a king. Not a dictator, not a power-hungry emperor, not a corrupt monarch or sadistic tyrant. They need a king. A man who is wise, just, and truly cares for each one of his people. A man who will put the needs and desires of the country above his own and those of his clan. A man who will make Taliban presence a thing of the past by being a figurehead and spokesperson of a new and peaceful ideology for the people to rally behind. He must be able to light a fire in the bellies of the Afghans with his words, and keep it burning with his actions. A good and wise king with a large circle of trusted friends, advisors, and officials who will not cave to bribe or coercion, is what is needed to restore Afghanistan to its former glory and drive it towards a prosperous future. Until we hear of the coronation of the king of Afghanistan, I expect BAF will remain full, along with the other FOBs [forward operating bases] in the country, of men fighting the skeleton of a conflict that should have died long ago.

Or perhaps I am wrong. There may come a day that the Afghan people will awaken to the reality of their predicament and livelihood and choose change for themselves. They may create their own form of self-government with cultural and family ties taken into account. The different tribes and peoples (Dari, Pashto, Uzbek, etc.) may take the unity they have found in fighting the Taliban alongside each other for all these years and create a more functional state (province) based mode of management that keeps the peace in all regions. Perhaps skilled and intelligent leaders will arise and help birth a new government, free of corruption, that will no longer fail in upholding the law and order it claims to stand for. It may be over two hundred years late, but there's no reason a proper political renaissance shouldn't rumble through Afghanistan now.

Either way I pray this people, this nation, finds peace.

Tuesday, February 20 to Monday, February 26, 2018

Between the 19th and the next entry on the 27th there were actually a few events of interest. However their blended effect was barely enough to break the monotony. Their only major effect was altering the form of boredom. Commandos were here until the 25th. During the time they spent here we went on two or three period of darkness missions. The first is chronicled above on the 18th. I think it was just two but I can barely remember, since all of those days blurred together in exhaustion, boredom, and aggravation. No combat, a couple explosions that didn't even raise my pulse, and miles of bumbling through the dark over terraces and walls, up and down steep hills, through water, through mud, etc., etc. And between those hellacious excursions, we sat in a truck for six hours a day pulling guard on the Afghan soldiers we were supposed to be building trust with. Good times.

Tuesday, February 27, 2018

We were supposed to be in Paktika today for round two. However, last night the advance convoy got ambushed and took casualties as well as damage to their trucks. We will see tonight if they decide to try again. If they do, we will fly out sometime around midnight for about a week of operations. I'm guessing it will be no more than two or three in total. I am longing for another proper firefight. I want to go back to my proving grounds and see what my actions there have wrought. I want to go back and make sure the Taliban are gone from that region for good. I want to do battle with the enemy in the physical once again. I want to witness YHVH's protection and might in battle again. I want to feel invincible again. One last hurrah.

After the next eight days, assuming Paktika is a go, deployment is practically over for me. No more missions. The next two months before we rip out will be time to work out, relax, and mentally prepare for the idea of returning to a place of freedom. Oh how I long for freedom. However the civilian world will no doubt look different to me now. I will adapt quickly as always, and probably within a week will fall back into old rhythms from before we left. Going home in June will be a bit of a shock as well. It will have been over a year since I have seen any of my family or friends. Life is simple here, despite its shortcomings, and returning to the chaotic complexity of normal life will be a burden initially. I guess in this too, I will adapt quickly. In fact, I may not even miss a stride. I will always remember this place, though, and the things I did here. And I will always miss parts of it.

I thank YHVH for giving me relief from the illness that crumpled me a couple days ago. I had extreme diarrhea four or five times a day minimum, a savage headache, stomach discomfort, body aches, and the dehydration and exhaustion that comes with all of the above. It was miserable. I asked my family to pray, and it was the next day that I felt much better. Today a mere cold lingers causing slight congestion and a mild dizziness/sensitivity of the eyes.

Prior to becoming sick, I fell miserably deep into an act I know to be a sin. It was far too easy. I believe the illness was a sort of retribution from my body and from YHVH. I know people say that's not how He works, but I know for a fact that every good father punishes his children with they stray from the light. I think YHVH retains this quality, and is not the effeminate softy that he is made out to be. There is punishment for sin. Its wages is death, and that is avoided through salvation through Christ Yeshua. So we no longer must pay in blood for removal of guilt; but in the same way a father will forgive and still discipline, so I believe YHVH uses discomfort to draw our attention to our actions and inspire a change. I have experienced this on a physical level many times. When I remain in a state of purity, of righteousness in spirit, my body retains impressive strength, resilience, and near immunity to disease and injury. However, when I slacken in my pursuit of righteousness and cave to the temptations of the id, my body breaks down an amount proportional to the sin. Exhaustion for minor, slight injury or pain for more severe, and a complete breakdown of all spiritual inhibitions resulting in a grave transgression yields the total incapacitation I experienced recently. Yet even in this, YHVH was merciful. He heard my cry and the prayers of my family and responded with compassion, cutting short the period of my suffering and allowing me to return to a place of spiritual cleanliness. Yesterday I was able to workout at full strength despite the congestion of a light cold. Today, though I am tired from having a night shift for TOC [tactical operations center] watch, I do not feel overly lethargic. This trend has exhibited itself many times throughout my life. So I must conclude that… YHVH loves me a whole lot. For a loving father disciplines his son, but a father who spares the rod ruins his child.

Our mission got rolled again. Now we aren't leaving until Friday night if we go at all. I want to go. I want at least one more good firefight. One more good taste of battle before I leave. And while that is true, I find myself increasingly homesick. Not in a heartbroken way, but in a longing way. Like the nostalgic ache of a fond memory. I am getting to the point where I am quite ready to go back. Still my desire for battle remains.

Deployment Journal 03/11/2018 – 03/27/2018

Sunday, March 11, 2018

We got back from Dahlke at about 4:00 AM today. I stayed awake to shower and brush my teeth for the first time in a week since I had forgotten to bring all my hygiene items to Dahlke. However, in true regular army fashion I borrowed an electric razor from Rogers to maintain a kempt facial appearance. Apparently it was not in vain since a female PSU soldier told one of the interpreters that I was beautiful. Although, he said that she had been talking about my demeanor being one of composed discipline, so maybe my face had nothing to do with it. Anyway, I stayed awake to shower and brush my teeth, following which ritual I elected to stay awake until breakfast so that I could spend a couple hours making phone calls home. I called Luke, but he didn't pick up so I will email him today. Then I called Heath, and we had a good talk about how life was going and our plans for the summer. Afterward I called my family for the first time in a few weeks and talked for about an hour and a half. We discussed how I believe YHVH is leading me toward the fight against human trafficking. It is a cause I find myself easily passionate about and I desire to aid in freeing the victims trapped by the sadistic psychos who abuse them for profit. I pray YHVH shows me the next step in joining that fight in both the spiritual, influential, and physical realms. I pray He sets up divine encounters for me that will yield the training and resources I will need to get involved in that righteous fight. I desire to see justice done upon the wicked men who victimize women and children. I desire to slay them where they stand if YHVH would allow violence on my part. I know not yet which form it will take; however, I can say with confidence that I will trust in YHVH and His guidance on the matter as all matters.

As for the singular mission we executed in Sharana while staged at Dahlke, it was uneventful. A nice stroll through a mountain valley by cover of night. I wish I could have seen it during the day. Not only would we have seen glorious battle, the valley being heavily Taliban infested, but the surrounding mountainscape that I could glimpse through my night vision and with the bright moon that night struck me as one of great freshness and beauty. It was similar to the region of Red Feather Lakes, though less forested (and far dustier of course). Overall, it was actually a good time. Leisurely, calm nearly to the point of whimsical, and without the aggravating distance or painfully challenging terrain as some of our other night missions. It was a good end to my missions in this country, (future Gabe: Ha, boy you thought!) though I still wish it would have been a blazing firefight.

As I enter the 70th page of these journals, I find myself looking back on all that has happened thus far in Afghanistan. I have grown substantially, seen much, and learned more. It has been one hell of an adventure, but with the curtains most likely closed on any further missions I look forward to a period of rest and peace that will extend to our return and through the summer. I am thankful for the experience I have gained here. I thank YHVH for His constant and evident protection, and gentle discipline. I am glad I came to this country. I did not accomplish all that I wished to, but I will return home with head held high and a new outlook on life. There are only two months left before we will definitely be home. It could be even sooner. My thoughts now turn to my tasks upon redeployment to Alaska. I can't wait for even the little boring things, like registering my truck. I long for freedom, … and weekends, dang do I miss weekends.

Thursday, March15, 2018

I had another dream about human trafficking last night. I wrote it in my phone, but I'll summarize it here as well. In the dream I infiltrated an organization that trafficked drugs and humans and were branching out to trafficking weapons in order to turn a larger profit. They cut me in as a partner and gave me drugs and grenades to sell. I thought about the long game, my strategy, and how I would use those grenades to kill those wicked men and free the humans they had enslaved. I am now more sure than ever that YHVH is calling me that direction. I pray YHVH will give me wisdom and insight when purchasing weapons in the physical (something I have been perseverating over for some time now) in preparation for potential fights. I pray that He will set me up with divine appointments for resources, training, and networking to build an organization that will fight with every weapon at our disposal to end slavery. I had another thought the other day that clicked in a way too perfect to ignore. The organization will be known as Goliath's Bane. For as YHVH used David to deliver Israel from the hands of the Philistines, so Goliath's Bane will follow YHVH's guidance to fight for the freedom of the oppressed and enslaved.

Thank you YHVH for the insight and confirmations. Thank you for placing this cause on my heart and giving me this glorious purpose in your Name. Please aide me in this mission, and bring friends to my side that will pursue the same goal. Please prepare me, and grant me success that Your Name may be glorified in the saving and freeing of innocent lives.

Sunday, March 25, 2018

I can't believe it has been so long since I've written here. Time has gone by quickly and slowly at the same time. Our leadership is on their usual kick still, pushing obnoxious training and stupid busy work over actual mission preparedness. It is especially annoying now that we have a month of what should be pretty gnarly missions coming up. Some of the training they've set up with the team is useful and should be entertaining which is a positive. However they are still pushing a retarded "mock board," and some pointless, irrelevant essays. I'm not even gonna do them probably. They aren't worth the time, and I don't have to prove my literacy to my leadership. If they want evidence of my linguistic competency, I'll be glad to show them samples from the plethora of essays from my time as a student.

Anyway, not much has happened since Dahlke. Same old shenanigans. But potentially some cool missions coming up. I pray that they are worthwhile and beneficial and full of ferocity.

Tuesday, March 27, 2018

I've spent a few days now once more seeking the physical and spiritual purity that has been so elusive at times during this deployment. It feels as though there is less grace than before. I sense a tension that I don't like. My companions have taken out their unknown, growing stress on me at times, as is the norm when I pursue things of the spirit. I am resilient to it, but annoyed with the frequency. Imagine a person saying an obnoxious or maybe even a slightly funny phrase. One time it is amusing, but after that it's just annoying. There's no way to make them stop, speak with reason, or even deflect it. I could completely ignore it, which I plan to do from now on. However, I have a bad habit of trying to enjoy the company of the people I am with, and attempting to hold conversation. I think I'm done with that now though. I'm honestly bored of these people. Seven months with no escape has been too long. I need a weekend.

The new ODA has moved in almost completely, and 0214 has almost fully moved out. I miss them. They didn't give a darn. They put people in their place. They shut down lame ideas. They didn't give us the time of day until a few of us proved ourselves on mission. They had a loud, rowdy dynamic that was entertaining to witness. The new team seems far too open to us already. The new 18C, is way too supportive of the LT and his stupid ideas. They almost seem as if they don't want to step on toes or hurt feelings. At the same time they seem super uptight, like a cordial librarian who has a scowlish smile that suggests she'll scold you over a sneeze. It kind of annoys me. They are also way too motivated. Don't get me wrong, I want to get out and kill the bad guys; that's why I am in this country. However, these new ODA dudes just seem a little bit too hooah for SF guys. I can see why Kevin had a bad impression of them early on. Disclaimer: These are first impressions of the group, I have not met everyone on the team yet, I'm sure a good portion of them are decent guys in person.

Either way, I am ready to go home or ready to go kill people. It's gotta be one of the two because I am growing exhausted of my circumstance.

He knelt with sword in hand

Wednesday, March 28, 2018

He knelt with sword in hand
A quiet prayer said
"Keep strong my arm and sharp
    my blade
So I do not join the dead"

His battle harsh and gruesome
Was one of many fought
And never did he question
What end his actions wrought

Some age and land apart
Far future from that deed
Another man took to knee
And with Providence did plead

"Make me swift and true
Give me courage and will
Keep my powder dry and feet
    the same
For tyranny to kill."

His war was one of anguish
To shrug off a royal yoke
A war of separation
Fought by common folk.

And onward throughout history
Such stories stemmed the tide
Of evil and of tyranny
And of foolish, haughty pride

Nation against nation
Brother against brother
Across the sea or across the street
One violence or another

Don't ask why
Don't ask who's right
Lest you lie
Awake at night

No answer can be given
No human mind can read
The cosmos in a moment
Or the effect of a single deed

But the Almighty up above
Does watch the ways of men
And guides those who honor him
To victory far from sin

But there is a master plan
That must not be disobeyed
And when bounds are overstepped
The hand of God will change
    the day

He hears the innocent cry
He sees the pain of
    those oppressed
Their sorrow breaks His heart
And their cause is there impressed

"Who will go?" He asks
"And be their mortal guide
To freedom and to joy
That with me they may abide."

A voice among thousands
Lifts unto His ears
"I will go, send me"
Echoes through the years

Until a man should find his way
To a dusty, wild land
Where evil men still roam
And the righteous cannot stand

Knelt he there, with gun in hand
A quiet prayer said
"Make my aim steady and true"
And proceeded to sling lead

The first battle of many
That the man would face
To follow the Call of Providence
And bring the lost to grace.

Deployment Journal 04/08/2018

Sunday, April 8, 2018

Once again it has been a while since I entered anything here. Deployment is winding down to its inevitable end, and I welcome it gratefully. Regardless, my soul aches for battle. As previously stated, I am torn. I crave home and freedom and relaxation, but voraciously I long for a final glorious fight in which YHVH's power is made evident. I am tired, but I want struggle. I am lonely, but I want to stand alone midst a corpse pile of wicked men. I desire still that cool, chaotic calm of justified violence....

I try not to care. I try to stay cool and collected. I try to ignore the petty annoyances around me that have grown to irksome pains. Yet I find myself hypocritical, oft taking the same attitudes and mannerisms which I detest. I am not them. I am not of them. I will not become them. I pray YHVH grants me grace, wisdom, and a stoic demeanor.

I have been informed I will not be on the first two missions this month. Fuss is supposed to be taking my SAW or an MK48 in my place. Our leadership is once again trying to please people rather than follow strategically sound choices. I trust YHVH will see His plan fulfilled for us, and His purpose accomplished, but the rejection stings nonetheless. I dislike saying publicly that I have earned or accomplished anything. I don't care for grandstanding. Yet my private thoughts are humming with indignation and offense. They scream outrage and injustice. I have earned my right to carry my machine gun into combat. I have proven myself. I belong on those missions. I am the one they need to choose and to send. Arrogance, the creeping pestilence, is ever at my door hissing and coiling with venomous intent. So too a myriad of other weaknesses, faults, sins, and transgressions. The enemy of my spirit would have no greater joy than to see me marginalized and sidelined due to the failure of my own flesh, the weakness of my own mind. I must not let that happen. YHVH save me. Forgive me for my wickedness, hard heartedness, corruption, hypocrisy, lust, arrogance, malaise, and all the other vile temptations of my mortal being. Wash me clean, and make me new by your blood that I may fight and be victorious over the unseen foe. You are my savior, my counselor, my advocate, and my God. YHVH, I trust you with all, and will follow your purpose for my life with all that I am. Show me the way, guide my steps, make true my path and my mission. Fill me with your Holy Spirit, and build me into the man you have destined me to become.

In olden days when men stood tall

Wednesday, April 11, 2018

In olden days when men stood tall
With sturdy build and
 mighty will
To shape the world and change
 it all
For God, for country, for sheer thrill

It was known and often taught
That men must learn and grow
 and fight
For justice, for freedom, or all
 for naught
Lest their names be lost in
 dying light

Honor was prized, and
 truthfulness too
Valor, compassion,
 mastery, strength
For what could be man,
 without virtue
For the sake of faith, go
 any length

And so it was that men were shown
The meaning of a life well spent
But in recent days, few men
 are known
To have their soul as yet un-rent

Now they're told, and often taught
That no man should seek
 out honor

Some men have it, and others not
It's all inside, so don't even bother

They're told to live a life of ease
To float and drift like dandelion seeds
Embrace the softer, sweeter self
Gone are the days of valiant creeds

Men who hone their bodies
Do so from fear and
 dangerous aggression
Real men only seek to please
Real men accept their
 inevitable depression

They live a life of gentle words
Never giving voice to their
 burning hearts
And so they're quenched with
 icy swords
Before ever they're given chance
 to start

And softer grows the world now
Because of this anemic trend
Weaker men make weaker vows
That once broken rarely mend

What can be done to change it
To right our rather precarious course
And who could ever arrange it
That men would reclaim their
 forgotten force

Indeed there is only one way out
One choice that must be made
To finally end our sorry rout
And once more take up
    mighty blade

To seek YHVH and learn
    His will
Is our only hope to recover
That virile joy and manly thrill
That's been traded for a
    sickly other

Deployment Journal 04/19/2018 – 04/28/2018

Thursday, April 19, 2018

YHVH has seen fit to honor me, to answer my prayers, and raise me up despite the wretchedness of my sinful flesh. Even now preoccupied with foreign thoughts and wanting, my mind aches of the constant struggle within. My spirit has been dull as of late. Weakened and muffled are the sound of its war cry, smothered by the mire of worldly temptations. However, never shall it be beaten. YHVH Himself has redeemed it by His Son Yeshua, Savior of the world and my God and King. In His mercy, he has seen fit to pardon my wickedness and set my eyes straight once more. I pray now for His continued mercy and grace, the strength to overcome the next test instead of faltering like one with no foresight or discretion. I thank Him for His kindness, goodness, compassion, forgiveness, and favor. I am humbled by His plan for me, and stand in awe of His ways.

Though I falter
Though I fall
I will remain
Through it all
To free the slave
And end their anguish
To fight for freedom, justice, and love
And evil shall be vanquished

Friday, April 27, 2018

Only three weeks before we are back in Alaska. Three weeks. One mission (ideally… outcome TBD). My mind now turns to what I will do when I get back. Register my truck, drone through the work days, drink alcohol for the first time in 8 months, go on hikes, go mountain biking (after buying a mountain bike), buy guns, go shooting. A short month after our return, I get to go back to Colorado for the first time in over a year.

But before that, a job must be done. A valiant quest must be undertaken.

There will be grueling hikes, dark paths, danger, and violence. I can't wait. Tomorrow evening is when it is supposed to go down, and I am stoked. My body well remembers the euphoria of combat and leaves me wired with desire. I have chosen to fast from video and social media so that I may focus my mind and heart on YHVH in preparation. The war of my spirit against my flesh rages in pitched battles, some of which I have lost recently, but through YHVH I will prevail and go into physical battle in a state of spiritual purity.

Within the past week, I have been given two more signs indicating that I will fight against human trafficking in the future. First, I watched Lethal Weapon 4 in which human trafficking was a main theme. Second, I had a dream that is written in my phone [added below]. It was about the start of the fight. The preparation. I gathered my friends and invited them to join me in combating the evil of human slavery in northern Colorado.

> Luke, Heath, Daniel, Preston, Ronnie, Jano, Tavo, Nate…, (Jason also?) I gathered them together for a proposition at an ISR [intelligence, surveillance, reconnaissance] drone airfield outside of Berthoud proper (on county road 17). I first asked Nate if he would be able to access the ISR drones once in a while to have eyes on a location of my choosing. He seemed unsure, but said he would give it a go. Then I asked the question. "Who here hates the idea of human slavery?" and Luke said to Daniel or Preston, "See I told you," as if he knew I was planning this. I continued "Who here hates the idea that there are innocent children being bought and sold for sex and it's happening all over the country. I am going to fight against it. In Loveland, Fort Collins, Longmont, Denver, and onward. Who will join me?" Those weren't my exact words but they were the gist. My friends all agreed and were moving before I even finished. They all seemed to know their roles already, and we began to prepare. They were all glad to help and excited that I had finally asked them.

I also had a dream about a girl that I only vaguely remember. I still pray that YHVH brings my future wife and I together soon.

Saturday, April 28, 2018

Gabe sent this dream to his dad on April 28, 2018, 14:39 in Afghanistan. It was his last text before his final mission

For your eyes only. Share at your own discretion.

Recently I dreamed that I was swimming and kayaking on a large body of water, similar to a lake in Missouri with many branches and sections. The section I was at was divided by a gate from the rest, and I had to pass some sort of test before I could move to the other parts. I wanted to explore the rest of the lake. Prill was swimming in the lake near the gate that sectioned off the part we were in. It went deep enough to prevent human passage but allowed fish to swim underneath. The water was incredibly deep and clear. There was a killer whale that swam under the gate, and I recall telling Prill something about it. She seemed in awe rather than afraid. It swam close under her and nudged her. The next thing I knew, her leg was in its mouth, and it was pulling her down as she struggled. I dove from the Cliffside I was on and grabbed her with an arm around her middle as the killer whale took her other leg in its mouth and began to inch up her body. I kicked it as I pulled upwards, hating my lack of strength. I called to YHVH and pulled with every ounce of strength I could, one leg on each side of the water (about 100 meters wide or more #dreamphysics). My whole body was weak, but I kept the whale at bay until I felt a surge of strength from YHVH, and it was as if there was no resistance at all. I yanked Prill from its jaws and set her on land (uninjured as far as I could tell). My machine gun appeared in my hand, and I held the trigger down for a long burst into the whale's head as I floated in the air above it. It died. After that, the rest of the lake was open to me and I ventured out in a kayak to explore, looking back once in a while to ensure the bay I had left behind was still safe from trouble.

I would like to hear any insight you may have.

Monday, April 30, 2018

[Shortly after 7:00 am local time, Gabe was killed in action in the Tagab District, Kapisa Province, Afghanistan.]

EPILOGUE

The whole of Gabe's twenty-two years on this planet was like a brief, refreshing gust of wind in light of eternity, yet he left a massive void in the lives of his family and friends who loved him. We thank God that he was such a prolific writer, and that he lived his dream of doing the work of a green beret. His mission in life was to free the oppressed, to defend the weak, and to crush evil. After reading this book, may the stirring in your spirit move you to continue your righteous cause, choose to live selflessly, take the hard road, and finish strong.

This brief glimpse into the soul of Gabriel David Conde concludes with his own words written on July 27, 2014:

> Here at the end of all things, what is reservation? What is control? What is restraint? They are nothing. And nothing and no one will stand in the way of what is to come. With holy rage and cleansing fire I decimate those who would harm the ones I love. I feel no remorse, no fear, no hesitation. My body will die, but my memory will live on, and my cause will be taken up by my successors. In that way, I will be immortal on the earth as in the spirit. Until then, however, my battle rages and my body fights. My enemies will fall before my gun and blade as grass before a scythe. The call me the reaper, the angel of death, the left hand of God. But to those whom I have destroyed and saved alike, I am a creature. An animal and an alien without equal. The Creature of moral standard and true justice. I am the blade of the guillotine, the hangman's noose, the rifle of the firing squad, the

millstone around your neck. Yet on top of this, I am the body guard's pistol, the hero's cape, the soldier's helmet, the rope that pulls you from the pit. And so here, at the end of all things, what is mercy? What is compassion? What is gentleness? They are everything. And everything and everyone shall meet their just end through what is to come. With holy fire and cleansing righteousness, I will save the oppressed, defend the defenseless, and destroy the wicked. I feel no pain, no fear, no worry. My body will die as I protect those I love, but my spirit will live on for eternity, and my memory will become legend. Until then however, I live, I fight, I prevail.

… and evil shall be vanquished.

Gabe at home in Colorado, January 2017

NOT THE END

GLOSSARY OF TERMS

ACU	Army Combat Uniform
ANA	Afghan National Army
BAF	Bagram Air Field
cal	caliber
CIB	combat infantry badge
CLS	combat lifesaver course
COER	commissioned officer evaluation report
COMSEC	communication security
CSM	command sergeant major
FOB	forward operating base
GB	green beret
HLZ	helicopter landing zone
ID	infantry division
IED	improvised explosive device
JBER	Joint Base Elmendorf-Richardson
KIA	killed in action
LT	lieutenant
LZ	landing zone
MATV	mine-resistant ambush-protected (MRAP) all-terrain vehicle
MWR	morale welfare recreation
NCOER	non-commissioned officer evaluation report
OCP	operational camouflage pattern ACUs
ODA	operational detachment alpha
OER	officer education review

PID	positive identification
PJ	pararescue jumper
PKM	Soviet general-purpose machine gun
PL	platoon leader
PLT	platoon
POD	period of darkness
PSU	Provincial Special Unit (Afghanistan)
PT	physical training
QRF	quick reaction force
RG	mine-resistant light armored vehicle
RPG	rocket-propelled grenade
RTO	radio telephone operator
SAW	squad automatic weapon
SF	special forces
SGT	sergeant
SOAR	Special Operations Aviation Regiment
SOC	special operations commandos (ANA)
SOF	special operations forces
UCP	universal camouflage pattern ACUs
YHVH	English spelling of God's name in Hebrew

CPSIA information can be obtained
at www.ICGtesting.com
Printed in the USA
BVHW030515301020
592177BV00015B/69